PRAISE FOR
Borderline Personality Disorder Demystified, Revised Edition

"Wonderful! A doctor's doctor speaks clearly and compassionately about a disorder he's spent his career treating and studying. The stigma of borderline personality disorder is countered by hope and advocacy. Readers will be enlightened and inspired."

—JOHN G. GUNDERSON, MD, Professor in Psychiatry
at Harvard Medical School and Senior Advisor,
Borderline Services at McLean Hospital

"Dr. Friedel's enthusiasm and life-long experience treating patients with BPD are evident on every page. This book is a well-balanced mixture of necessary information for patients and families and up-to-date overviews of relevant fields, from neurobiology to treatment."

—CHRISTIAN SCHMAHL, MD, Professor and Director of the
Department of Psychosomatic Medicine and Psychotherapy,
Central Institute of Mental Health (Mannheim, Germany)

"This informative and compassionate book dispels myths and replaces misunderstanding with a wealth of knowledge so patients can get effective help. Clear, concise, and readable, *Borderline Personality Disorder Demystified* is helpful not only to those with BPD and their loved ones but also mental health professionals who want to know more about this disorder and what it is like to suffer from it."

—JOHN LIVESLEY, MD, PhD

"This book is a sensitively written, scientifically informed overview of borderline personality disorder. Both caring and authoritative, Dr. Friedel is a rare academician who combines a touching humanistic perspective on this challenging clinical syndrome with a deep and wide grasp of the rapidly growing relevant scientific literature."

—KENNETH S. KENDLER, MD

"This is an outstanding book. It is must reading for those with border-line personality disorder and must reading for those with loved ones with this disorder."

—EMIL F. COCCARO, MD, E.C. Manning Professor, University of Chicago Department of Psychiatry and Behavioral Neuroscience

Praise for the First Edition

"Dr. Friedel provides a concise and nicely organized compendium of the latest, up-to-date information on everything you need to know about the medical causes and treatment of borderline personality disorder. This book is easy to read and filled with useful information and engaging vignettes."

—LARRY J. SIEVER, MD, professor of Psychiatry and director of the Mood and Personality Disorders Research Program at Mt. Sinai Medical School

"Dr. Friedel has personally cared for patients with BPD, conducted significant pharmacological research with patients with the disorder, and organized numerous national symposia to teach others about this illness. As readers will discern as they move through this volume, Dr. Friedel has 'lived' with the problem and brings it clearly to light."

—S. CHARLES SCHULTZ, MD, Professor and head of the Department of Psychiatry, University of Minnesota

"Help at last! People with borderline personality disorder, their families and friends can now easily understand this perplexing medical-neurobiological condition and how to find help for it. Dr. Friedel has condensed decades of research and clinical experience into this information-packed book. Readers will be delighted with chapters on diagnosis, possible causes, disturbed neural circuits, medications, psychotherapy, and a hopeful future."

—BERNARD D. BEITMAN, MD, professor and chairman of the Department of Psychiatry, University of Missouri at Columbia

"This book should be required reading for everyone with borderline personality disorder and for the families, spouses, friends, and mental health professionals who are involved with them."

—KENNETH R. SILK, MD, professor and associate chair, Clinical and Administrative Affairs, Department of Psychiatry, University of Michigan Medical School

"Dr. Friedel's book uniquely demystifies the challenging clinical puzzle that is borderline personality disorder, resulting in a much-needed message for patients and their loved ones—there is hope—and the scientific data is emerging to back it up!"

—WARREN T. JACKSON, PhD, ABPP, Borderline Personality Disorder Program, Department of Psychiatry and Behavioral Neurobiology, University of Alabama at Birmingham

"This is a clinically rich and honest description of borderline personality disorder that allows us to experience the devastating effects of this illness on the lives of the people who have it as well as their families. It will help those with borderline personality disorder understand not only their illness, but themselves."

—STEVEN SECUNDA, MD

"Truly, as Dr. Friedel states, in dealing with this condition, 'knowledge is the edge.' And knowledge is precisely what he has provided so well in this book."

—DON R. SCHULTE, MD

"Borderline is a complex and heterogeneous disorder, but Dr. Friedel succeeds in weaving a coherent story that demystifies the disorder for the reader."

—HAGOP S. AKISKAL, MD, Professor of Psychiatry and director of the International Mood Center, the University of California, at San Diego

"This book is a great guide for patients and the people close to them. It will also help professionals working with these patients improve their knowledge of and therapeutic interventions for the disorder."

—SABINE HERPERTZ, MD, Aachen Technical University, Germany

Borderline
Personality
Disorder
Demystified

ALSO BY ROBERT O. FRIEDEL

Current Psychiatric Diagnosis & Treatment
Cognitive and Emotional Disturbances in the Elderly: Clinical Issues

Borderline Personality Disorder Demystified

An Essential Guide for
Understanding and Living with BPD

Robert O. Friedel, MD

with Linda F. Cox, LCSW, and Karin Friedel

Go

hachette
BOOKS
New York

In memory of
Denise

Contents

Foreword

Donald W. Black, MD, and Nancee Blum, MSW

UCH HAS HAPPENED SINCE 2004, WHEN THE FIRST EDITION
of *Borderline Personality Disorder Demystified* was published.
The good news is that since Dr. Friedel's guide was first
published, the amount and quality of research on borderline personality
disorder has exploded. Now, instead of a single evidenced-based treatment program (as was described in the first edition), Dr. Friedel describes
seven programs that have been specifically developed to treat borderline
personality disorder. Pharmacotherapy has also advanced, leading to a
much better understanding of the role of medication in treating our
patients with BPD. In addition, we have learned much more about the
disorder itself, including its course, risk factors, and possible causes. The
search is on for its genetic roots, a search that will only accelerate over
the next decade. More information about children and adolescents with
borderline personality disorder is available, giving hope to parents who
are at a loss for how best to cope with their child's disorder.

Happily, careful work by our colleagues Mary Zanarini, John Gunderson, and others shows that a disorder once thought chronic (and
even hopeless) actually improves significantly, even over the course of
a few years. Despite this good news, we still don't know enough about

why people develop the disorder, nor can we predict which treatments will be most effective for a given individual. And even when our patients improve, most still don't function as well as they (and we) would like. Thus, the work continues.

So where does this leave us? Borderline personality disorder remains a challenge for our patients and those who treat them. All too often, attempts at treatment are stymied by ongoing stigma, well documented in the literature. We recently conducted a study about attitudes held among mental health professionals toward borderline personality disorder. We were shocked that many psychiatrists and therapists continue to harbor negative attitudes toward these patients, and to denigrate and devalue their disorder. Many say they prefer not to work with borderline patients. There is no justification for these attitudes, especially among those charged with their care. We often wonder how our patients survive with a disorder they don't want and that causes them untold misery. Our patients deserve much better.

And that brings us back to *Borderline Personality Disorder Demystified*, because the best way to combat negative attitudes, as we have learned through our work, is by educating professionals about the disorder. Dr. Friedel's masterful book was written to teach everyone, lay persons and professionals alike, about BPD. We were impressed by this book in 2004, and have been enthusiastically recommending it to our patients and their family members ever since. While much has been written about borderline personality disorder in the professional literature, most of that information is not accessible to the nonprofessional audience. Now, after fourteen years, the book has been revised to include the most up-to-date research and to present it in a way that makes even the most difficult concepts understandable.

One of the lessons learned from developing and researching the Systems Training for Emotional Predictability and Problem Solving (STEPPS) program at the University of Iowa is that patients must be empowered to take responsibility for and to participate in their care. We teach them how to manage their symptoms, but it is up to the patient to practice, and then to reinforce, their newly learned skills. An equally important lesson is the positive impact achieved from providing education to family members and mental health professionals to allow them to respond to the patient in a way that further reinforces their skills. This book amply supports those goals. *Borderline Personality Disorder Demystified* will become an important resource for our patients and those in their support network, enabling them to better understand borderline personality disorder and its treatment. The book is authoritative yet readable. It provides compassion for patients and their families who have received little. Last, it provides hope, where there may have been none. Thank you, Dr. Friedel.

Foreword

Jim and Diane Hall

AFTER OUR VISITS WITH OUR ELDERLY AUNT, A RETIRED LI-brarian in Mentor, Ohio, she always dispatched us to Barnes and Noble with a list of new books she needed—so that's what took us to the bookstore one day in the summer of 2004, armed with her latest list. That task completed, we wandered into the psychology aisle, as we had been searching for quite awhile to see if something had reached the shelves on borderline personality disorder.

At that time, our family was in the midst of despair with the recent yet long overdue diagnosis of BPD for our beloved adult daughter. Our lives had been consumed for the past fifteen years with turmoil and chaos, as we tried to understand her tormenting illness while she worked and sought therapy yet suffered to survive. The diagnostic criteria seemed to clearly fit her symptoms, but skilled and informed treatment was scarce. So we were ever hopeful to find a resource but had never found much—until that summer day, when there it was: *Borderline Personality Disorder Demystified* by Robert O. Friedel, MD. With one glance at the Table of Contents, starting with "You Are Not Alone" and ending with "The Ultimate Reason for Hope," we bought and read it immediately.

Dr. Friedel's book began to unravel the nagging questions: What really was borderline personality disorder? What treatment and medications address the misery? What caused it? How can we help as family members? Our questions and deep concern for our loved one had developed into what felt to be an insurmountable mountain.

To us, this book was a sturdy ladder, and we started to climb.

Dr. Robert Friedel had an email address listed in his book, and we began to communicate. With the resources in his book plus the corresponding website, bpddemystified.com, our education on borderline personality disorder began in earnest.

Fortunately, our daughter lived on the East Coast, where some therapies existed for BPD. With extensive searching and a household move, she began in-depth dialectical behavior therapy (DBT) treatment. She has chosen to continue to anchor her life with the guidance and principles of DBT in conjunction with targeted medications.

Dr. Friedel's book contained the inherent and essential concepts that borderline personality disorder is indeed a serious mental illness, that effective therapies do exist, and—most important for us—that families matter! This was a revelation to us. When a family seeks education about the illness, they can help change their family's dynamic to support and facilitate their loved one's treatment.

We began to seek out support, and the knowledge we gained through this book and through learning more about mental illness has held our family together. We first attended meetings of the National Alliance on Mental Illness (NAMI) and the National Education Alliance for Borderline Personality Disorder (NEA-BPD). NEABPD offers a program called Family Connections. It includes current information and research on BPD and family functioning, individual coping skills based on DBT, family communication and problem-solving skills, and group support that builds a network for family members. Family Connections gave us the specific tools for change, and through our efforts to learn and use the skills taught in the course, our family dynamic began to change, starting with us. NAMI has a wonderful free family course called Family-to-Family, which is structured to help caregivers understand and support individuals with serious mental illness while maintaining their own well-being. It is specifically designed for parents, siblings, spouses, adult children, and significant others of people with severe and persistent mental illness, including borderline personality disorder. (For more information, see www.nami.org/programs.) After taking these powerful courses, we took training to teach them, learning more about ourselves with each class.

Through this process of learning and training, we became active volunteers and family educators working to combat the stigma and biases about this illness that persist despite decades of research. Today, we head a local chapter of NAMI in Corpus Christi, Texas.

Families are extremely important in the lives of our loved ones with mental illness. We're all in this together, and as the individual works on a wellness path, the family can help or hurt. In many cases, families are the constant for our loved ones. Learning how to build the right family support system can be life-changing, and if you have picked up this book, we'll bet you're looking for change.

As we have worked to educate families and increase awareness of BPD, we have remained devoted fans of Dr. Friedel, carrying his books to meetings, conferences, and conventions.

A highly respected clinician, professor, researcher, and editor, Dr. Friedel continues to present on borderline personality disorder worldwide. We have had the privilege of being present with him at congressional briefings involving NEA-BPD and NAMI, NEA-BPD conferences, NAMI conventions, and the NAMI Expert Focus Group Meeting on BPD. Like us, Dr. Friedel has devoted his life and work to helping people who have experienced a mental illness, and sharing essential knowledge with their loved ones. His popular presentations reveal not only his wisdom but his deep sense of caring and considerate respect for those with the diagnosis and their families. We're confident his patients recognize his kindness and concern as well as his ability to interpret their pain and gently guide their growth into wellness.

Dr. Friedel's life and exemplary career have been dedicated to those who struggle to understand and throw off the shackles of BPD. Driven by familial love and a special fondness for his sister Denise, he has continued his work even into retirement—and shared the continuing research and new findings on BPD in this wonderful revised edition of his book. And so we will now begin another fulfilling ten years or more carrying this new edition to meetings, conferences, and conventions. Thank you, Dr. Friedel, for reinforcing our ladder!

Introduction

URING THE FOURTEEN YEARS SINCE THE FIRST EDITION OF *Borderline Personality Disorder Demystified* was published, many significant advances have been made in our knowledge about borderline personality disorder (BPD), including the genetic and environmental **risk factors** of BPD, the neurobiological underpinnings of the disorder, and changes in its diagnosis and treatment. The total body of information has resulted in a major increase in interest and research about this disabling and potentially fatal disorder, which affects an estimated 4 to 6 percent of the general population in the United States. For example, the number of research citations listed under "borderline personality disorder" by the National Library of Medicine search engine (PubMed) has approximately doubled during this fourteen-year interval. That increase is even more striking when you consider that the initial 50 percent of articles on the topic were published over a period of seventy years. The federal and private funding of research grants allocated to the study of various aspects of the disorder has increased as well. In addition, the methods of treatment of BPD, which we will refer to as borderline disorder, with pharmacological, psychotherapeutic, group, and educational interventions have undergone significant change and improvement.

It's not just the medical community that has taken more notice of BPD. The awareness and acceptance of the diagnosis of borderline disorder has increased dramatically in the general population, accompanied by the number of healthcare providers who are skilled and experienced in treating the disorder. Finally, patient and family advocacy organizations such as the recently established Black Sheep Project, the National Education Alliance for Borderline Personality Disorder (NEA-BPD), and the National Alliance on Mental Illness (NAMI) have widely distributed current information about BPD to those individuals much in need of hope for improvement in their lives, as well as to their loved ones. The Black Sheep Project is also developing a private foundation to focus on borderline personality disorder where additional information can be translated promptly into increased awareness and improved, more readily available treatment for the disorder.

My main intent in writing this book is to provide a comprehensive review of this maligned and frequently misunderstood medical disorder. The many myths about it are seldom challenged, and when they are, the realities are often unheeded. To some extent, myths about BPD are becoming less frequent and are more often discredited, but many of them remain. Among the most damaging of them are that borderline disorder is almost always severely disabling and untreatable and that the diagnosis cannot be made in individuals who are younger than eighteen, when symptoms are likely to first appear. (Other psychiatrists and I have evaluated and treated many patients with BPD who meet the diagnostic criteria for the disorder in their teens and early twenties.) The effects of these and other myths cause unnecessary and intolerable suffering and an overwhelming loss of hope for those affected directly or indirectly by the disorder.

My younger sister suffered from borderline personality disorder, so I have also personally experienced just how damaging misunderstandings of the disorder can be and the resulting heartache for every member our family (Chapter 2). In my sister's case, the manifestations of the disorder were initially thought to be willful, causing additional harm. However, experiences with other patients and families have shown me that this disorder *is* significantly more treatable now than it was two generations ago and manageable with proper care. Since the first edition of this book was published, there is even more reason for hope.

It has been very gratifying to receive communications from readers of the first edition who rediscovered hope and the motivation to find the help of skilled professionals that ultimately enabled them to live happy and productive lives. It is my hope that this updated version of the book will help you achieve the same results.

ONE

What Is Borderline Personality Disorder and How Is It Diagnosed?

T HE CAUSES OF BORDERLINE PERSONALITY DISORDER OFTEN vary in type and degree from one person to another, so it makes sense that the symptoms also vary considerably in type and severity. In other words, there's not a one-size-fits-all description for why any one person has BPD or how it causes them to feel, think, and act. Even so, once the basic symptoms are understood, it usually becomes apparent to the individual and family that borderline personality disorder (BPD) is present, and that it is a major contributor to the difficulties they are experiencing. Simply recognizing that you have BPD is the critical first step in gaining control over your life.

There is very good research evidence that borderline personality disorder (referred to as borderline disorder) is the result of physiological and chemical disturbances in certain pathways in the brain that control specific brain functions. You are born with these disturbances, and they usually are amplified by events that occurred after birth. According to the most recent survey conducted in the United States, borderline disorder affects approximately 6 percent of the population. It appears to be more common than schizophrenia and bipolar (also known as manic-depressive) disorders. Borderline disorder was once thought to occur more frequently in women than in men, but that data is now in question. Therefore, it may now be estimated that approximately one in every seventeen people in the United States suffers from borderline disorder.

THE SYMPTOMS OF BORDERLINE DISORDER

To be diagnosed with borderline disorder, you must experience and demonstrate a minimum of five of the nine symptoms listed in Table 1.2 on page 20. These symptoms are separated into four different groups (Table 1.1), or as many experts in the field of personality disorders refer to them, behavioral dimensions or domains.

TABLE 1.1

THE FOUR BEHAVIORAL DOMAINS OF BORDERLINE DISORDER

1. Poorly regulated emotions
2. Impulsivity
3. Impaired perception and reasoning
4. Markedly disturbed relationships

Most people with borderline disorder don't have all of the symptoms in each of the four domains of affected behaviors listed above, but most do have at least one symptom from each. Many of my patients find that the arrangement of the symptoms of the disorder into these four domains makes it easier for them to recognize and remember their symptoms and the consequences. Overall, individuals with borderline disorder may be characterized as appearing dramatic, hyperemotional, and erratic.

DOMAIN 1: POORLY REGULATED EMOTIONS

A number of experts in the field believe that an inherent difficulty in regulating emotions is the driving force behind many of the other symptoms of borderline disorder. If you have borderline disorder, your emotions may change quickly, and you may find it difficult to accurately perceive and express your emotional responses, especially to unpleasant events. You may often overreact emotionally to daily events. However, at other times your emotional responses may seem blunted, only to be followed by hyperemotional reactions at a later time. Descriptions of other major symptom indicators of poorly regulated emotions in borderline disorder follow.

Mood Swings and Emotional Lability

The emotions of people with borderline disorder are often very unstable and undergo rapid changes that are difficult to control. This is referred to as **emotional lability**. These labile emotions can include negative feelings of anxiety, anger, fear, loneliness, sadness, and depression. Less often, labile emotions can also include positive feelings such as happiness, joy, enthusiasm, and love. Your emotions may fluctuate quickly from feeling good to feeling bad, sometimes for reasons that are obvious to you but at other times for reasons that are not apparent. Because of these rapid fluctuations in mood, and because you are more likely to develop feelings of depression and episodes of **major depressive disorder** than individuals who do not have borderline disorder, at some point you may have been diagnosed as having bipolar disorder (which psychiatrists previously referred to as manic-depressive disorder).

Your feelings may also be **hyperreactive**; that is, you may significantly overreact to some situations. For example, you may become very upset over constructive criticisms, unavoidable separations, or disagreements that other people seem to take in stride. Such events may cause a wave of anxiety, sadness, anger, or desperation. In addition, you may find that you have great difficulty calming down your emotions and soothing yourself by focusing on reassuring thoughts or by engaging in usually pleasant and healthy activities. During these periods of severe hyperemotionality, or "emotional storms," as they're called, you may feel so desperate that you turn to alcohol or drugs for relief, lash out in anger or rage, or engage in other destructive behaviors such as cutting.

Recent research also suggests that people with borderline disorder have difficulty in accurately identifying their emotional responses and those of other people, cannot appropriately balance mixed feelings, and have intense responses to negative emotions. For example, you may find that you overidentify with the emotions of others and may become overly upset when they have negative experiences. You may even feel as if these events are occurring to you. In other words, you react too strongly to the plight of others, such as their living situation, their difficulties, or any negative situation they are experiencing.

One patient told me that at such times "it is like someone is putting a dagger in my heart." This person also told me that the situation did not even have to be happening to real people; it could affect her if she were watching a movie or even a television commercial. She knew the situation was not real, but she felt as if it were and that it was happening to her. She added that at these times, the pain from her emotional involvement in these situations lasted for quite some time. This is another characteristic of emotional dyscontrol in borderline disorder. In addition, you may find that once upset your emotions do not return to their normal level as quickly as they do in people who don't have the disorder.

You may also be hypersensitive to the real or perceived negative behaviors of others toward you: you're always on the lookout for the slight frown, raised eyebrow, or minor change in a person's tone of voice that indicates that they are irritated or angry with you. When you believe you detect such critical reactions, no matter how subtle, your response may often be considerably out of proportion to the situation. You may feel anxiety, self-recrimination, and anger that are simply not warranted under the circumstances. While you may be vaguely aware that you are overreacting, the feelings are just too real and too strong to ignore.

Anxiety

Episodes of severe anxiety are common symptoms of borderline disorder. One of the first psychiatrists to write in detail about borderline disorder believed that "anxiety is the motor" that drives the other emotional symptoms of the disorder, such as anger, and behavioral symptoms such as impulsivity. Anxiety can produce tension-related physical symptoms, including a migraine headache, backache, stomach pain, irritable bowel, rapid heartbeat, cold hands, hot flashes, and excessive sweating.

Anxiety may even reach the level of the massive and disabling symptoms referred to as **panic attacks** that are so severe you feel you are dying and may go to the emergency room for immediate care. When less severe than a panic attack, the anxiety may be more pervasive and last for a longer duration. Or the anxiety may evolve into anger, despair, and physical symptoms. You may also attempt to relieve the anxiety by engaging in impulsive behaviors that I discuss below.

Intense Anger or Difficulty Controlling Anger

Poorly controlled anger is one of the most common and destructive symptoms of borderline disorder—so much so that it occurs in *two* of the nine diagnostic criteria of the disorder. You may feel irritable and angry much of the time, and you often can be argumentative, quick-tempered, and sarcastic. You may even become furious, or sometimes enraged, in circumstances that do not warrant such responses. The slightest event or exchange can result in an angry outburst. You may then say and do things that are quite destructive and later regret that you did so. Individuals with borderline disorder have more numerous and intense episodes of anger and depression than other individuals, and their emotions may fluctuate between anger, anxiety, and other emotions more readily as well.

You may realize in the midst of these outbursts of anger that you are overreacting, but seem unable to control the strong emotions sweeping over you. As one patient put it, "I know my husband does not deserve all of the anger and abuse that I heap upon him, but he's the one around most of the time and I'm fairly sure he won't leave me. I don't seem to be able to control the anger. At the time, I think he deserves it—so he gets it." Your family, your spouse or partner, and others close to you have learned that they must be very careful about what they say or do. Many comment, "It's like I'm walking on eggshells all the time. I never know what I will do to cause her [or him] to blow up." This apprehensiveness on the part of your family can result in a persistent, elevated level of tension in your home. Because you are very sensitive to the negative feelings of others, this can make an already tense living situation even worse.

Chronic Feelings of Emptiness

Another strong feeling you may experience is a sense of persistent emptiness. This sense of emptiness is often accompanied by feelings of boredom and loneliness. In turn, these feelings may lead to dissatisfaction with the people in your life and with your life in general. Dissatisfied with your life, you may be prone to change friends and jobs frequently, and even to engage in brief affairs. For a time, these changes can feel very exciting and temporarily relieve the emptiness, loneliness, and boredom. But the feelings return after a while, and the life patterns of inconstancy repeat themselves.

During our initial meeting, one young patient told me that these feelings of emptiness and boredom were so strong that she felt as if she had a big hole inside her that wouldn't go away. It did diminish when she was involved in a relationship with a young man, at least for a while, but then would return in full force when they fought or when he left her. She added that, when severe, this feeling was so emotionally painful she would do almost anything to relieve it, even cut or burn herself, although the emotional pain always returned shortly thereafter.

Another patient, whom I describe in more detail in Chapter 2, told me early in her treatment that when she felt empty and bored for a long period, she would leave her husband without notice and travel to another city. There she would see a former teacher for a brief two- or three-day affair, then fly home again. Although she temporarily felt excited, desired, and satisfied by these escapades, ultimately she was plagued by guilt and remorse for her behavior, and she dreaded having to deal with her husband about her absences. Nonetheless, the pattern continued until she was able to understand the nature of the feelings and the life situations that triggered this behavior, then take measures to gain control over it. Fortunately, her husband was able to tolerate the behavior until she was able to develop much more effective responses to the emptiness and boredom she often felt.

DOMAIN 2: IMPULSIVITY

The tendency toward impulsive, self-damaging behavior is so common and so strong in people with borderline disorder that some experts in the field consider it the most harmful symptom of the disorder. They believe it is more damaging than the symptoms of emotional instability and impaired reasoning. Impulsivity alone, as well as the overall severity of symptoms, appear to be the best predictors of the long-term outcome of the disorder. Untreated, people with borderline disorder who are very impulsive tend to have a worse **prognosis** than those who are not as impulsive. Research suggests that impulsivity in people with borderline disorder is the result of an imbalance between the **neural** systems (nerve cell pathways) of emotion and reasoning that regulate impulsive behavior (Chapter 6). Following are the major groups of symptoms of borderline disorder that are included in the category of impulsivity.

Impulsive Self-Harming Behaviors

If you have borderline disorder, there are many ways that you may behave impulsively, such as binge eating and spending money recklessly on clothes or other items. You may also engage in more harmful, impulsive acts like uncontrolled gambling; excessive drinking and drug abuse; unprotected sexual promiscuity; violent, aggressive acts or repetitious, illegal acts such as speeding, driving while intoxicated, and shoplifting.

For example, when one of my patients felt especially anxious and empty inside, she would go shopping at expensive stores and then steal clothing and other items, even though she could easily afford to buy them. Before these actions could be brought fully under her control, she was arrested for shoplifting and convicted of a felony. When another patient felt particularly neglected and abandoned, or was criticized by her husband, she would go to bars, drink excessively, and strike up conversations with men. She stated that she did this in an attempt to feel better about herself and to "get even" with her husband. These episodes would occasionally lead to brief sexual encounters that were very destructive to her self-esteem and to her relationship with her husband. These episodes also exposed her to a considerable risk of being seriously harmed, as she knew little about the men she picked up, and she did not protect herself properly from sexually transmitted diseases.

There is considerable research on the prevalence and consequences of impulsive behavior in people with borderline disorder. However, there is a scarcity of research on the events and warning signs that lead up to such behavior, and on why some people with borderline disorder are more impulsive than others. In general, impulsive behaviors often follow episodes of emotional storms and disrupted close relationships, especially real or threatened abandonment. They also appear to be more common in people with borderline disorder who have been physically or sexually abused as children. To meet this particular diagnostic criterion, you would exhibit a pattern of impulsive behaviors in at least two of the self-destructive ways that I mentioned above.

Recurrent Suicidal Behavior, Gestures, and Threats or Self-Mutilating Behavior

Recurrent suicidal behaviors, gestures, and threats or self-mutilating or injurious behaviors are a particularly striking group of impulsive symptoms that occur among many, but by no means all, individuals with borderline disorder. They are referred to as **parasuicidal acts**. The severity of these behaviors ranges from very serious acts that may inadvertently be life-threatening to less serious acts that are often attempts to control painful symptoms or a situation, gain attention, or seek help. You may physically hurt yourself by hitting yourself; cutting or scratching your wrists, arms, thighs, or other parts of your body; burning your skin with cigarettes; or taking overdoses of medications. At times, you may do these things in the desperate desire to have others take care of you, to "get even" with them, or to impose your way on them.

Most often, you may hurt yourself to help reduce the emotional pain you feel when it reaches an intolerable level. As one patient who frequently cut her thighs with a razor blade explained to me, "When I see the blood and feel the pain, somehow the pain and dead feelings inside go away for a while, and I'm again back in control and in contact with the world." At these times, these acts may seem to alleviate, at least to a degree, the severe internal pain you are feeling.

For those of you who engage in one or more of these manifestations of borderline disorder, they are most likely very distressing to you, and to family members as well. It's also such a striking type of behavior that, in its rare extreme, it has been dramatized in movies. For example, the character played by Glenn Close in the classic 1987 movie *Fatal Attraction* demonstrated this and many of the other symptoms of borderline disorder. She engaged in cutting behavior twice in the movie. In an early scene, she cut her wrists when the character played by Michael Douglas attempted to end their relationship. This persuaded him not to do so then. In the final scene of the movie, the Glenn Close character absentmindedly poked at her leg with the point of a knife until it bled, while she was talking with Michael Douglas's wife before attacking her. For dramatic purposes, this movie presents the symptoms of borderline disorder in their most severe form. Please realize that these are extreme rather than typical behaviors exhibited by people with borderline disorder.

I often ask patients who engage in self-injurious behavior if they recall when they first did so, where they got the idea to do it, and under what circumstances it occurred initially. Their responses are frequently quite similar. The first event usually occurred when they were teenagers; it was often in response to a serious argument with their parents or the threat of abandonment by a boyfriend or girlfriend. Surprisingly, a number of my patients cannot account for what prompted them to commit such an unusual act; the idea just came to them. Others report that doing so is common knowledge. Once done, the immediate result is typically a decrease in emotional pain and an increase in attention and concern by others when they learned of it. These two responses to their self-injurious behaviors reinforced them and made the patient more likely to do so again in response to periods of high stress and emotional turmoil. I think it is striking as well as distressing that such behavior should occur spontaneously to a young person. I don't believe that the idea to hurt oneself in these ways and under these conditions spontaneously occurs to many individuals without borderline disorder, but it does occur.

There is no single symptom of borderline disorder that indicates with certainty that a person has the disorder. But if you engage in self-injurious behavior of the types mentioned, I recommend that you see a psychiatrist who is well trained and experienced in borderline disorder to determine if you suffer from it.

Munchausen Syndrome (Factitious Disorder Imposed on Self)

A very striking and serious form of self-injurious behavior that may occur in people with borderline disorder is Munchausen syndrome. People with this disorder hurt themselves intentionally, but in a way that looks like a bona fide medical disease. For example, they may place a drop of blood in their urine to make it appear they are bleeding from their urinary tract, or create a serious skin infection and then seek medical help. Tests are then performed to determine the mysterious nature of the illness, often over a great length of time and at great expense. During these episodes, the person receives a considerable amount of medical care and attention.

Many people with Munchausen syndrome have some direct familiarity with the medical profession, so they are quite knowledgeable about the symptoms and signs of diseases that are especially difficult to diagnose. More dramatic cases involve severe self-injurious behavior such as injecting a vein with infected material, thus causing widespread, internal infections of unknown origin throughout the body that require extensive medical diagnostic studies and treatment. In the extreme, people with Munchausen syndrome who are highly knowledgeable about the practice of medicine are able to produce symptoms that result in multiple, unnecessary operations.

Munchausen by Proxy (Factitious Disorder Imposed on Another—Previously, Factitious Disorder by Proxy)

A particularly severe subtype of Munchausen syndrome is Munchausen by proxy. In this disorder, a parent or caregiver of a child, usually the mother, will repeatedly inflict a medical illness on the child and then seek medical care and attention for the child. In this way, the caregiver will also receive attention, support, caring, and sympathy from medical professionals, family, and friends. Tragically, some of these children die before the correct cause of their illnesses is discovered. Again, I want to emphasize that Munchausen syndrome and Munchausen by proxy occur in only a small percentage of individuals with borderline disorder. However, when these serious conditions are recognized, it is essential that borderline disorder be considered as a strong contributory factor. Unfortunately, if the underlying problem of borderline disorder is missed and not treated, the behaviors are likely to continue, regardless of the potential medical, legal, and personal consequences. However, if the diagnosis of borderline disorder is made and the person enters treatment, there is hope for recovery.

Note: The *Diagnostic and Statistical Manual of Mental Disorders*, 5th edition (DSM-5), states, "Deliberate physical self-harm in the absence of suicidal intent can also occur in association with other mental disorders such as borderline personality disorder. Factitious disorder requires that the induction of injury occurs in association with deception." The issue of intentional deception in DSM-5 is specified to differentiate this behavior in individuals with borderline disorder from those with the diagnosis of somatic symptom disorder, in which the behavior is proposed to be unintentional. I know of no evidence to support this distinction. The lack of evidence is not surprising, considering the number of primitive psychological mechanisms, such as **dissociative episodes**, **paranoid thinking**, and other brief **psychotic episodes**, observed in patients with borderline disorder.

Suicide Risk in Borderline Disorder

The most extreme case of self-injurious behavior is suicide. The risk of successful suicide attempts is significantly elevated in those individuals with borderline disorder. Obviously, some people with the disorder do intend to commit suicide. If you have borderline disorder, you may have already thought of ending your life, or you may have wished you had never been born. It is important to recognize the difference between hurting yourself for the reasons I discussed above and the clear intent to commit suicide. There is a typical stage-by-stage progression from nonsuicidal, self-injurious behavior to a high level of suicidal risk. The duration of these stages may vary from one individual to another, but their content is reasonably consistent. The first stage in the process is having the thought that life is not worth living, that it's simply too painful. The next stage is thinking about suicide itself, at first occasionally, then more and more frequently. You may then find yourself planning how you would do it and may even acquire the means to do so. (Typically, women commit suicide by overdosing with drugs; men by a more violent act such as using a gun.) This is a very dangerous stage in the progression toward suicide by a person with borderline disorder, as the next stage is the final one, the suicide attempt itself.

Certain circumstances increase your risk of suicide if you have borderline disorder. These include a family history of suicide; your engaging in highly impulsive acts, especially the frequent abuse of alcohol or other substances; previous self-injurious behaviors; and unsuccessful suicidal attempts. If any of these are present, your risk of suicide is estimated to be between 4 and 9 percent. Whether or not you fall into this high-risk category, if at any time you recognize the above symptoms of the suicide process, or you do not feel safe for any reason, you need to know how to get help quickly. If you believe you are at risk for attempting suicide, you should immediately contact the National Suicide Prevention Hotline at 1-800-273-8255 or call 911, and then your physician or clinician, if you have one. If you can't make contact, go to the closest hospital emergency room.

There are a number of other reasons why you may be at higher than average risk for suicide. For example, major depressive disorder and bipolar disorder are common in people with borderline disorder. There is a higher risk of suicide for a person with borderline disorder who is being treated for one of these disorders but who is not receiving effective treatment for borderline disorder. I discuss these disorders in detail in Chapter 8, including how they relate to borderline disorder. In addition, those people with borderline disorder who were physically or sexually abused as children or teenagers, or are being abused currently, are more likely to commit suicide than those with the disorder in the absence of these experiences. Not surprisingly, those who are most impulsive are at most risk.

Finally, if you have no suicidal intent but perform acts of self-injurious behavior to reduce emotional pain and to deal with difficult situations, it is easy to overlook a real threat to safety. Like "the boy who cried wolf," repeated parasuicidal acts may result in any or all of your caregivers mistaking your reports of a real suicidal situation for parasuicidal behavior and not providing you with the emergency help you need.

Therefore it is essential that you learn how to recognize the triggers of parasuicidal behaviors and stop them. You should discuss your triggers with your therapist and psychiatrist, and they should work with you to develop and implement a specific treatment plan. It's also important that you and your family learn the risk factors for suicide in borderline disorder, participate in developing your plan, and remain constantly alert to your increased risk of suicide (see Chapter 8).

DOMAIN 3: IMPAIRED PERCEPTION AND REASONING

Individuals with borderline disorder often report that they have difficulty with their memory, especially under stress. You may also misperceive experiences, expecting the worst thoughts or behaviors from others, even when none are intended. You may have difficulty with your concentration and with organizing your thinking and actions. You may not be able to think a complex problem through adequately and determine reasonable alternatives and the consequences of impulsive actions you undertake. In addition, approximately one-third of people with borderline disorder experience episodes of auditory **hallucinations**—that is, hearing sounds and usually negative, conspiring voices that are internally produced. These difficulties with the perception of reality and important events, as well as thinking and reasoning, may result in faulty decisions with highly detrimental consequences. Although these problems are not listed as such in the diagnostic criteria for borderline disorder, careful psychological and neuropsychological testing demonstrate that they are present and constitute important features of the disorder.

For example, problems in remembering and reasoning seem to be related to the emotional state of most individuals, whether or not they have borderline disorder. Most of us have had moments when we're unable to recall clearly the details of an event that occurred while we were under great emotional stress, such as a house fire, a dangerous automobile accident, or any incident that provoked severe anxiety or anger. We realize that our reasoning ability at these times is also impaired. When we are at the point where we panic or are very angry, we're not able to make as rational and thoughtful decisions as we do otherwise. If you have borderline disorder, you may have difficulty with memory, thinking, and decision making in the face of even minimal stress. Your tolerance of stress is often much lower than it is for people without the disorder.

We have discussed previously the difficulty that people with borderline disorder have in the area of emotional control. Therefore, it's not surprising that you may have difficulty in participating in reasonable conversations to solve problems when you are in a hyperemotional state, or to remember accurately the content of these situations afterward. In other words, the emotional hyperreactivity common in borderline disorder often gets in the way of normal reasoning in social or interpersonal situations. This difficulty in social reasoning seriously impairs your ability to learn and develop the skills necessary to have mature, successful, and sustained personal relationships. The section below on impaired relationships deals with this problem in more detail.

Split Thinking: Living in a Black-and-White World

Many people with borderline disorder report that they see themselves, other people, and the world in general as black or white and as good or bad. They have difficulty in dealing effectively with the gray areas, especially those involving relationships. You may have a difficult time accurately evaluating positive characteristics in yourself and others and comparing them reasonably with characteristics you don't like. This difficulty is often due to your tendency to overrespond emotionally to negative occurrences, underrespond to positive occurrences, and have problems with social reasoning.

These gray areas of life, of course, constitute the vast majority of human experiences. Consequently, it may be difficult for you to reach a balanced, reasonable, and well-integrated opinion about people, especially those important to you. This makes it hard for you to deal with close relationships in positive ways that enable you to adapt to the reasonable frailties of other people. It follows logically that you may also find it a challenge to determine effective ways to help others adapt to your own shortcomings. To some degree, this may be because, when you're symptomatic, you believe unrealistically that your problems are mainly the result of the behaviors of other people, not your own.

Some experts in the field of borderline disorder consider "split thinking" to be the core problem of the disorder.

Brief Episodes of Paranoid Thinking and Auditory Hallucinations

Individuals with borderline disorder are often suspicious. They typically expect others to be overly critical of them and to behave more negatively to them than to people who do not have the disorder. When exposed to severe stress (usually criticism), or imagined or real abandonment, when under the influence of alcohol or drugs, when treated with certain classes of stimulants such as **amphetamines**, or with certain antidepressants, some people with borderline disorder become so suspicious that they have difficulty thinking rationally. During these brief episodes of paranoid thinking, you may falsely believe that others are planning to harm you or that an intimate partner is cheating on you. These episodes may last from a few hours to several days, or even longer.

There is recent evidence that approximately one-third of people with borderline disorder may also experience auditory hallucinations, such as hearing strange voices, music, or other sounds.

Dissociative Symptoms

You may notice that there are periods of time during which you can't recall anything. These are referred to as **dissociative episodes**. At their extreme, dissociative episodes can be so severe that the person actually splits off part of their feelings, thinking, and behavior and temporarily creates one or more separate personalities. When this occurs, it is referred to as "multiple personalities." Dissociative episodes are fairly common in borderline disorder, but I have only recognized clear evidence of multiple personalities in fewer than ten individuals during my career. Some experts do not believe that this condition exists, which may be why it is still not mentioned in DSM-5. I believe that this important issue will be addressed in a future edition of the DSM.

Magical Thinking

You may have odd thoughts, such as unrealistic and magical thinking. **Magical thinking** is the use of highly unrealistic thoughts and beliefs to solve the challenges and problems in your life. For example, you may believe that somehow you will become a lawyer or architect, although you barely succeeded in completing high school. Or you may believe you are clairvoyant. You may begin to act in ways consistent with these beliefs.

Depersonalization and Derealization

During episodes of depersonalization, you feel unreal, as if in a dream, and strangely detached from the world or outside of your body. I have had patients report that at times they feel numb or hollow. An unusual example of depersonalization was recounted to me by a patient who said that she often incorporates characters and situations from books or television into her thinking, as if these characters or incidents are real.

In derealization, *you* feel normal, but your surroundings, or the people in them, seem distorted in shape, color, motion, or behavior.

Unstable Self-Image or Sense of Self

You may feel frequently that you have little self-worth and that your self-concept depends mainly on the attitudes and behaviors of people close to you. If they seem loving and attentive, you feel good about yourself. But their minor, constructive criticisms may cause you great anxiety and to have feelings of worthlessness and despair. Regardless of what you have accomplished, it doesn't seem to counterbalance the opinions of others. In other words, you may feel as if your self-esteem is almost totally dependent on the attitude of others toward you.

It is probably not uncommon for you to feel unsure of your identity, who you really are, what values you truly believe in, what career you should pursue, and what causes you should support. You may have difficulty in feeling "centered," in developing a constancy of purpose in your life that serves to stabilize you and provides integrity and predictability to you, your peace of mind, and your behaviors. As one patient put it, "I feel as if I too easily adopt the characteristics of the people I am with. I am desperate that they like me. I quickly adopt their mannerisms, their way of speaking, and their attitudes, even the ones that I don't usually agree with. Other people's opinions of me are much more important to me than my own opinions and convictions. I feel as if I have an emptiness inside of me that only other people can fill."

At times, this tendency to be overly flexible in one's values, attitudes, and preferences in order to please others may extend to sexual relationships and result in multiple sexual encounters. Especially when you're under stress or the influence of alcohol or drugs, it may seem that your central beliefs do not hold and that your internal touchstones are not enough to guide you to the appropriate courses of action. I want to emphasize that the presence of these qualities is a characteristic of borderline disorder and does not mean that you are without morals or ethical convictions. People with borderline disorder just don't seem to be able to consistently withstand their very strong need for approval.

There may also be times when you swing to the other extreme. Then you may be very critical, inflexible, and dogmatic about certain beliefs, to the point that you offend others. As a result of these difficulties, it's understandable that you may do better in stable, highly structured situations, especially with people whose behaviors and personal values are solid and reliable.

DOMAIN 4: MARKEDLY DISTURBED RELATIONSHIPS

Given the three domains of symptoms of borderline disorder already described, it's not surprising that your life may be marked by tumultuous relationships. Usually, the closer the relationship, the greater the turmoil. During a person's childhood and early adolescence, the major problems in relationships usually occur with parents, other family members, teachers, and friends. Later in adolescence, difficulties can also occur with boyfriends or girlfriends, and in adulthood, with spouses, children, coworkers, and employers.

A Pattern of Unstable and Intense Personal Relationships

Individuals with borderline disorder have significant difficulties in establishing trusting, consistent, interdependent, and balanced relationships with parents, other family members, peers, associates at work, and so forth. Disturbances in perceiving realistically their own emotions and value systems, and empathizing with those of others, present major challenges in this area. You may have noticed that you fluctuate dramatically and quickly in your feelings and attitudes toward those people who are most important to you. As a result of split thinking, at times you may perceive someone to be more wonderful than anyone reasonably could be—capable of making you feel happy, safe, important, and alive under any circumstance. In other words, you unrealistically overvalue and idealize this person who is so central to your sense of well-being. You may find that you cling desperately to these people and worry continually about their happiness, success, and faithfulness to you. You may even call them often to reassure yourself that they're all right because you believe your happiness and success depends so much on them.

Of course, no one is able to live up to these unrealistic expectations. Feeling disappointed that the relationship cannot stabilize your emotions and your life, you may have an abrupt change in attitude that moves to the other extreme. For example, after a small slight, you may perceive the other person to be uncaring, unsupportive, selfish, and even punitive, to a much greater degree than is actually the case. In doing so, you devalue the importance of that person, finding fault with them at every turn. You won't be able to tolerate this situation for very long, so you may either leave them or abruptly swing back to the other extreme, only to find that the cycle repeats itself, again and again. Eventually, this stressful pattern of behavior typically results in a very painful end to most of your relationships, thus validating and reinforcing your fear of abandonment.

Frantic Efforts to Avoid Real or Imagined Abandonment

People with borderline disorder find themselves caught in a bewildering, frustrating, and stress-provoking dilemma. On the one hand, you may have a strong, often unrealistic and uncontrollable fear of being abandoned. Even brief separations from people who are important to you and on whom you are dependent are traumatic and may result in a severe flare-up of your symptoms. On the other hand, at times you may have an equally strong fear of becoming too closely involved with another person, of losing your sense of individuality and self-control, or of being hurt should the relationship go badly. You may feel as if you are going to fall apart or cease to exist if you become too close to other people.

For example, one patient, Mrs. Davis, who is discussed in the next chapter, complained to me frequently that her husband was away in class or studying much of the time, leaving her alone. When she felt this was the case, she felt abandoned, anxious, and angry. At these times, she wouldn't go to work, which put her job in jeopardy, or she had brief encounters with another man, which placed her marriage at risk. Mrs. Davis spent months looking forward with great anticipation to a vacation during which she and her husband planned to drive across the country together. By the third night of the trip, she felt confined and trapped in the situation. While her husband slept one night, she left their motel room in the middle of a rainstorm, dressed only in her nightclothes. After walking several miles along a deserted road, she came to a telephone booth and somehow managed to call me. Only after considerable discussion was she able to gather herself together and return to the motel and her husband, and to complete the trip. After they returned home and to their usual routine, she again became anxious, lonely, and angry much of the time, because he was away from her so often.

For some people with borderline disorder, the issue of separation, abandonment, aloneness, and closeness can be even more complex than this example. As one patient explained to me, "Sometimes I have the strong urge to be alone, to move far away from everything and everyone I know. I don't think it's because I'm afraid of becoming too close to someone, or that I will lose my individuality. This urge occurs when I have strong feelings of anger, hopelessness, or even regret and shame. I feel that I've messed up this life and want to start a brand-new one, in a place where no one knows me and I can't get into trouble again. Most of the time I realize that these strong feelings and this impulse are unrealistic. I know my difficulties would simply go with me. But at the time, the feelings seem very real, and escape seems the best solution."

The implications for individuals with borderline disorder of the above difficulties with relationships obviously cut across most areas of life. One that may not be readily apparent to you is appreciating how they affect your relationships with those clinicians who attempt to help you understand your disorder and to cope with it in more effective and realistic ways. Because of this problem, many of the psychotherapeutic approaches used in the treatment of borderline disorder focus on establishing and continually improving the therapeutic alliance between the patient and the treating clinician. The effectiveness of your treatment is dependent to a significant degree on your ability to engage in such work and to become increasingly flexible in your thinking and behaviors in and out of therapy. (These issues are raised in detail in Chapters 9–12.) For example, your tendency to engage in all-or-nothing or black-and-white thinking and behaviors with your treating clinicians is counter-productive to your treatment; avoiding such tendencies is paramount.

TABLE 1.2

DIAGNOSTIC CRITERIA OF
BORDERLINE PERSONALITY DISORDER

This table lists the symptoms of borderline disorder as described in the *Diagnostic and Statistical Manual of Mental Disorders* of the American Psychiatric Association, 5th edition (DSM-5), published in 2013. This is the official listing of mental disorders in the United States prepared by experts in each disorder under the auspices of the American Psychiatric Association. It includes the diagnostic criteria for each of these disorders and is considered the gold standard across much of the world. According to the definition of borderline personality disorder in this manual, people with the disorder have a broad spectrum of symptoms, listed below, but each individual does not necessarily have all of the symptoms listed.

A pervasive pattern of instability of interpersonal relationships, self-image, and affects, and marked impulsivity beginning by early adulthood and present in a variety of contexts, as indicated by five (or more) of the following criteria:

1. Frantic efforts to avoid real or imagined abandonment. Note: Do not include suicidal or self-mutilating behavior covered in Criterion 5 (below)

2. A pattern of unstable and intense interpersonal relationships characterized by alternating between extremes of idealization and devaluation

3. Identity disturbance: markedly and persistently unstable self-image or sense of self

4. Impulsivity in at least two areas that are potentially self-damaging (e.g., spending, sex, substance abuse, reckless driving, binge eating). Note: Do not include suicidal or self-mutilating behavior covered in Criterion 5

5. Recurrent suicidal behavior, gestures, threats, or self-mutilating behavior

6. Affective instability due to a marked reactivity of mood (e.g., intense episodic dysphoria, irritability, or anxiety usually lasting a few hours and only rarely more than a few days)

7. Chronic feelings of emptiness

8. Inappropriate, intense anger or difficulty controlling anger (e.g., frequent displays of temper, constant anger, recurrent physical fights)

9. Transient, stress-related paranoid ideation or severe dissociative symptoms

SOURCE: *Diagnostic and Statistical Manual of Mental Disorders*, 5th ed. (Arlington, VA: American Psychiatric Association, 2013).

two

You Are Not Alone

MANY OF MY PATIENTS HAVE TOLD ME THAT WHEN THEY were very young, they realized there was something different about them or wrong with them. Regardless of the specific ways in which they thought they were different, and how their lives eventually seemed to confirm these differences, the end result is the same. They think that no one truly understands them and they feel painfully isolated. If you have borderline disorder, you may think and feel this way too: that you are alone and at the mercy of the symptoms that plague you, your emotional storms, impulsive behaviors, unusual thoughts, self-doubt, and tumultuous relationships. You may believe that these problems separate you from everyone else. Even worse, you may believe that you have caused or deserve this condition.

In this chapter, you will read the true stories of two people with borderline disorder. I hope that these stories will help you understand that you are not alone. They are personal and have great meaning to me. One is of my sister, Denise. The other story is of "Mrs. Davis," one of my first patients with borderline disorder. In order to maintain confidentiality, I have changed a few details in her story. These details are unimportant to our purposes here, but they might serve to identify her. Although you will see similarities in these stories, there are significant differences as well. Somewhere in them, I think you may recognize some features of your own life.

DENISE

My sister Denise was born a year and a half after I was. I can't recall clearly specific memories of her as a young child. Photos of her during this period, as well as stories told to me by my parents and immediate and extended family, seem to blur out personal recollections. But given the purpose of this story, it's probably more fitting anyway to begin with some of my memories of our mother, who was a central figure in Denise's life.

As I described in Chapter 1, pervasive feelings of emptiness and a negative self-image are among the main symptoms of borderline disorder. In the next chapter, I discuss the early opinions proposed by psychoanalysts that these symptoms are the result of poor nurturing by a mother who was incapable of providing warmth and affection to her children. It's difficult for me to reconcile that proposal with my observations of and experiences with our mother. One of my most vivid memories of her was the way her face would light up whenever she saw one of the family. It made me feel good to my core to be caught in the radiance of Mom's smile and the warmth of her embrace. I would observe her bestow the same love on every member of our family, down to the youngest great-grandchild, and watch them respond as I did. There was never any doubt: Mom loved us all deeply and unequivocally.

Everyone seemed to feel and understand this except Denise, who often appeared uncomfortable with Mom. Of course, my mother knew this too. Later in her life, she tried to explain to me why she thought Denise was often so unhappy and had so many difficulties. She believed that the main cause of Denise's problems was that Mom had received a mild anesthetic during her delivery and that the medicine had affected Denise's brain. She had not been given an anesthetic during the delivery of my older brother or me, and she certainly refused any during the births of our sister and brother who were born after Denise. When I asked Mom why she believed this so strongly, she said it was because Denise behaved differently from the rest of us from the day she was born. She went on to explain that, by comparison, Denise cried more, did not eat as well, was more easily upset by any change in routine, and was more difficult to soothe and comfort when she was upset.

In her early childhood, Denise clung to my mother when relatives or neighbors would visit. She frowned frequently and didn't smile warmly or often. I believe there is only one picture taken of Denise as a child when she was smiling. It was the only childhood picture of her that Mom would display. Years later, Denise told me that as a child she always felt that she was different from the rest of us, that she was more anxious and less happy. She also believed that Mom and Dad loved her less than they loved us, and she resented it.

Denise's difficulties became more apparent as she grew into adolescence. Her disposition and behavior gradually worsened. Most obvious and disruptive to the family were her outbursts of anger that could quickly grow into full-blown episodes of rage. When this occurred, nothing was safe. She would lash out verbally and physically at all of us, including Mom and Dad. My sister Beatrice, younger than Denise by two years, was a frequent target of her anger and abuse. Denise would also throw or break anything at hand, even pieces of Mom's fine china. Particularly disturbing was the fact that no amount of reasoning or appropriate threats of punishment, or even punishment itself, seemed to have any effect on these or future outbreaks. If anything, appropriate discipline seemed to make the situation worse. To the rest of us children, it appeared there were two standards of behavior in the family: one for us and the more lenient standard for Denise.

Not surprisingly, the family thought Denise was simply willful, and we hoped that she would grow out of it. We were worried, though, because she also had episodes of anxiety accompanied by complaints of severe stomach cramps that prevented her from attending school. When Denise was anxious, she would wring her hands and twist and pull strands of her hair to the point that she developed bare spots on her scalp. The doctor reassured my parents that Denise was just "high-strung."

When I think back on those years, I remember vividly two incidents that changed my impression of, and my attitude toward, Denise. We were in our mid-teens when they occurred. At the time of the first, it was winter, and there was snow on the ground. I was cleaning my golf clubs in preparation for the spring, but one was missing. I looked everywhere in the house—no club. Denise walked by, so I asked her if she had seen it. She calmly said yes; she had broken it in two and thrown the pieces into the snow behind the house. It seemed we had argued over something a few weeks earlier, and she had done it then. At first, I thought she was taunting me. She knew that I had worked and saved to buy those clubs. Surely no one would do such a thing, not even Denise. Then I remembered the broken china. Even though to me, at that age, there was little comparison between the value of a golf club and fine china, I knew how much my mother valued the china. Later, when the snow melted and I found the broken club, I realized that something was truly different about Denise, and that it was probably best not to provoke her in any way, for any reason.

My impression that Denise had serious problems was reinforced a few months later. In the midst of a big argument with Mom, Denise impulsively announced that she was leaving home. This was a new threat, so Mom didn't know how to handle it. Not that it would have made any difference, because Denise was out the door in a few moments. When she didn't come home for dinner that evening, my mother and father left in the car to find her. Given the drastic lengths to which she would go when angry, I didn't think they would locate her until she was ready to return home. That turned out to be two days later. Denise had found a small church that remained open all night, and she stayed there, existing only on water. She then came home and explained where she had been, and life went on as before. Denise was about fifteen years old at the time. After that, I attempted to not have any serious arguments with Denise. Possibly in part because of this, as the years passed we grew close to one another.

One of the things that perplexed us about Denise was how well she seemed to do between her episodes. During these periods of relative calm, she would excel in school, be pleasant, caring, and even fun at home, get along with her friends, and became a member of her high school cheerleading team. Yet it all hung on a thread. Within moments, it could be gone. At her best, Denise was bright, creative, sensitive, attractive, and intent on doing good things for others. What a shame it was that she could not remain at that level consistently.

Denise tried many ways to hang on, to stabilize her life. After high school, she commuted with Dad to New York City to work for the same company as he did for about a year. That seemed to go fairly well for a while, but eventually she became bored and dissatisfied. Her demons were still plaguing her.

Ultimately, Denise decided she needed a quieter, more structured and disciplined life. So, at the age of nineteen, she entered a Catholic convent (this was in about 1957). Because of communication restrictions during the first year, Mom and Dad received a letter from her, and visits with her were limited to once a month each. As I read her letters later, it occurred to me that this may have been the most tranquil period of her life. After five months in the convent, Denise wrote to us:

"It just doesn't seem possible that it's been that long since I left home, and yet in other ways it seems to me that I've never known or could ever hope for any other life than this. Not that I haven't missed you either, on the contrary, it seems that I love, appreciate and feel much closer to you all now than I ever did at home. I've found so much peace and happiness here."

A year after she entered the convent, she sent the following note to Dad as a "Spiritual Bouquet."

Dear Daddy,

After living with you for approximately nineteen years, it was only last summer, traveling back and forth with you (to and from work) and visiting you at odd moments during the day that I came to really know and love you.

I've often told you since last September that I think of you and pray for you every day. Well, it's true, I do, and when I think of you I realize I love you so much because you're so like God in one of His most loving ways—His completely unselfish love of His children. And since He has promised that as you've done to the least of His brethren (your family) as do you also to Him, you can be assured Daddy of a place in Heaven very close to the heart of God.

Prayerfully, in the Sacred Hearts of Jesus and Mary,

Your loving daughter, Sister Denise

Three months later, the letters stopped in accordance with the regulation of the convent to limit outside communication during the second year of training. Though she remained in the convent that year, there is no record of what she was thinking or feeling during this period. Then, one year before taking her final vows, Denise concluded that her life in the convent was too restricted, and she returned home.

At this point, Denise decided that she would like to be a teacher. In spite of her lack of formal baccalaureate and postbaccalaureate education and training, she was appointed to a position in a Catholic grade school badly in need of teachers. Denise also dated, but she was not happy with herself or with her life for very long. She had a close but troubled relationship with one young man of whom she was fond. However, after about a year, he broke it off. Within six months, at the age of twenty-three, Denise decided to accept a proposal of marriage from a man she had known since her mid-teens.

Denise's marriage and relationship with her husband seemed to provide her with some stability for several years, until their first child was born. Although she worked hard at being a good wife and mother, over time the responsibilities and stresses were too great. She lacked the resilience to meet them. The episodes of anger, anxiety, and depression returned. Arguments with her husband increased to the point that they separated soon after the birth of their second child. Denise took the two children and lived with our parents. But within a year, she returned to her husband, and they soon had a third child.

By this time, Denise was about thirty years old. I had married; my wife and I had four children, and I was in residency training in psychiatry at Duke University, some five hundred miles away from Denise and our childhood home. The phone calls from her began during this period. Two sentences into the first of these calls, I realized that Denise was in serious trouble. Her voice was a low monotone, devoid of life or enthusiasm. On occasion, she had suffered from several days of depressed mood when something had gone badly for her, but this was different. Denise offered little information spontaneously. I had to ask her questions to keep the conversation going.

After a few minutes, I noticed that Denise was slurring her words slightly, so I asked her if she had been drinking. She said she had had a few glasses of wine. She gradually revealed that she had become increasingly depressed over the prior few months and was now suicidal. After much coaxing, and a discussion with her husband, Denise agreed to go to the hospital, where she could obtain safe and proper care. She seemed well enough to return home after two weeks, though she was far from recovered.

From that time on, it was rare that a month passed and I didn't receive a phone call similar to the one I just described. Denise began psychotherapy, but the psychiatrist, as was then common, had not received any specific training in borderline disorder, and Denise made little improvement. The only antidepressants available at that time caused her to gain weight, which she hated. They also made her suspicious, and sometimes even paranoid, so she refused to take them. According to her husband, she was now drinking daily and beginning to neglect the children and the house, though until then she had been a fastidious housekeeper and a loving mother. The situation was deteriorating so rapidly that I suggested to Denise and her husband that she come to visit my family so that she might undergo an evaluation at Duke. She agreed.

One of the senior faculty in the department of psychiatry, a man whose clinical skills I admired greatly, evaluated Denise. He told her that she needed to stop drinking for several weeks so that he could examine her thoroughly and arrive at a more valid diagnosis. She did so, but the depression did not improve. Because Denise had failed to respond to multiple antidepressants, her psychiatrist suggested a course of electroconvulsive therapy (ECT).

ECT is most often used for patients who have severe depression or manic episodes and who don't respond to medications, or for whom medications cause serious side effects. A course of ECT typically consists of eight or more individual treatments. During each treatment, patients are administered a quick-acting anesthetic, and then a carefully controlled amount of electric current is applied to the head, resulting in an intentional seizure of controlled severity and duration. The muscle contractions associated with the seizure are eliminated by the simultaneous use of a muscle relaxant. It's not known how ECT causes its therapeutic effect, but it is somewhat comparable to applying electric current to the chest of a person who is having a medication-resistant cardiac arrest or arrhythmia to restore normal heart rhythm. After a course of ECT, Denise's depression improved considerably, and she seemed to be herself again, so she returned home.

Again, Denise appeared to do well. At the age of thirty-four, she and our younger sister, Beatrice, enrolled in a local community college to obtain nursing degrees. It was during this period that Denise wrote a number of poems, a few of which were published. The following one suggests that she was still struggling each day, but with considerable insight.

IDENTITY

Because mother's she—I'm me.
Because father's he—I'm me.
Because of them, I am what I am,
In spite of them, I am me.

Because of my schooling—I'm me.
Because of church ruling—I'm me.
Because of the norm, obey and conform,
In spite of the norm, I am me.

Because of three wars—I'm me.
Because of bomb lore—I'm me.
Because of the fear, year after year,
In spite of the fear, I am me.

Because of the times—I'm me.
Because of the clime—I'm me.
Because of the pall, wrapped over this ball,
In spite of the pall, I am me.

Because there is caring—I'm me.
Because there is sharing—I'm me.
Because there is fate, indifference and hate,
In spite of my fate, I am me.

Accepting, rejecting the mold.
Accepting, rejecting don't fold.
Accepting, rejecting man and his earth.
Is this all I am, all I'm worth?

Within this sum total I see
A more basic awareness that's me
To be fought for each day, lest it wither away,
The true me—if I want to be free . . .

Denise graduated at the top of her class and gave the valedictory address. She worked as a nurse for a few years, but then the slow, relentless slide began.

When Denise was in her late thirties, I received a phone call similar to those of a decade before—same tone of voice, but the words were more slurred. We talked, and she promised to stop drinking, though she believed there was no point to it. She did stop drinking for a while, but even then she was barely holding on. Her husband and children were withdrawing from her, and she felt increasingly abandoned.

At these times, Denise would contact Mom, who lived nearby and would do as much as she could to help Denise clean her house and offer her encouragement. Denise would also contact Beatrice, who would also try to help as best she could. It was difficult to know what helped and what didn't. She would have a few good weeks, maybe even one or two months, but overall, the slide continued. Although both Denise's family and ours remained very concerned and distraught, we had no idea of the horrors that awaited Denise and us.

About eleven o'clock on the night of Denise's forty-third birthday, I received a phone call from my mother. (Dad had died some nine years earlier.) Denise had been out to dinner with her husband and children, celebrating her birthday. She had been drinking since late afternoon. Midway through dinner, she choked on a piece of food. This is not an uncommon event in people who have had too much to drink, because alcohol inhibits the gag reflex. Denise hurriedly went to the ladies' room, signaling she was okay, but was found unconscious on the floor ten minutes later.

Denise was immediately taken to the closest hospital, where she was found to have suffered massive brain damage as the result of a lack of oxygen to her brain. She remained unconscious and was placed on all of the necessary life support systems. A team of neurologists evaluated Denise and gave her husband and the rest of the family the tragic news. Denise would most likely never regain consciousness.

After months of round-the-clock care, Denise was weaned off the respirator and nourished through a feeding tube. She was moved to a long-term care facility where she had worked as a nurse, and the family's vigil continued. The entire family would visit regularly, but my mother would go to see Denise every day, bathe her, change her nightgown, and talk to her softly. Indications that only the deepest survival systems of her brain functioned were the regular, autonomous beat of her heart, her breathing, and the occasional contortions of her muscles, including those of her face that made her appear to be smiling or grimacing in pain.

It was impossible to persuade Mom to take a day off. She spent a large part of each visit praying for Denise's recovery. Mom said that being with Denise was not a burden. Actually, she said, she was finally able to give Denise the love and care she had always tried to extend but that Denise had resisted. Months passed with no positive change. Instead, her general condition deteriorated gradually but noticeably.

It is a measure of the agony and desperation experienced by the loved ones of people so afflicted that my brothers, sister, and I began to discuss our own thoughts and feelings about what should be done. Other than me, Denise's family and most of our family lived in northern New Jersey at the time. The legal debates about the fate of Karen Ann Quinlan had recently concluded with the decision by the New Jersey Supreme Court to allow the removal of extraordinary life support systems from people who are brain-dead. Therefore, this alternative was fresh in our minds. During the period surrounding our father's death years before, Denise herself had mentioned that she would never want extraordinary measures taken to keep her alive if she were brain-dead.

Ultimately, we decided to speak with Denise's husband. He and the three children, now teenagers, were suffering terribly. I can only imagine the toll it was taking on each of them. With great reluctance, he revealed that he thought Denise's feeding tube should be removed. He knew this would result in Denise's death, but he was increasingly concerned about the children. We told him we supported his belief and offered to approach our mother with him.

Mother prayed, spoke with the priest, and agonized over the issue. With great emotional pain, she agreed that it was cruel to her children and to Denise to allow Denise to die by inches in front of their eyes. We were now in agreement about what needed to be done, but we did not realize that the legal and moral problems were to be decided by others.

There were two major difficulties. First, Denise was under the care of a devout physician in a Catholic hospital. He and the administration of the hospital opposed our decision on moral grounds. We were forced to hire a lawyer in order to obtain relief from the court. Second, the Quinlan decision did not provide a crystal-clear precedent in cases such as Denise's.

The entire family testified in open court, and the newspapers carried the story. The judge spoke with Denise's children. The family testified in court verifying Denise's wishes regarding not wanting any extraordinary measures to be taken to keep her alive if there was no hope for recovery. Our plea to the court was unanimous: "Declare her incompetent and make her husband legal guardian. Allow this suffering to end." The judge granted the petition but did not rule specifically on the removal of the feeding tube. Although asked to remove it by her husband, the doctor refused. Denise died seven months later at the age of forty-five. She was in a coma for one year and eight months from the time of her accident until the time of her death.

I thought another perspective on Denise would be of value, so I asked Beatrice to write some of her own memories. Beatrice was closer to Denise in many ways than my brothers and I were.

Denise was two and a half years older than I. In order to understand our relationship, you have to know my personality and my place in the family. I was fourth of five children, the second girl, and had two older brothers and one younger.

My parents and grandparents told me I was a happy and contented child from the moment I was born. Relatives and strangers gravitated toward me, and I loved my parents and siblings.

In retrospect, I now realize that on some level I was aware of the upheaval in the family caused by my sister's temper and that I always tried to make everyone laugh to ease the tensions of the moment. My personality became very accommodating because of Denise's flare-ups. I became the peacemaker.

I believe that my sister loved me deeply, but her feelings were conflicted as we grew up. During her "healthy" periods she was a loving, nurturing person who gave me great advice and would even iron my clothes for me when I wanted to go out. She was a joy during these times, a wonderful older sister for whom I would do anything.

However, I wasn't always aware of the changes taking place when her dark side would emerge. Sometimes I would borrow an article of clothing without asking first. She never said a word. But later I would discover that one of my favorite skirts or blouses had disappeared. I quickly learned not to cross her. As we grew older and entered high school, we were not close. On weekends, I would stay at one of my friend's homes, while Denise slept all day in our room with the shades drawn.

Later, when our children were young, we did have good years. We were as close as you could be with Denise, but she hated separations. If I were planning one for whatever reason, she would begin her own separation from me days or even weeks before I left.

Together we entered nursing school, when I was thirty-two and she was thirty-four. She excelled and was a highly motivated, A student, while I was a B+ average student and not nearly as dedicated or zealous. From 1972 to January 1975, we drove together in her car and spent four to eight hours at school, where we developed a nice group of friends in labs and at lunch. Things appeared to be quite normal, but then in February 1975, just a short time before we were scheduled to graduate, without a word or phone call, she failed to pick me up one day. I finally got to class that day, only to find Denise sitting in her usual seat. She never looked up or acknowledged my arrival. After class, when I tried to approach her, she ignored me and walked out without a word. Calls to her home later went unanswered. While I attended the "capping" ceremony held by the nursing school, I did not attend the graduation exercises where Denise gave the valedictorian's address. We both began working at the same hospital that fall, but never addressed what had happened at school. Before long we slipped back into our old sister routine—I gave of myself; Denise took what she wanted and rejected everything else.

Denise became a highly respected nurse, specializing in geriatrics, and was loved by her patients.

As the years passed, Denise gradually drank more and more routinely and heavily. She began to call me at all hours of the night, and I would listen to her incoherent rantings until she hung up. Then she began to call to tell me she was going to commit suicide. I would rush over to her home to find her overdosed on drugs or, on several occasions, with her wrists slashed. She was hospitalized after these episodes, with little apparent improvement.

Just before her forty-third birthday she became very angry with our mother, refusing to see her or even talk to her. My mother was terribly hurt, and I could hear the anguish in her voice when she called me. I realized how futile it would be to try to change Denise's mindset, but I called her anyway to tell her that if she could not give Mother the time she deserved, I would no longer have time for her. I told her not to call me again.

She never did. At dinner celebrating her birthday she choked on a sparerib. Rather than cause a scene in the restaurant, she went to the ladies' room, where she collapsed. Deprived of oxygen, she had a seizure, and when she arrived at the hospital forty or so minutes later, she was declared to be brain-dead, and put on a respirator.

Denise had so much to give, and when able, she gave it with generosity of spirit. Although everyone in our family often worried about her and sometimes were angry with her, we knew she suffered greatly through her life, and we loved her deeply. No one in our family emerged without emotional scars. She died much too young, and I still miss her greatly.

MRS. DAVIS

Specialty training in psychiatry typically begins with clinical rotations on psychiatric inpatient units. Here, the **residents** (physicians enrolled in a formal training program in a medical specialty) are responsible for much of the daily care of patients, under the supervision of a member of the faculty.

After spending a year and a half to two years of training on a number of inpatient services specializing in psychiatric disorders, psychiatry residents continue their education in the psychiatry outpatient clinics. It is in these clinics that residents learn to treat patients who are chronically ill but don't require inpatient care. A very important part of this training is learning the skills of various types of psychotherapy. **Psychodynamic psychotherapy** involves learning and applying a specific body of knowledge about complex psychological processes and behaviors. To learn these skills, a resident must engage simultaneously in two tasks: first, a series of seminars and readings on the topic, and second, the treatment of patients using the knowledge the resident has acquired, all under the careful direction and supervision of a member of the faculty. Not all psychiatric patients are suitable candidates for psychodynamic psychotherapy. Therefore, residents must carefully select a few patients, from among those assigned to them in the clinic, who they believe would benefit from this type of psychotherapy.

I was a resident involved in this process when I first met Mrs. Davis. She came to the Duke Psychiatric Clinic, which was staffed by residents, because she couldn't afford the regular fees of a fully trained therapist. When I first interviewed Mrs. Davis, she was a twenty-two-year-old medical technician and the wife of a first-year law student. She was a well-groomed, nicely dressed, and attractive young lady who was in mild to moderate distress, mainly from anxiety. During the initial interview, she told me that she was seeking help for frequent episodes of anxiety and depression.

Mrs. Davis said that she had experienced these problems off and on since her early teens. However, they had increased in frequency and severity since she and her husband had moved, three months earlier, from a city in the Midwest so that her husband could enter law school. They were married a few months prior to the move, and she had never been that far from her family for such an extended period. Mrs. Davis had been hired at Duke Hospital, and she and her husband depended on the income to pay their bills. She had finished her training a few months before her marriage, and this was her first full-time job.

As I took and recorded Mrs. Davis's medical history and performed a psychiatric examination, I detected no indications of psychotic episodes or behaviors suggesting a lack of self-control. She was intelligent, appeared insightful and reasonable, and was intent on finding out why she suffered from anxiety and depression and on making whatever changes necessary to live a better life. In short, Mrs. Davis seemed to be an ideal patient for psychodynamic psychotherapy. I reviewed my notes with my faculty supervisor, who suggested that projective psychological tests might help determine if we were missing something important.

There are several categories of psychological tests that are used to evaluate an individual's psychological status. Projective tests are employed to gain insight into a person's areas of concern and internal conflict, and to determine the types of psychological adaptations or "defenses" that they typically use to deal with life's challenges (an indication of their resilience). Some of these psychological coping patterns are more effective than others. In other words, some people can tolerate more psychological stress than others before developing symptoms such as anxiety, depression, and even more primitive symptoms such as paranoid thinking. The two most frequently used tests of this type at that time were the Thematic Apperception Test (TAT) and the Rorschach test. The TAT consists of a set of thirty pictures depicting one or more individuals. The patient is asked to make up a story based on each picture. The Rorschach is the well-known inkblot test.

Mrs. Davis readily agreed to the testing. Afterward, I met with the psychologist who had administered and interpreted these tests, a senior faculty member with an excellent reputation. The examining psychologist reviewed the results with me and assured me that she could not determine a reason to avoid using psychodynamic psychotherapy in the treatment of Mrs. Davis.

With these assurances, I reviewed with Mrs. Davis the ground rules of therapy. It was expected that she come to every fifty-minute session twice a week and that she come on time. It was also expected that Mrs. Davis, to the best of her ability, talk about whatever came to her mind, no matter how painful or difficult and without editing her thoughts. Additionally, Mrs. Davis was expected to pay the clinic charges each month. I believe they were one dollar per session.

In turn, I explained that my responsibilities in therapy were to be there on time for every session, and to listen to and record carefully what she had to say. Finally, I told her that we had a mutual responsibility, in the last ten or fifteen minutes of each session, to attempt to understand the meanings of what she had talked about that day. I indicated that early in treatment, I would probably make more comments (interpretations) of the information than she did, but that she would become more skilled in the process as treatment progressed.

Our work together began with both of us slowly learning the process of psychotherapy. Each week I met with my supervisor and read to him every word Mrs. Davis had said that I was able to record, plus my rare comments and questions during the session. I also reported our thoughts on the meaning of the material that Mrs. Davis and I discussed prior to the termination of each session. My supervisor would then try to help me to understand better the different conscious and unconscious layers of meaning of my patient's words and the themes of the sessions.

Everything appeared to go well for about six weeks. Then, during a session that seemed initially no more remarkable than any other, Mrs. Davis increasingly expressed suspicions of her section head at work, her husband, and finally me. She claimed that the three of us were conspiring against her and that I had broken my pledge to her of confidentiality. No amount of reassurance that I had not spoken with either person made any difference. Mrs. Davis was becoming paranoid and increasingly agitated right before my eyes. There had been no warning signs that I could detect with my limited knowledge and skills. I vividly recall being surprised, confused, and more than a little anxious. What had caused this response in my patient?

I quickly tried to divert Mrs. Davis's attention from her paranoid thoughts to routine issues at work and at home. Remarkably, within about five minutes, she began to calm down and became much less suspicious. By the end of the session, Mrs. Davis seemed no different from the way she was when the session began. She assured me she was fine. After careful consideration, I thought it safe for her to leave.

Fortunately, I was scheduled to meet with my supervisor later that day. He listened carefully to my report, asked me several questions, then sat back in his chair, and reflected on what had occurred. A few minutes later, he leaned toward me and gently said, "Welcome to the mysterious world of borderline personality disorder." He went on to tell me about the characteristics of the disorder, as well as they were known in the late 1960s. I don't recall having heard of the diagnosis before then, in spite of my many rotations on the inpatient services. He told me to go to the medical school library and do some serious and extensive reading on borderline disorder before my next therapy session with Mrs. Davis.

This reading assignment was not an easy chore. The usual sources of information were of little help. Most of the leading psychiatric textbooks at that time contained minimal useful information. The American Psychiatric Association's *Diagnostic and Statistical Manual of Mental Disorders*, then in its second edition (DSM-II), did not even include the disorder. I was left with the time-consuming prospect of performing a literature search from primary sources, that is, from original articles in scientific journals and the rare academic books written about the disorder.

My initial readings of this material left me confused about the diagnosis of borderline disorder and somewhat discouraged about the prognosis for Mrs. Davis. There was no clear agreement among a number of experts about what symptoms defined borderline disorder. A few even referred to the disorder as "a wastebasket diagnosis for patients who do not meet criteria for any other disorder," which may have been why the DSM-II did not include borderline disorder. As confusing as this was, there was even less clarity about the specific treatments for borderline disorder, other than **psychoanalysis**, which was considered to be ineffective by most authors and even harmful by some.

I returned to report my findings to my supervisor and to ask for his guidance before my next visit with Mrs. Davis. From what I had read, I knew that her brief break with reality in our therapy session occurred in some patients with borderline disorder who were treated with psychodynamic psychotherapy or psychoanalysis. Indeed, it was one of the hallmarks of the disorder, in the view of some clinicians. Clearly, the significant change in Mrs. Davis's diagnosis indicated that a different therapeutic approach was necessary. My supervisor instructed me to reduce the number of our therapy visits to one a week and to change to supportive psychotherapy. He also suggested that I be careful about the use of medications, as they were rarely helpful for patients with borderline disorder and might make her worse.

And so our work together began again. First, I had to speak with Mrs. Davis about her potential new diagnosis and our change in treatment strategy. I was uncertain how to raise the issue of the diagnosis, as I was concerned it would make her more anxious, especially because I was unable to clearly describe to her the confusing diagnostic and therapeutic problems. However, I thought it best to tell her what I had learned about the disorder and deal with the results as well as we could. Second, we would then discuss the changes in treatment.

When we met next, I told Mrs. Davis what information I had gathered. Initially, she was frightened and upset. Then, to her credit, after some discussion she calmed down, and we talked about the possible changes in treatment. We reduced the frequency and changed the type of therapy. I suggested that we meet only once a week and focus on those issues that currently were most relevant in her life, with less emphasis on her past. I explained that I would ask more questions and make more comments during the session, and that we would focus on problem-solving strategies. Then I raised the possibility of using a little medicine, if it seemed appropriate at some time in the future. Mrs. Davis agreed to the change in therapy but was concerned about medication. I told her we would not rush into the use of a medication but wait until we had more information. That was fine with her.

As therapy progressed, I slowly gained a clearer picture of the complexity of Mrs. Davis's problems. A pattern gradually emerged from the ways she dealt with her daily life, her relationship with her husband, challenges at work, and her "homesickness." For example, as we knew, she was often angry with her husband for not devoting more time to her in the evening and on weekends, rather than studying the law. This was a main source of many arguments with him. In part, she understood that he needed to study to do well in school. However, she had difficulty in resolving her conflicting feelings about this issue, as she was rarely able to overcome the empty feeling that this caused and the fear that he didn't care about her. These feelings would grow stronger and stronger, until she reached the point where she was extremely angry and desperate for attention.

Occasionally, at these times, Mrs. Davis would go to the airport, fly back home, and have a two- or three-day affair with an old boyfriend from college. She told me after one of these impulsive trips that this young man was very kind to her, appreciated her, and spent quite a bit of time with her. Then she and I discussed the consequences of this trip on her relationship with her husband—and on her job if she left during the workweek. We also discussed what alternatives were available to her to deal with her loneliness and sense of desperation in ways that were not harmful.

It took many months of work in therapy for us to recognize when Mrs. Davis was at greatest risk for making these trips. We struggled to help her find better ways to deal with her feelings of rejection by her husband, the sense of abandonment, and other feelings that put her at risk. Also, she and I agreed that she would call me at any time of the day or night *before* she left. But nothing seemed to help.

Another recurring problem was Mrs. Davis's relationship with her section head at work. As Mrs. Davis described her, the supervisor seemed to be a well-intentioned, competent, and highly motivated woman, but one who ran a pretty tight ship. Mrs. Davis consistently perceived her as being nonsupportive and overly critical. Mrs. Davis's responses to any real or perceived criticisms from her were either sullen withdrawal or temper outbursts. She told me that during one such incident, in a fit of uncontrollable anger, she went to the hospital parking lot to look for her section head's car so that she could put a few dents in it. Fortunately, she could not find it. As usual, she and I discussed the incidents leading up to the outburst of anger, how much she needed the job, and alternative ways of dealing with these situations. Again, Mrs. Davis understood the issues involved, but this did not seem to have any clear effect on how she felt or how she behaved. By now, I was getting a little desperate myself, because her behaviors were understandably placing both her marriage and her job in great jeopardy. My therapy supervisor was supportive but could not offer me any treatment alternatives. He did counsel me to not become discouraged and to press on in therapy with my patient.

At this point, I recalled a patient I had treated the previous year on the inpatient service. This man, a dentist, suffered from recurring anxiety attacks so severe that he was left unable to work or even to care for himself. Psychotherapy did not reduce these episodes, nor did the usual anti-anxiety agents or antidepressants available at the time. Therefore, he required frequent short-term hospitalizations until he was functional again. Because he had never been tried on a major tranquilizer (we now refer to them as **antipsychotic agents**), I proposed to my faculty supervisor then that we do so, but at very low doses. The treatment worked well, reducing this patient's symptoms and the number of hospitalizations, as well as improving his work performance. I describe this patient in more detail at the end of Chapter 10.

Based on that experience, I thought that this class of medications (antipsychotic agents), in very low doses, might help Mrs. Davis bring her behavior under better control, although this result had not been resolved in the scientific literature. I raised the issue with Mrs. Davis and told her that I had reviewed the scientific journals thoroughly, searching for some help for her. Most studies on the use of these medications at doses higher than I proposed reported negative results in people with borderline disorder and were very pessimistic. Medications just did not seem to help people with this disorder. If anything, many people with borderline disorder abused the anti-anxiety agents (then called minor tranquilizers) such as Valium, Librium, and meprobamate. The standard doses of antidepressants and antipsychotic agents typically produced only intolerable side effects.

However, because of my experience the year before, I suggested to Mrs. Davis that it may be worth trying a very low dose of a major tranquilizer, especially because she had experienced one break with reality early in her treatment with me. She asked more about the medicine and then said "absolutely no" when I told her that the class of medicine I was recommending was usually used for people who suffered from schizophrenia or severe manic-depressive (bipolar) disorder, although at much higher doses.

Therapy continued for several more months with little improvement. Then, for reasons that are still unclear to me, Mrs. Davis agreed to try the medicine. After carefully describing the potential side effects of the medication, I started her on a very low dose of a medicine called Stelazine (trifluoperazine), one milligram each morning. The usual dose of this medicine is twenty to forty milligrams a day. After one week, she reported she felt a little less anxious and angry. We waited another week. There was no further improvement, so we increased the dose to two milligrams a day. She then reported a noticeable decrease in her emotional reactions, angry outbursts, and impulsive behaviors, and some improvement in her ability to have fairly calm and reasonable discussions with her husband about their problems.

Our first breakthrough in psychotherapy occurred not too long thereafter. She called me late one night from the airport just before boarding the plane for one of her trips. She had never done that before. We talked for some time about the events that had occurred over the previous few days, the consequences of her leaving, the need for an emergency therapy session the next day, and anything else I could think of to keep her off that plane. Finally, she agreed to return home and to see me the next day. She made very few unscheduled flights after that.

Progress in other areas also occurred. There were fewer flare-ups at work, and she missed fewer days resulting from severe headaches and other physical symptoms of stress. Her impulsive buying sprees, another source of difficulty at home, decreased in frequency and degree. She seemed better able to recall and apply the work we did in therapy.

As Mrs. Davis progressed in therapy, she would report the impulsive things she had thought of doing but had not yet done. "Before I do it, I can hear you say, 'Well, what problems are you currently encountering in your life, what are your alternative solutions, and what are their consequences?' Then you will ask, 'Which one do you think is the best choice?' So now I try to figure that all out before I see you, and try to do it."

After another year in therapy, Mrs. Davis reached the point where her emotions had stabilized quite well, and most of her decisions were appropriate. Mrs. Davis and her husband had worked out a mutually satisfactory relationship; she was doing well at work, and she no longer felt as desperate living so far from her parents. She had made a number of friends at Duke and in her neighborhood.

I suggested that we gradually reduce the frequency of therapy sessions, but was careful to let Mrs. Davis know that we could always increase them again if needed. In another year she was seeing me only for medication checks, when she had a problem that needed my help, or just to touch base with me to assure herself that I was available if necessary. (By then, I had completed my training and was a member of the faculty at Duke.) This pattern of treatment continued for several more years. I then accepted a faculty position at the University of Washington in Seattle. I was fully aware by now of the extraordinary sensitivity that Mrs. Davis, and other people with borderline disorder, have to separations. Therefore, months before I was scheduled to move, I asked her to come in to discuss my leaving. We spent the next few months working through her feelings and concerns about my departure. I recommended a few of my colleagues to her so that she could continue her medicine and get other help when needed. Fortunately, she seemed to feel comfortable with one of these psychiatrists and permitted me to brief him on our work together.

I still think of Mrs. Davis from time to time, hope that she and her family are doing well, and remain very grateful for all that we learned together about borderline disorder.

I think you may now understand why these two stories are important to me. Although there are similarities in them, the outcomes are very different. Denise's illness was not treated successfully and ultimately resulted in her premature death. Now it would not have to be that way. I wonder what course Denise's life would have taken if she had received the medications and therapy now available for people with borderline disorder. Most were not available to patients at that time. Denise also eventually turned to alcohol in an attempt to reduce her suffering. Mrs. Davis did not reach this level of desperation. This was a critical difference, as we will discuss later in this book.

If you receive proper help, it is very unlikely that you will reach Denise's level of desperation. You have a much better opportunity to receive effective treatment for your disorder than has ever been available before. Chapters 10–12 discuss the treatment processes involved in making this happen. However, in order to make full use of the information on treatment, it will be helpful for you to learn more about the history, causes, and nature of borderline disorder.

THREE

The History of
Borderline Personality Disorder

W HEN MY PATIENTS AND I ARRIVE AT THE DIAGNOSIS OF borderline disorder, they become quite concerned about the meaning of the name of the disorder and its nature. It's not uncommon for them to have researched the topic online and come across terms like "borderline psychotic," "borderline schizophrenia," and "**pre-schizophrenia**." Understandably, these terms can be frightening and therefore require an explanation.

The meanings of the term "borderline" and the diagnostic criteria of borderline disorder have changed considerably over the past eighty years. Borderline psychotic, borderline schizophrenia, and pre-schizophrenia, as well as other terms and different definitions of borderline, have been used at some point during this evolution. In this chapter, I trace the development of the main concepts about the diagnostic characteristics of borderline disorder to distinguish those ideas that have stood the test of time from those that have been discarded as the result of further experience and research. I also contrast the concepts of the main diagnostic issues involving borderline disorder with those currently under review by experts in the area.

I realize that some of the material in this chapter at first may seem a bit abstract and not particularly relevant to dealing with the problems that borderline disorder causes in your life. Trust me here for a while, as I will continue to use and build on this information in many of the chapters that follow. I believe that the effort you devote to learning as much as you can about borderline disorder ultimately will be well rewarded by your gaining a great deal more control over your life than you have experienced in the past. In most areas of life, knowledge is the edge that gives you an advantage.

THE EVOLUTION OF THE DIAGNOSIS
OF BORDERLINE DISORDER

The term borderline personality disorder came into official use in 1980, when it was included in the third edition of the *Diagnostic and Statistical Manual of Mental Disorders* (DSM-III). However, the symptoms of the disorder have been recognized for almost three thousand years.

The late Theodore Millon, a psychologist at the University of Miami and Harvard, and an expert in the evaluation of personality and personality disorders, uncovered a number of early historical literary and medical references that describe individuals with symptoms we would now consider to be consistent with borderline disorder. Some of these descriptions appear in the writings of Homer, Hippocrates, and Aretaeus. Aretaeus is renowned for his symptomatic description of diseases and his diagnostic skills. More recently, Theophile Bonet in 1684, Samuel Schacht and Ernst Herschel in the eighteenth century, and Jules Baillarger, the Fabrets, and Karl Kahlbaum in the nineteenth century described medical conditions that closely resemble borderline disorder. However, during this period, there was no consistent descriptive or diagnostic term for the behavior of these patients.

In the early decades of the twentieth century, there was a modest increase in attention by the medical community to those individuals for whom we now use the diagnosis of borderline disorder. In 1921, the German psychiatrist Emil Kraepelin, noted for his brilliant work in describing and classifying mental disorders, defined a group of patients who demonstrated the core symptoms of borderline disorder. Two years later, the European psychiatrist Kurt Schneider provided another description of patients who now would probably be diagnosed with the disorder.

THE PSYCHOANALYTIC ORIGINS OF BORDERLINE DISORDER

Simultaneously, the psychoanalytic concepts of the Viennese neurologist and psychiatrist Sigmund Freud, the founder of psychoanalysis, were dominant in American psychiatry. It is not surprising, therefore, that psychoanalysts made the next significant contributions to our understanding of borderline disorder.

During this period, psychoanalysts recognized a population of patients that did not fit into any existing diagnostic category. These patients were treated with psychoanalysis because they initially appeared to suffer from anxiety, depression, and other symptoms that were thought to be **neurotic** in origin. At that time, all mental disorders that did not have psychotic symptoms fell into the category of neuroses. Although patients with the symptoms of borderline disorder at first appeared the same as neurotic patients, their therapists noticed several important differences as treatment progressed. For example, some of these patients developed psychotic features for brief periods during and outside of treatment. In addition, they did not seem to improve from psychoanalysis. Although they appeared to understand the meanings of the information and the general concepts that arose in treatment, and did seem to improve at times, the improvement was temporary. So, if progress did occur, relapses were commonplace and usually complete.

Based on these experiences, some psychoanalysts began to report their observations in the medical literature. In doing so, they speculated on the diagnostic category, nature, and causes of the disorder that affected these patients. It was during this period that terms like "borderline **psychosis**," "pre-schizophrenia," "**pseudoneurotic schizophrenia**," and "**latent schizophrenia**" emerged in attempts to accurately classify this group of patients. These disorders overlapped at the boundaries

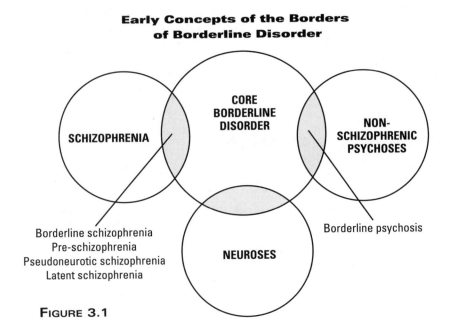

Early Concepts of the Borders of Borderline Disorder

CORE BORDERLINE DISORDER

SCHIZOPHRENIA

NON-SCHIZOPHRENIC PSYCHOSES

NEUROSES

Borderline schizophrenia
Pre-schizophrenia
Pseudoneurotic schizophrenia
Latent schizophrenia

Borderline psychosis

FIGURE 3.1

between the core symptoms of borderline disorder described previously and other disorders (see Figure 3.1). However, no clear consensus developed in the field regarding the proper diagnostic name and criteria, the causes, or the most effective treatments of borderline disorder. Some psychoanalysts at the time even suggested that the borderline diagnosis lacked validity and integrity. They called it a "wastebasket diagnosis" and suggested it was only used because people with these symptoms did not fit neatly into any existing diagnostic classification. Unfortunately, there are still some mental health professionals who don't believe that borderline disorder is a distinct mental illness. The evidence that it is one is contained in the remainder of this chapter, and in other chapters of this book.

Adolph Stern and the Border Line Group

In 1938, in the midst of this confusion, the American psychoanalyst Adolph Stern published a landmark article. In it, he defined what he believed were the main characteristics and nature of borderline disorder;

described why he thought these patients reacted the way they did, both in and out of therapy; and provided modified guidelines for their treatment that he found were more effective than traditional psychoanalysis. Stern referred to these patients as the "border line group." Because of his clear and comprehensive description of these patients, Stern is credited by many as the person most responsible for the popularization of the disorder, defining its major characteristics, and the continued use of "border line" (now "borderline") as a diagnostic term for these patients.

Stern listed ten characteristics of his border line group:

1. Narcissism
2. Psychic bleeding
3. Inordinate hypersensitivity
4. Psychic and body rigidity—"the rigid personality"
5. Negative therapeutic reactions
6. Constitutionally rooted feelings of inferiority, deeply embedded in the personality of the patients
7. Masochism
8. A state of deep organic insecurity or anxiety
9. The use of **projection** mechanisms
10. Difficulties in reality thinking, particularly in personal relationships.

Because Stern's article was written primarily for other psychoanalysts, the meanings of some of these terms are probably not clear to you, but I think it would be helpful for you to understand them as Stern meant them, for several reasons.

First, you'll see a considerable number of similarities between these characteristics and the current diagnostic criteria and characteristics of borderline disorder that I described in Chapter 1. The consistency of the symptoms of borderline disorder over an eighty-year period of careful observation and research provides partial evidence that this diagnosis has validity and integrity.

Second, Stern's article was the first of very few articles that significantly influenced and stimulated later thinking and research on borderline disorder. This is referred to in the research literature as a **seminal article**. For example, when discussing the possible causes of borderline disorder, Stern wrote "this group never develops a sense of security acquired by being loved, which is the birthright of every child. These patients suffer from affective (narcissistic) malnutrition." The word "narcissism" refers to one's capacity to value or love oneself. Those who regard themselves too highly are above the normal range of self-value, and we refer to them as narcissistic. People plagued with chronic self-doubt and poor self-esteem are generally below the normal range of narcissism. The concepts of early parental deprivation and other early traumas were noted by Stern as risk factors for developing borderline disorder. Since then, these concepts have been supported by a number of research studies.

Third, Stern believed that one of the underlying causes of the disorder was an *inherent or inborn tendency* for an individual to develop it. In doing so, he correctly anticipated by fifty years the identification of genetic and other biological risk factors for borderline disorder. The heritability of the disorder is now estimated to be 60 percent, which means the degree to which the symptoms of the disorder are attributable to genetic factors. The remaining 40 percent are attributable to environmental factors, as noted in Chapter 4.

Fourth, Stern believed that identifying the border line group of patients was essential if psychotherapy was to be successful. Although he maintained that psychoanalysis was still possible, he believed several modifications in therapy were required. He stated it was important that the therapist be very supportive of the patient and be very careful not to appear critical. He stressed that attention should be focused on the relationship issues between the patient and therapist, not on historical issues or interpretations of feelings or actions. This meant the issues of excessive dependency, clinging behaviors, unrealistic expectations, and overly negative reactions had to be dealt with consistently and in a non-judgmental manner. Many of these principles are incorporated into the borderline disorder–specific treatments that have been developed over the past several decades (see Chapters 11 and 12).

The following is a description of the characteristics of borderline disorder as Stern defined them in 1938:

1. **Narcissism.** Stern reported that at least 75 percent of his patients in the border line group did not receive wholesome and spontaneous affection from their mothers in the early years of their life. He believed that this, either alone or with other early deprivations, resulted in a fundamental deficit in the self-assurance and self-worth of these patients that made them much more prone to high levels of anxiety in response to stress. Stern considered the anxiety resulting from this fundamental deficit in self-assurance to be "the motor" that produced the other symptoms of patients in the border line group.

2. **Psychic bleeding.** Stern coined this term to describe patients in the border line group who were not resilient to painful and traumatic experiences, who collapsed under pressure.

3. **Inordinate hypersensitivity.** Patients in Stern's border line group were "consistently insulted and injured by trifling remarks . . . and occasionally develop mildly paranoid ideas." He considered the hypersensitivity to be the result of the deeply rooted insecurity in character noted above, which "necessitated undue caution and awareness to danger." This characteristic clearly resembles the symptoms of emotional instability and stress-related paranoid ideation included in the current diagnostic criteria of borderline disorder (Table 1.2 on page 20).

4. **Psychic rigidity or "the rigid personality."** Stern's border line group reacted to external and internal anxiety-producing stress with both physical and psychological rigidity, manifested by repetitious responses of perceptions, thoughts, emotions, physical actions, and pain. He emphasized their lack of tolerance to change and inflexible responses to stress, conditions present from childhood.

5. **Negative therapeutic reactions.** Stern observed that his patients in the border line group operated within a very narrow margin of security. This caused patients to respond with anxiety, anger, discouragement, and depression to any comments by the therapist that they perceived as harmful to their self-esteem. Patients more often reacted negatively (as though they'd been rejected) rather than favorably to potentially helpful discoveries

and comments made by the therapist in therapy. Many therapists are still reluctant to treat patients with borderline disorder because of this common response in therapy. This characteristic is similar to the symptoms of inappropriate anger and affective instability that are current criteria of borderline disorder (Table 1.2 on page 20).

6. **Feelings of inferiority.** According to Stern, patients in the border line group had persistent feelings of inferiority that affected almost the entire personality. These feelings of inferiority were not influenced by any accomplishments, no matter how significant, and created a wide gap between the normal expectations of mature performance and their own perceived abilities. This gap resulted in severe anxiety, protests of inability to perform, and then collapses into inaction.

7. **Masochism.** Stern noticed that self-inflicted harm of all types was prevalent in the personal, professional, and social lives of this group of patients. Self-destructive behaviors and self-injurious or parasuicidal acts ("any non-fatal, serious, deliberate self-harm with or without suicide intent," according to J. M. G. Williams) now constitute diagnostic criteria of borderline disorder (Table 1.2 on page 20).

8. **"Somatic" insecurity or anxiety.** This refers to a lack of self-assurance or self-confidence that appears to have always existed in this group of patients. Stern implies that it appears to be of "somatic"—that is, biological—origin. This inherent deficit would explain the difficulties that patients with borderline disorder have in developing self-assurance through experience, improved performance, and personal growth. This characteristic has some similarities to the criterion on identity disturbance in the current diagnostic criteria for borderline disorder (Table 1.2 on page 20).

9. **The use of projection mechanisms.** In Stern's view, this was the link between people in the border line group with those patients who suffer from psychotic disorders (Figure 3.1). Projection is the unconscious psychological attempt to deal with

anxiety by attributing one's own unacceptable attributes to the outside world. In the border line group, this could result in an expectation of malevolence in others and, when under severe stress, in paranoid thinking. This characteristic is related to the paranoid ideation listed in current diagnostic criteria of borderline disorder (Table 1.2 on page 20).

10. **Difficulties in reality thinking.** Stern suggested that the border line group had considerable difficulty in perceiving their environment accurately and thinking realistically. The chief examples he used to illustrate this difficulty were the distorted attitudes and behaviors of his patients toward the therapist. He found that on the one hand, the border line group viewed the therapist as an omnipotent, all-knowing, and extremely powerful figure who made them feel happy and secure, and to whom they would cling with desperate dependency; on the other hand, they responded very negatively to any clarifying or instructive comments by the therapist, which they usually perceived as an attack on their fragile self-esteem or identity. Under these circumstances, the patients often responded with anxiety, anger, discouragement, and emotional withdrawal from the therapist. You probably recognize these responses as being similar to the pattern of unstable and intense interpersonal relationships that is a current criterion of borderline disorder (Table 1.2 on page 20).

Seven of the nine criteria we now use to diagnose borderline disorder are included in these ten characteristics described by Stern in 1938. I think it's remarkable that he based his conclusions mainly on the sparse medical literature existing then and on his personal clinical observations.

In the decades following Stern's article, a small but growing number of other articles and book chapters about borderline disorder appeared and made significant contributions to the medical literature. I believe you'll find that the evolution of thinking about borderline disorder is an informative and interesting story. At the very least, it will dispel a number of myths about the disorder, especially the myth that there is no validity to the diagnosis of borderline disorder.

Robert Knight and Borderline States

The next major contribution to our recognition and understanding of borderline disorder was made by the psychoanalyst Robert Knight in the 1940s. Knight introduced concepts from the field of **ego psychology** into Stern's psychoanalytic conceptual framework of borderline disorder. Ego psychology addresses those mental processes that enable us to integrate and deal effectively with our thoughts, feelings, and responses to the events of everyday life. These are called **ego functions**.

Knight believed that the ego functions impaired in borderline disorder include emotional regulation; rational thinking; integration of feelings, impulses, and thoughts; realistic planning; successful adaptation to the world around us; involvement in mature relationships; and effectively subduing and rechanneling the energy from primitive and basic impulses. He also believed that other ego functions were spared in borderline disorder, including memory, calculations, and certain habitual performances. We now know that these latter functions are also subtly impaired in individuals with borderline disorder. Knight referred to the symptoms of these patients, and the ego dysfunctions he described, as "borderline states."

Otto Kernberg and Borderline Personality Organization

Two decades later, the American psychoanalyst Otto Kernberg proposed that people with borderline disorder represented a distinct population of individuals who could be defined by the characteristic organization of their personalities. He suggested using a model of mental illness, which was determined by three distinct personality types: *psychotic personality organization*, consisting of individuals predisposed to psychotic disorders such as schizophrenia; *neurotic personality organization*, comprised of those individuals predisposed to less severe mental illnesses such as anxiety and depressive neuroses; and *borderline personality organization*, represented by people who fell between the first two types and show the symptoms that we now refer to as borderline personality disorder. His work further elaborated on Knight's conclusions that borderline personality organization represented fundamental and persistent impairments of ego functions.

In addition, Kernberg remains more optimistic about the effectiveness of modified psychoanalytic psychotherapy for patients with borderline personality than many of his colleagues. He believes that if treated properly in psychoanalysis, positive and lasting changes can be made in the fundamental organization of the personalities of people with the disorder. The combination of Kernberg's model, his optimism about treatment, and his lucid contributions to the medical literature sparked a badly needed increase in interest in borderline disorder among psychiatrists.

HOW BORDERLINE DISORDER BECAME A VALID DIAGNOSIS
Roy Grinker and the Borderline Syndrome

The next important contribution to our understanding of borderline disorder was made by Roy Grinker and his colleagues in 1968. In that year, they published the results of the first **empirical research** involving people with borderline disorder. Rather than base their research on psychoanalytic concepts and strategies, Grinker and his research team decided that verbal and nonverbal behavior are the basic data of scientific psychiatry. So they attempted to describe, classify, and quantify in behavioral terms the ego functions that are disturbed in borderline disorder.

From their data, Grinker and his colleagues concluded that specific impairments of ego function differentiate the "borderline syndrome," as they named it, from other mental disturbances. These ego dysfunctions were manifested in four behavioral characteristics that best identify patients with the disorder. They are: (1) a predominant emotional state of *expressed anger*; (2) a defect in *emotional relationships*; (3) impairments in *self-identity*; and (4) *depressive loneliness*.

The four behavioral characteristics of Grinker's borderline syndrome remain valid criteria of borderline disorder, as you can see from Table 1.2 in Chapter 1. The empirical research of Grinker and his colleagues was critical because it provided a research model for the identification of characteristics of borderline disorder, and it inspired further research to clarify and validate the main diagnostic features of the disorder.

John Gunderson and Borderline Patients/ Borderline Personality Disorder

John Gunderson is a psychiatrist at Harvard's McLean Hospital. His first major contribution to the field of borderline disorder was in 1975, when he published, with Margaret Singer, a critically important article called "Defining Borderline Patients: An Overview." This widely acclaimed article reviewed and synthesized all of the relevant literature that then existed on borderline disorder and redefined the main characteristics of the disorder. The enthusiastic response to the article prompted Gunderson and his colleagues to develop a structured research instrument, the Diagnostic Interview for Borderline Patients (DIB). This instrument enabled researchers around the world to conduct studies with a more homogeneous population of borderline patients than had been possible previously and to more validly compare results from these studies. This was a major research breakthrough, and it stimulated a significant amount of research of all types on borderline disorder.

Much of the initial research conducted by Gunderson and his colleagues focused on defining a set of diagnostic criteria of borderline disorder that clearly distinguished it from other mental disorders.

This work was followed up by a large empirical research study led by Robert Spitzer, a psychiatrist from Columbia University. Together, these studies provided the initial scientific rationale for confirming the validity of borderline disorder and its inclusion in the third edition of the *Diagnostic and Statistical Manual of Mental Disorders* (DSM-III) published in 1980.

This listing of borderline personality disorder (its official name) in DSM-III was the culmination of the efforts of the psychiatrists I have mentioned above, and of others, to define and authenticate the existence of a mental illness that causes much suffering but had not yet received adequate attention by the medical community.

An indication of the growing recognition of borderline disorder as a valid clinical entity is the increasing number of research articles about the disorder in the medical literature. In the mid-1970s, about one hundred peer-reviewed research articles on borderline disorder were cited by the National Library of Medicine. By the mid-1980s, the number had jumped to approximately one thousand articles; in 2004 it was almost three thousand; and as of this writing it is now over eight thousand.

RECENT CHANGES IN THE BORDERS
OF BORDERLINE DISORDER

A major result of the research inspired by Gunderson's diagnostic rating instrument for borderline disorder has been the changes in the borders— the overlap of symptoms—of borderline disorder with other mental disorders. Initially, the borders with schizophrenia and nonschizophrenic psychotic disorders were considered most important (Figure 3.1). This remained the dominant concept until the late 1970s.

Data produced by a number of different research strategies, including genetic, epidemiologic, and descriptive studies, have dramatically altered our thinking in this area. First, it now seems clear that borderline disorder is not related to schizophrenic disorders. Second, borderline disorder appears to have some fundamental, but as yet unknown, connection to or correlation with other mental disorders such as affective disorders (major depressive disorder and **bipolar II disorder**); alcoholism and other substance use disorders; **posttraumatic stress disorder**; **attention deficit hyperactivity disorder (ADHD)**; and other personality disorders, especially **antisocial, schizotypal, histrionic, and narcissistic personality disorders** (see Figure 3.2 for more information). I discuss many of these mental disorders in detail in Chapter 8.

THE NEUROBIOLOGICAL UNDERPINNINGS
OF BORDERLINE DISORDER

In the 1980s, a large number of neuroimaging, biochemical, and genetic studies indicated that borderline disorder is associated with specific neurobiological disturbances in specific neural pathways in the brain (Chapter 7). For example, neuroimaging studies have demonstrated alterations in structure and function in brain areas related to a

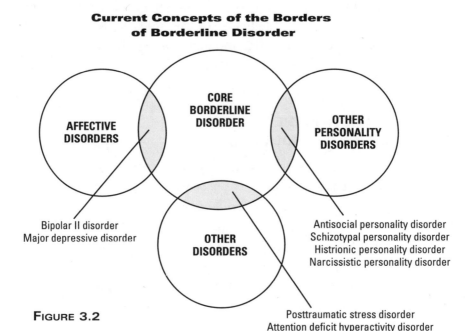

**Current Concepts of the Borders
of Borderline Disorder**

CORE
BORDERLINE
DISORDER

AFFECTIVE
DISORDERS

OTHER
PERSONALITY
DISORDERS

OTHER
DISORDERS

Bipolar II disorder
Major depressive disorder

Antisocial personality disorder
Schizotypal personality disorder
Histrionic personality disorder
Narcissistic personality disorder

FIGURE 3.2

Posttraumatic stress disorder
Attention deficit hyperactivity disorder

number of the symptoms of the disorder, such as emotional response, emotional and behavioral regulation, and thought integration and reasoning. Disturbances in the levels of critical brain **neurotransmitters** and **neuromodulators** have also been identified.

Although the heritability of the different diagnostic traits of borderline disorder varies considerably, the overall heritability of the disorder is estimated at approximately 60 percent. This fact has significant implications for our understanding of the interaction of the genetic and environmental risk factors for each of these diagnostic traits (see Chapter 4).

THE INTRODUCTION OF MEDICATIONS INTO THE TREATMENT OF BORDERLINE DISORDER

In 1979, John Brinkley, Bernard Beitman, and I challenged the prevailing notion that medications were of no value in the treatment of borderline disorder. We provided evidence from five case studies that low doses of **neuroleptics** (now referred to as first-generation antipsychotic agents—FGAs) appeared to be effective in reducing some of its symptoms (see Chapter 10). In 1986, my research team published support for this proposal in the first of two placebo-controlled studies of medications in individuals with borderline disorder.

A similar finding was reported in the subsequent article by Paul Soloff and his colleagues, who used a different neuroleptic agent. Since then, controlled studies of similar agents have supported and extended the original findings. In addition, medications in other classes have been reported to have efficacy in treating the symptoms of borderline disorder (see Chapter 10).

THE INTRODUCTION OF BORDERLINE DISORDER–SPECIFIC PSYCHOTHERAPIES

In 1991, Marsha Linehan introduced dialectical behavior therapy (DBT), a specific and now well-investigated form of psychotherapy for patients with borderline disorder who are prone to self-injurious behaviors and who require and request frequent, brief hospitalizations. Since then, other forms of psychotherapy have been developed that are specifically designed for borderline disorder (Chapter 11).

THE DEVELOPMENT OF ADVOCACY, EDUCATIONAL, AND SUPPORT ORGANIZATIONS FOR INDIVIDUALS WITH BORDERLINE DISORDER AND THEIR FAMILIES

Over the past twenty years, a number of lay support and advocacy organizations have been founded, or expanded their interest, to enhance awareness of, knowledge about, and treatment for borderline disorder. The most prominent ones include the National Education Alliance for Borderline Personality Disorder (NEA-BPD), the Borderline Personality Disorder Resource Center, the Treatment and Research Advancements Association for Personality Disorder (TARA APD), the Black Sheep Project (BSP), and the National Alliance on Mental Illness (NAMI) (see Resources starting on page 263). In general, the mission of these organizations is to increase the awareness of borderline disorder and its treatments, provide the names of clinicians skilled in the diagnosis and treatment of borderline disorder, and provide support and educational opportunities to those suffering from the disorder and to their families and friends. For example, the Borderline Personality Disorder Resource Center was developed to assist individuals who may have borderline disorder and their families with locating clinicians skilled and experienced in its diagnosis and treatment and to provide other helpful information. Some (such as the BSP and NAMI) also strive to increase federal and private research funding dedicated to borderline disorder and to decrease the stigma associated with the disorder.

IN SUMMARY

After three thousand years of recording symptoms of patients with an affliction that was labeled with various names, the term "borderline personality disorder" evolved. Finally, the current diagnostic name was synthesized in the twentieth century from Stern's border line group, Knight's borderline states, Kernberg's borderline personality organization, Grinker's borderline syndrome, and Gunderson's Borderline Patients/Borderline Personality Disorder. In addition, the legitimacy of the current criteria for borderline disorder, and of the disorder itself, are supported by a number of well-conducted empirical research studies.

Other important advancements in the field of borderline disorder have been a marked improvement in understanding its prevalence and disabling effects, its fundamental nature, and the development of specific and effective methods of pharmacological and psychological treatment. These issues will be discussed in detail in subsequent chapters of this book.

Four

The Causes of Borderline
Personality Disorder

A FTER PATIENTS ARE REASSURED THAT THEY ARE NOT SUF-
fering from a disorder that will result in their developing
schizophrenia or another severe psychotic disorder, many of
them and their families want to know what causes borderline disorder.
You may have read or heard that this disorder is caused by the way
you were raised—that you didn't receive enough love and affection
from your mother or that your father was too cold, critical, and distant. You may have also learned that the parents of people with borderline disorder don't provide a consistent, supportive, nonchaotic
home life for their children, and that there are frequent arguments
and angry outbursts in the family, much of it focused directly or indirectly on the child with borderline disorder. In addition, it's often said
that emotional, physical, and sexual abuse in childhood are common
experiences of individuals with borderline disorder and are serious
risk factors for developing the disorder. Unfortunately, you may have

even suffered from one or more of these traumas as a child and have concluded, quite reasonably, that your early experiences are the sole causes of your current difficulties.

These early concepts of the causes of borderline disorder prevailed for many decades, in spite of the fact that they were based mainly on unverified reports of patients to their therapists, and that there was little empirical research to support these beliefs. When studies in this area were conducted, the results only partially validated the original observations. It is the case that about 50 percent of people with borderline disorder have experienced one or more of these early traumas. However, the other 50 percent with borderline disorder have not, yet they have also developed the disorder. In addition, many children have experienced these traumas but *have not* developed borderline disorder. What are we to make of these findings?

DOES BORDERLINE DISORDER HAVE ENVIRONMENTAL OR BIOLOGICAL CAUSES?

Research studies examining this issue over the past several decades have uncovered biological alterations in specific neural pathways of people with borderline disorder compared with people without the disorder. These pathways are known to control the core behaviors that are impaired in individuals with the disorder, such as emotional regulation, impulse control, perception and thinking, and relationships. This work has revealed consistent and specific structural and functional changes in these critical pathways in people with borderline disorder. There is evidence that genetic factors also contribute a significant risk to the development of the disorder. Finally, studies have found that individuals who experienced serious and sustained emotional, physical, and/or sexual abuse during childhood are at higher risk of developing borderline disorder than those who were not abused. It's important that you and your family understand that both biological and environmental factors contribute to the risk of developing borderline disorder.

These findings do not address the question, Which one is more important than the other? The problem with this question is that it suggests a split between the functions of the *mind* and the *brain*. Despite René

Descartes's popular theory of a mind-brain split, there is no such thing. *All psychological and nonpsychological functions of the brain depend on the activity of specific neural pathways in the brain.* Later in this book (Chapter 7), I will describe some of the main relationships between the psychological functions that are disturbed in borderline disorder and the specific neural pathways controlling these functions. From this information arises another question: If the above italicized statement is true, how do environmental risk factors for borderline disorder predispose individuals to the disorder through neurobiological mechanisms?

RISK FACTORS VERSUS CAUSES

Based on current research evidence, it's reasonable to conclude that borderline disorder is the result of the interplay between biological *and* environmental risk factors. Risk factors are not the same as causes. When situation A *causes* situation B, a linear, one-to-one relationship is implied. Each time situation A occurs, it will result in situation B. For instance, if someone inherits the gene for Huntington's disease, a fatal, degenerative disease of the brain, to the best of our current knowledge, they will inevitably develop the disorder. In this case, a single defective gene *causes* the disorder. It, alone, is necessary and sufficient to do so. It does not appear that other genes or environmental risk factors contribute to the development of the disease.

But that is not true for most medical disorders. For example, in the case of diabetes, we know of more than twenty genes that, if abnormal, place a person at risk for developing the disorder. It appears that the combination of at least four or five of these abnormal genes is required to put an individual at serious risk for diabetes. In addition, it is possible that some people with a significant loading of genetic risk factors will develop diabetes, and others with a similar genetic makeup will not. In part, developing diabetes also depends on the behavior of these individuals. Those individuals with additional environmental risk factors for diabetes, such as a poor diet, excessive weight, and little exercise, will have an added risk of developing diabetes. In some instances, these environmental factors appear to make the difference between developing and not developing the disease.

In other words, there is either an additive or an interactive effect of the degree of multiple genetic and environmental risk factors. The more severe the genetic risk, the less environmental risk is required to develop the disorder. The less severe the genetic risk, the more severe the environmental risk that is required. Most experts now agree that mutations in a number of genes appear to be necessary to develop many medical disorders, including borderline disorder. These are referred to as **multigenic disorders**, that is, disorders that require the interaction of a number of genetic mutations before the disorder manifests itself.

Therefore, it now seems likely that the additive or interactive effects of genetic and environmental disturbances serve as the total risk factor for developing borderline disorder.

BIOLOGICAL RISK FACTORS

When I was about twenty years old, I remember asking my maternal grandmother why she thought there were such significant differences in the personalities of the members of our family—my brothers, my sisters, me, our cousins, and other members of the extended family. She said, "Robert, I have seen almost one hundred babies born into the entire family over my lifetime. [She was raised in a large French-Canadian, Roman Catholic family.] With very few exceptions, the way you were as babies is the same you were as children, then adolescents, then adults. I have not seen any of you change very much throughout your lives. I believe that to a large degree, we are the way we were born."

My grandmother was taken out of school at the age of twelve to cook, clean, and care for her father and six older brothers. Family lore held that her mother had left them to provide better care for one of their severely disabled siblings. It seems that what Grandma lacked in formal education, she made up for with keen observational skills and astute insights. We now know that many of the characteristics we use to define personality can be attributed to genetic and environmental factors.

There are two types of biological risk factors that contribute to the development and course of any medical illness. They are inherited (genetic) factors and factors resulting in abnormal development of the fetus during pregnancy. Either of these biological factors affecting the brain could place a person at risk for developing borderline disorder, but in most instances genetic factors predominate.

Genetic Risk Factors

A number of studies published during the past two decades provide evidence that there is a significant genetic predisposition to borderline disorder. Although the degree of genetic predisposition varies among personality traits, the different behavioral manifestations of borderline disorder appear to have a total heritability of approximately 60 percent (recall that "heritability" here refers to the degree of genetic influence on behavior). Experts now believe that what is inherited are genetic mutations, which impair one or more components of the normal functions of the specific neural systems controlling the core behavioral characteristics of borderline disorder: regulation of emotions, impulse control, perception and reasoning, and relationships. The number and importance of each of these genetic alterations are believed to place individuals at more or less risk for developing the disorder.

Therefore, borderline disorder is more common in families with members who have borderline disorder and/or other disorders that share some of the behavioral traits and genetic mutations associated with borderline disorder, such as bipolar disorder, posttraumatic stress disorder, alcoholism and other substance use disorders, and several other personality disorders. These disorders also appear to be genetically transmitted and have been associated with abnormalities that occur in some of the same neural pathways as those affected in borderline disorder. (See Chapter 7 for more information on the neural pathways that appear to regulate the characteristics affected in borderline disorder.)

Developmental Risk Factors

In addition to genetic risk factors, it's also possible that the neural systems associated with the major symptoms of borderline disorder develop abnormally in some people with the disorder, either before or shortly after birth. These developmental abnormalities may then increase the risk for developing borderline disorder if they affect the neural systems that control the traits of the disorder. But what could cause such alterations of intrauterine and early infant development? There are at least two possibilities.

First, it's estimated that the brain contains approximately one hundred billion neurons (nerve cells). In order for the brain to carry out all of its functions properly, these nerve cells must be anatomically arranged in a specific way. They must be lined up precisely in each of the many pathways and circuits that control all of the functions of the brain, such as vision, hearing, motor activities, emotion, motivation, and thinking. Developmental disorders (for example, some forms of intellectual and learning disabilities) occur when certain neural pathways are not aligned correctly and do not function properly. Considering the enormous number of neural pathways and connections in the brain, it is understandable that some of these pathways and connections do not always develop correctly. The greater the number of incorrect neural connections in the brain, the greater is the likelihood that a developmental disorder will occur.

Second, such developmental abnormalities may be caused by external physical factors that impair normal brain development during pregnancy or near the time of birth. These factors may include nutritional deficiencies; congenital infections; the use of substances by the mother that are toxic to the fetus, such as alcohol, nicotine, and certain medicines; and decreased blood flow to the fetus. There is a small possibility that my mother may have been correct in her belief that the use of an anesthetic during the delivery of my sister Denise contributed to her developing borderline disorder, though there is no experimental evidence I know of to support this conclusion.

As noted above, there is evidence that genetic disturbances affect the neural systems that control the behavioral characteristics of borderline disorder. Genetic disturbances would then account for the reports by some parents of children with borderline disorder that these children were "different" since birth or early childhood.

Environmental Risk Factors

It's clear that biological risk factors alone predispose people to borderline disorder. Multiple studies have shown repeatedly that environmental risk factors also increase the risk of individuals to the disorder.

The environmental risk factors most frequently observed among people with borderline disorder are early separations or loss, sustained abuse, ineffective parenting, and possibly adverse social customs.

Early Separations or Loss

A large percentage of people with borderline disorder have a history of early childhood separation from one or both of their parents. In these families, parents separate or divorce, or one parent dies or deserts early in the child's life. Some parents of patients with borderline disorder have genetically transmitted mental disorders themselves, including bi-polar disorder, severe depression, alcoholism, or antisocial behaviors, including criminality. These disorders clearly affect the capacity of these parents to provide good parental care and can cause them to separate physically and/or emotionally from their child.

Childhood Abuse

Early emotional, physical, and sexual abuse are among the most commonly occurring traumas experienced by individuals with borderline disorder. Repeated sexual abuse is more common in women than men with the disorder, while long-term physical abuse is more common in men. Such abuse can occur by a member of the family or by a person outside of the family. Sustained sexual abuse, especially incest, is associated with a high incidence of self-injurious behavior and suicide in people with borderline disorder.

Ineffective Parenting

There is considerable evidence that many people with borderline disorder have suffered from poor parenting. In these cases, there is a broad spectrum of parental failures. They include unresponsive, unloving, inconsistent, and unsupportive care from one or both parents. Poor parenting also includes providing a poor role model for the child. Frequent arguments, fights, and separations fail to provide children with a safe and secure harbor at home. They also fail to equip children with examples of how to deal effectively with life's problems, and with strategies and skills to deal with their own internal emotional tensions and conflicts. Finally, poor parenting can involve the failure to protect the child from repeated abuse by the other parent, another member of the family, or an outsider.

It should be noted that these identical environmental risk factors might result in different mental and physical disorders, based on the person's unique set of genetic risk factors. Also, in the absence of significant biological risk factors for mental disorders, some children, possibly because they have a high level of inherent resilience, can tolerate even severe environmental stress without apparent serious long-term psychological consequences.

Adverse Social Customs

The late psychosocial academician Theodore Millon proposed that two social and cultural trends in Western culture place people at additional risk for borderline disorder. These are: (1) social customs that worsen rather than remedy damaged parent-child relationships and (2) a decrease in the capacity of institutions to compensate for the harm done by these impaired relationships.

Children with inherent difficulties integrating information and feelings, and with negligent and inconsistent parenting, may be subjected to constantly shifting cultural styles and values that add to their lack of a coherent and stable view of themselves and their lives. Their relationships may also be less stable than in former generations. Societal and technical changes have resulted in children having less understanding of the value of their parents' work, and the work of others, than was true in the past. These changes have also made it more difficult for parents to help encourage appropriate behavior and support a stable environment than in previous generations. Society itself rarely provides children at risk for borderline disorder with values that they can emulate and that would help stabilize their precarious view of life. In such an unstable environment, these children are unable to feel secure about their fate and what the future holds for them. The brief and often disruptive images on television are probably, on balance, more harmful than helpful in establishing clear and consistent boundaries of behavior for children who are desperately in need of such boundaries. It is estimated that the typical eighteen-year-old American teenager has spent more time online than interacting with his or her parents or attending school. Finally, the availability of drugs and the lax attitude about them by their peers further decreases the capacity of these children and adolescents to properly modulate their emotions and impulsive behaviors, to think clearly, and to develop increasingly mature and sound relationships.

Traditional social customs meant to back up those of home customs no longer do so with consistency. Peer groups are also unlikely to succeed in this area. For example, members of the extended family, who are now often dispersed across the country, as well as neighbors, schools, churches, and other community organizations, no longer play the pivotal roles in helping mold children's value systems, as they did in prior generations. In modern American society, they do not provide the same safety net for children at risk as they did previously.

As is the case for all environmental risk factors, it is not suggested that sociocultural risk factors *cause* borderline disorder. However, it's possible that they add to or interact with the total environmental burden of risk for children and adolescents already at an elevated inherent risk for the disorder.

HOW ENVIRONMENTAL RISK FACTORS AFFECT THE BRAIN

Are there permanent consequences on brain development for children who are exposed to long-term harmful experiences very early in life? More specifically, does the early occurrence of continuous environmental stress irreversibly alter the critical neural systems of individuals who develop borderline disorder? Answering these questions requires some knowledge of how the brain develops and is affected by experience.

The human brain continues to develop well into the second decade of life. It is now known that the brain has many more neurons during childhood than even a few years later. This early "surplus" of neurons appears to provide exceptional adaptability and survival value to humans. We use, and thereby highly develop, those neural pathways critical to survival in our peculiar environments. Under certain circumstances, these pathways may be the ones that control physical abilities that enable us to hunt, fight, plant, or build. In an environment requiring such skills, the neural pathways mediating these functions will develop more than ones that are used less. Also, people with superior inherent talents in these areas will have a better chance at survival and procreation than individuals less naturally gifted.

In other societies, intellectual abilities are more in demand and better rewarded than are physical talents. In these societies, as a result of environmental need and emphasis, the neural pathways that control intellectual processes will develop preferentially, and those individuals most inherently gifted in these brain functions will, on average, do better than those with less inherent intellectual talents.

Regardless of the degree of inherent ability, the brain responds to the demands of the environment by diverting nourishment from underused neural pathways to those in greater use. This process "prunes" the less frequently used neural pathways in the brain, thus conserving energy for growth and development and assuring optimal learning and performance in the more critical areas. The development of essential abilities and the pruning of less essential abilities enable the brain to function most efficiently and effectively in multiple environments.

Now let's return to the question raised above: What effects do environmental risk factors have on brain function in children? The answers to this question are currently under investigation. For example, it has been demonstrated that there is abnormal brain function in certain regions of the brain of women with borderline disorder who have been sexually abused as children. Such abnormal function is not present in women who have also been abused but do not have the disorder. Although there are different interpretations of this finding, it raises the possibility that long-term changes in critical neural pathways may be the result of early traumatic experiences interacting with inherent risk factors of borderline disorder. These and similar changes in brain function resulting from other harmful environmental experiences could serve as one mechanism by which environmental risk factors interact with inherent biological risk factors. Other environmental risk factors would increase the probability that individuals who have been exposed to these harmful experiences may develop borderline disorder.

From a biological perspective, unsupportive, invalidating behavior by the parent may cause the fear system of the child to become permanently hypersensitive and overreactive. In addition, long-term abuse may damage the function of certain memory pathways and thus protect the child from the emotional pain of thinking about these assaults. However, later in life, suppressing unpleasant events from memory may be maladaptive and even result in dissociative episodes during which critical experiences are not remembered.

Early separation from, or impaired parenting by, one's mother or father may result in a lifelong dread of separations and an impaired capacity to develop a proper sense of self-worth. Although changes in the brain caused by repeated negative experiences appear to be difficult to totally reverse, they can be modified considerably. There are a number of ways to produce these modifications in people with borderline disorder, and I discuss them at greater length in Chapters 10 and 11.

HOW BIOLOGICAL AND ENVIRONMENTAL RISK FACTORS INTERACT

For the most part, environmental stresses such as those described above are harmful to children, including those who are born without any genetic or developmental impairments. When added to genetic risk factors for borderline disorder, environmental risk factors appear to significantly enhance the risk of these children developing the disorder and of increasing its severity. This is referred to as a **stress–diathesis model**.

One question raised by the stress–diathesis model is: Which life experiences most increase the risk of developing borderline disorder? As mentioned earlier, the long-term psychological consequences of harmful experiences for people with borderline disorder are controlled by changes in the neural pathways involved in the symptoms of the disorder. In addition, it seems that the extent to which each of the environmental risk factors is harmful varies with the nature, duration, and severity of the stress and the specific symptom of borderline disorder in question. Each is different in severity from one child to another.

To complicate the issue further, there is disagreement about which specific biological and environmental risk factors are most critical. For example, Marsha Linehan, a psychologist at the University of Washington who developed a specific form of therapy for borderline disorder (see chapter 11), believes that people with the disorder have a biological predisposition for dysregulated emotions. She contends that this inherent biological deficit is aggravated by parents who punish or demean these children, rather than attempt to understand them and help them deal with their poor emotional control (that is, validate their problem).

However, Mary Zanarini from Harvard and Paul Links at the University of Western Ontario suggest that inherently impaired and poorly learned impulse control is the main feature of the disorder. Otto Kernberg and colleagues from Cornell, and Patricia Judd and Thomas McGlashan from Yale, assert that the main disturbance resulting in the development of borderline disorder is faulty bonding to the parents, bonding that fails to maintain the infant's safety and survival by caring and nurturing parental protection. Such a defect results in the split thinking and cognitive incongruity that are hallmarks of borderline disorder.

Until recently, there were no objective data to support or refute any of these hypotheses. However, in 2013, Ted Reichborn-Kjennerud, Ken Kendler, and their colleagues provided evidence suggesting that criteria 4 and 5, making up the impulsive dimension of the disorder, had the highest heritability. Their evidence also suggested that the genetic risk factors making up the interpersonal dimension (criteria 1, 2, 3, and 9) had the lowest heritability. They also found a general borderline disorder factor that had a strong inherent effect on all nine criteria of the disorder, while five of the nine criterion-specific genetic effects were zero or negligible. These findings appear to support the hypothesis of Zanarini and Links and not those of Kernberg, Judd, and McGlashan, as noted above. The implications of these findings are still to be determined, as other studies must replicate these findings.

It's very important for those with borderline disorder, as well as their parents, siblings, and families, to understand that none of the environmental risk factors I've discussed have been shown to *cause* borderline disorder. Recall that many people who are exposed to the same abuse, separations, and poor parenting do not develop borderline disorder, and some patients with borderline disorder have experienced few, if any, of these environmental risk factors. It now seems most likely that some critical combination, interaction, and balance of biological and environmental risk factors are necessary for a person to develop borderline disorder. Much more research is needed to tease apart the precise interactions and influences of these risk factors on the development of each of the specific symptoms of the disorder. Such knowledge will enable more specifically targeted pharmacological and psychotherapeutic treatment programs.

THE MAIN IMPLICATIONS OF THESE FINDINGS

Clearly, there is a growing body of evidence indicating that both biological and environmental factors increase the risk of developing borderline disorder. One of the important conclusions that we can draw from these findings is that they provide a scientific basis for the use of both medications and psychotherapy in the treatment of patients with borderline disorder.

It's very important to fully recognize the significance of this point. I treat some patients with moderate to severe borderline disorder who are initially opposed to the use of appropriate medications. These include patients with a high degree of impulsivity, which, as noted above, is significantly influenced by biological variables. One could logically assume from this finding that these largely biologically influenced symptoms would be more effectively treated with pharmacological intervention than with psychotherapy.

As I described in Chapter 2, Mrs. Davis significantly increased the duration of her recovery by resisting medication during the early phase of her treatment. Interestingly, it was her impulsive activity that most impaired her progress. As a result, she was not able to benefit adequately from the issues worked on in psychotherapy until the appropriate medication for her reduced the severity of her symptoms to a level that enabled her to apply effectively the information she learned in therapy.

The data on the degree of heritability of other symptoms also supports the need for psychotherapy. I see patients with borderline disorder who are quite willing to take medication, hoping for a rapid and painless cure of their difficulties. They are resistant to engaging in psychotherapy and the difficult work and changes that therapy involves. Consequently, they fail to learn the information and develop the skills they would normally have acquired when they were younger, but were not able to because their symptoms interfered.

Finally, it has been my experience that many patients become less resistant to pursuing either form of treatment when they understand the importance of both the biological and the environmental factors associated with borderline disorder that we have discussed in this chapter. This is why I take the time to carefully explain to new patients the rationale underlying this critical, dual therapeutic component of our working agreement. It's not a deal breaker when a patient refuses initially to agree to this treatment strategy. As was the case with Mrs. Davis in Chapter 2, I find that most patients ultimately agree to employ both methods when our patient-doctor relationship is more fully developed and they trust the recommendations I am making. After all, it would be unfair and inconsistent of me to suggest to patients in therapy that they be flexible and consider making big changes in their behavior when I have not demonstrated a reasonable degree of flexibility myself.

FIVE

Tracing the Course of the Disorder

ONE OF THE FUNDAMENTAL FEATURES OF ANY MEDICAL ILL-
ness is its natural course. That is, its usual progression through a
number of stages to its ultimate outcomes with and without
treatment. The course of a disorder is determined by several characteristics: the **etiology** (the specific group of genetic and environmental
risk factors affecting the vulnerability of each individual); the age of
onset; the nature, severity, and progression of symptoms; the acute,
chronic, or episodic occurrence of the symptoms; the responses of
the disorder to treatment; and the prognosis or likely outcome of the
disorder in general.

PRECURSORS OF BORDERLINE DISORDER IN CHILDREN

The growing body of evidence that borderline disorder has genetic and
environmental risk factors has enhanced our interest in reports of similar
behavioral disturbances in children. Early behavior may be a precursor
of the disorder in adolescents and adults. Such disturbances in children,

and their implications, are complex and not well understood. (They are described in detail in the following chapter.)

BORDERLINE DISORDER IN ADOLESCENTS

If some behavioral symptoms resembling borderline disorder develop in children, which is not uncommon, they usually continue to evolve as these children enter preadolescence. These behaviors do not inevitably develop into borderline disorder. The full spectrum of symptoms of borderline disorder most often appear to manifest themselves during the early teenage years and young adulthood. This is a very vulnerable period of life for those people who are at risk for developing the disorder. The symptoms that mark the onset of borderline disorder in teenagers closely resemble those seen in adults (Chapter 1). Therefore, mental healthcare clinicians knowledgeable about borderline disorder are often able to accurately diagnose the disorder during adolescence.

As an aside, it is worth noting that when the first edition of this book was published in 2004, the prevailing opinion among many mental healthcare practitioners was that it was inappropriate to diagnose borderline disorder before the age of eighteen. This view was taught in many training programs and prevailed among practitioners in spite of the clear presence of the criteria in DSM-IV-TR (*Diagnostic and Statistical Manual of Mental Disorders*, 4th edition, Text Revision, published in 2000) for making this diagnosis in adolescents. The disconnect between this erroneous position and the facts was so extensive and harmful that Andrew Chanen and his colleagues published a scientific article under the title, "Personality Disorder in Adolescents: The Diagnosis That Dare Not Speak Its Name." The article presented a case study of a young girl with borderline disorder. Although the resistance to making this diagnosis in adolescents has abated somewhat, be aware that it is still common. If you hear this erroneous statement from a practitioner, get an opinion from one who has more knowledge and experience in the field.

Although adolescents with borderline disorder typically have symptoms that are similar to adults, they are modified in age-specific ways. In a study of hospitalized adolescents with borderline disorder, two-thirds of them demonstrated symptoms of emotional instability, uncontrolled anger, feelings of emptiness or boredom, impulsiveness, and suicidal threats or gestures. Surprisingly, in this study, only one-third were reported to manifest unstable relationships, and even fewer were thought to have identity disturbances. However, having cared for many adolescents with borderline disorder in a residential treatment center, I have observed that the majority of them do demonstrate these difficulties. Because these are such important symptoms of borderline disorder, a large and representative sample of adolescents with the disorder should be studied to resolve this discrepancy in anecdotal observations and reports. Other than in this area, the rate of occurrence of borderline disorder among all admissions, and the symptom profiles of individuals with the disorder in this study, were similar in adolescents and adults.

As adolescents diagnosed with borderline disorder grow into young adulthood, follow-up studies suggest that less than half of them still meet criteria for the disorder. This does not mean that those who no longer meet criteria are without symptoms; they just do not have as many symptoms as are necessary (five) to meet the categorical criteria of DSM-5. They may have three or four of the nine criteria in Table 1.2 on page 20 that cause disabling problems, but they do not meet the full criteria for the diagnosis. For example, in one study, three symptoms of borderline disorder were found to be more persistent and stable over time than other symptoms. They are: emptiness or boredom; inappropriate, intense anger; and emotional instability. These symptoms can be quite disabling, yet the patient may not meet the required number of diagnostic criteria of the disorder. Required treatment may not be initiated or will be discontinued. This is one of the flaws of the categorical system of diagnosis of personality disorders that has been employed in DSM-III to DSM-5.

Poor Emotional Control

In adolescents with borderline disorder, arguments with parents and siblings may occur more frequently than they did in childhood and become very heated and far out of proportion to the content of the disagreement. In addition to severe outbursts of anger, other symptoms of poor emotional control may appear, such as significant episodes of moodiness, sadness, or anxiety.

Another feature of emotional dyscontrol in borderline disorder is that once an emotional hyperreaction has occurred, it takes a significant amount of time to return to baseline. This is certainly the case in adolescents with borderline disorder. Some may show great initial enthusiasm with an activity, followed by a tendency toward rapid boredom. Interests will shift readily from one area to another. Additionally, adolescents often have difficulty in completing projects that require persistence. As noted below, these characteristics of borderline disorder result in difficulties establishing friendships that are wholesome and that endure. With some exceptions, most relationships are made and terminate abruptly. Note that some of the above symptoms overlap with those of ADHD, a disorder that occurs five times more frequently in individuals with borderline disorder than it does in the general population. This can be confusing to the diagnostician and is addressed in Chapter 8.

Impulsivity

Serious and generally rebellious misbehaviors may first appear in adolescents who already have been diagnosed with borderline disorder, or who will develop symptoms. These may include reluctance, and even refusal, to do homework; driving the family car before obtaining a license; drinking and taking drugs; staying out past curfew; stealing; dressing and appearing in hair styles, bodily ornaments, and clothes that are at, or beyond, the margin of what's acceptable for the family or for social norms; sexual misconduct; truancy from school; and developing friendships with other teenagers who engage in similar behaviors. Some teenagers with borderline disorder may perform destructive acts such as breaking furniture or other people's possessions, or physically attacking peers, siblings, and even parents.

Adolescents with borderline disorder may also demonstrate self-injurious behavior for the first time. These behaviors are usually scratching or cutting their wrists, arms, or legs with sharp instruments, physically hurting themselves in other ways, or taking overdoses of aspirin or other medications that are available at home. These and other harmful actions are often in response to arguments with parents or a significant other; actual or threatened separation from these and other people important to them; or being caught engaging in, and held accountable for, serious misbehaviors. When parents attempt to modify these behaviors, their children often escalate rather than improve. Therefore, parents must find alternative ways of dealing with such behaviors. This issue will be discussed later in this book (Chapter 13).

Impairment of Perception, Reasoning, and Other Cognitive Functions

There are very few studies that have examined this group of symptoms in adolescents. These studies and anecdotal reports suggest that identity disturbance, suspiciousness, paranoid thinking, and dissociative episodes may occur in adolescents with borderline disorder, though they may not be as apparent as in adults. Clinical experience suggests that adolescents with borderline disorder also have difficulty with their ability to reason at a level equal to that of their peers, especially in social situations and when under emotional stress.

Impaired Relationships

As a group, adolescents are caught in a major dilemma of normal development. On the one hand, they continue to be dependent on their parents and others for many of their daily essentials. On the other hand, they strive for increasing independence, often beyond their capacity to use this independence wisely. During this period of development, it is important to reinforce the concept that the most solid and enduring relationships are built on *interdependence*, not on either dependence or independence.

Gradually achieving mature interdependence in relationships is a difficult task for all adolescents, even those without borderline disorder. Because major characteristics of the disorder include severe conflicts over dependency and a significant impairment of forming sound and balanced relationships with anyone, it is not surprising that adolescents with borderline disorder have even more difficulty with these normal processes of maturation than do those without the disorder.

As a result, relationships with parents, other family members, friends, and boyfriends or girlfriends may become increasingly tumultuous. Parents often become "the enemy," seemingly overnight, as adolescents with borderline disorder shift their dependent, clinging, and ambivalent relationships from parents to one or more of their peers. They may first develop one or two very close friendships with other teenagers of the same sex. However, it is usually not too long before the relationships shift to boyfriends or girlfriends. These relationships are often intense and brief, may involve premature sexual activity, and, when over, for whatever reason, often result in dramatic functional "meltdowns." For example, the adolescent may not be able to attend school or do his or her homework, may withdraw from interacting with family and friends, and may develop physical symptoms such as headaches and abdominal pain.

BORDERLINE DISORDER IN EARLY ADULTHOOD

For some people, the symptoms of borderline disorder don't significantly disrupt their lives until their late teenage years, their early twenties, or even later. In the early twenties, life for everyone becomes more complex and challenging. The stresses of leaving home and the demands of higher education, work, marriage, and child rearing require increasing self-reliance, self-discipline, and the capacity for healthy interdependence. To succeed, we must trust and share our burdens with others and assist them with theirs. People with borderline disorder typically have great difficulty developing these adaptive skills before and during this critical period in their lives. This inability to deal effectively and consistently with the normal stresses of maturity is the result of the emotional, impulsive, cognitive, and physical symptoms of the disorder. These symptoms may occur for the first time, or if they were already present, they may become more severe or more frequent with age. The severity of these symptoms of borderline disorder can vary considerably among young people with the disorder, and therefore will cause varying degrees of disturbances in their lives.

Before starting treatment, most of my new patients in their early to mid-twenties with moderate to severe borderline disorder report that life seems to be passing them by. They observe their friends completing college, obtaining good jobs with promising careers, getting married, and even having children while they achieve few, if any, of these life markers. When asked why they think that this is so, common responses are lack of motivation, the absence of a credible life plan, an incoherent sense of who they are, and only a vague sense of their value system, their strengths and their weaknesses, their likes and dislikes, with no clear path forward. They often live with their parents, many are not employed, and they use alcohol and marijuana as means of soothing themselves when particularly distraught. They have few close friends as would be defined by their peer group and have an elevated sense of suspiciousness of others. Many of these symptoms and behaviors can be summed up with the term "severe impairment of identity."

The Episodic Nature of Symptoms

Regardless of when and which symptoms of borderline disorder first appear, and their severity, they often occur episodically on a background of otherwise fairly normal or marginal behavior. These episodes are usually precipitated by stressful experiences involving significant personal losses or disagreements. At other times, they are in response to severe consequences of behaviors such as failure at school or work, stealing, reckless driving or driving while intoxicated, and alcohol and drug abuse. Family gatherings at holidays, or other occasions, are particularly stressful and may also result in a flare-up of symptoms. Sometimes it is not clear to the individual or family why they occur, but a common theme is that the individual with borderline disorder typically sees themselves as the black sheep of the family, someone so distant and different from other family members that they just don't fit into the family. This self-perception results in feelings of anger, anxiety, sadness, and jealousy. Such a strained atmosphere results in the feeling by family members and friends that they must continually walk on eggshells to prevent a major incident on what otherwise should be a day of celebration and joy.

The family of the person with borderline disorder gradually learns under what circumstances symptomatic episodes are most likely to occur, and begins to dread these occasions. For example, family gatherings during the holidays or at special celebrations often provoke a relapse of symptoms in an individual with borderline disorder, even one in treatment. Other triggers are arguments or a breakup with their partner. It becomes increasingly frustrating and discouraging for the person with the disorder and their family to repeatedly go through these experiences, which usually worsen and occur more frequently over time. It's especially bewildering because between episodes, the person with borderline disorder may be relatively free of symptoms and appear to be doing very well. These periods of symptom-free behavior make it more difficult to endure the next relapse, because it appears that the relapses are deliberate and intentionally provocative.

Different Levels of Severity of Borderline Disorder

The symptoms of borderline disorder and their severity are not the same for everyone who has the disorder. Some people have very mild forms and respond promptly and well to treatment. Others have more severe forms. For them, the treatment plan is more complex, and treatment takes longer. This difference in severity is a common characteristic of many illnesses. For example, some people with mild forms of diabetes may respond well to changes in diet and require only oral medications to markedly reduce the consequences of their illness. Other diabetic patients require severe dietary restrictions and multiple daily injections of insulin, and may still remain in poor control and develop serious secondary medical problems. As Paul Links and Ronald Heslegrave discovered in their study (see below, page 90), severity is an important indicator of the long-term outcome of borderline disorder. It's important to remember that if you or a loved one suffers from severe borderline disorder, the situation is not hopeless. It does mean that you'll have to expend more effort and patience to do better.

Regardless of the severity of borderline disorder, psychiatrists and other physicians and mental health professionals who specialize in the treatment of people with this illness are now much more optimistic about successful outcomes than they were even a decade ago. This optimism is based, in part, on the research findings on treatment that I discuss later in this and other chapters. In addition, our understanding of the fundamental nature of borderline disorder is increasing more rapidly now than in the past. Advances continue to be made in treatments specifically designed for people with borderline disorder, and we now know that significant improvements can result from the combined efforts of the person with borderline disorder and their family.

I understand that it can be frustrating for parents of adolescents and young adults who appear to have borderline disorder to not be able to find a local psychiatrist or other mental healthcare clinician who is experienced in treating people with borderline disorder. If you are having this difficulty, please refer to the Resources starting on page 263; the Black Sheep Project and the Borderline Personality Disorder Resource Center may be particularly helpful to you.

THE MISDIAGNOSIS OF BORDERLINE DISORDER

Many people with borderline disorder or their parents first seek medical help during the period of their lives that begins with puberty and continues into early adulthood. Some parents consult with psychiatrists or other mental health professionals about emotional and behavioral symptoms, while others go to their primary care physicians with complaints of physical symptoms. Unfortunately, the core illness of borderline disorder is often initially unrecognized. If this is the case, the person with borderline disorder then begins a frustrating and unsuccessful series of psychiatric and psychosocial evaluations and medical tests. These often result in incorrect diagnoses and ineffective treatments that bring, at best, only partial and temporary relief, frustration, and a growing sense of hopelessness.

At this point, people with borderline disorder are at a critical juncture in their lives. If the correct diagnosis is made, and if skilled clinicians provide effective treatment, the prognosis can be quite good. The symptoms of the disorder may be brought under control, and individuals with borderline disorder can be stabilized, having determined their true identity and their strengths. In the absence of the correct diagnosis and effective care, the outcome is less favorable.

THE PROGNOSIS OF BORDERLINE DISORDER

Until recently, many psychiatrists and other mental health clinicians thought that the prognosis for patients with borderline disorder was very poor or "guarded." This pessimism was based, in part, on the chronic, episodic, and recurring nature of the symptoms of the disorder. Also, this prognosis was supported by the apparent failure of many patients to respond well to the standard uses of psychotherapy and medications that had proven helpful to patients with other mental disorders, such as depression and anxiety. Finally, the widely held perception of a poor prognosis for individuals with the disorder may have been due to a variety of flaws in the design of early research studies evaluating the treatment outcomes of borderline disorder. For example, these studies typically involved relatively few patients who had severe borderline disorder who were initially in inpatient treatment, and the studies often did not include a comparison group. These factors would be expected to bias the results in a negative direction. In general, the findings from these early studies were that many patients with severe borderline disorder did poorly in the short term but somewhat better over the long term.

Recent sophisticated, population-based, quantitative genetic studies have shed new light on the prognosis of borderline disorder (see Chapter 3). Twin studies from adolescence to adulthood of individuals with borderline disorder suggest that the contribution of genetic factors increases with time, as the impact of environmental factors decreases proportionately and then remains constant. This means that as a patient gets older, genetic predisposition to borderline disorder is more likely to play a role than environmental factors. Also, there is clear evidence of a gene-environment interplay. For example, a lower heritability of borderline disorder (24 percent) was found in individuals with a history of sexual abuse, while a higher rate of heritability of the disorder (47 percent) was found in individuals who had no history of such abuse (see Chapter 3). Such studies have also found that different symptoms of borderline disorder have different rates of heritability. These findings have significant implications for the use of specific treatment interventions for the disorder (see Chapters 10 and 11).

Other recent studies suggest that prognostic pessimism is not warranted. These studies demonstrate that many people with borderline disorder respond well to specific medication regimens and to special forms of psychotherapy designed specifically for the treatment of the disorder. Some evidence suggests that 60 to 75 percent of people with borderline disorder improve significantly over time as the effects of treatment are realized. This doesn't mean that they no longer have any symptoms, but that the symptoms are significantly reduced in severity, and that they cause less disruption and disabilities in the patients' and their families' lives.

THE EFFECTS OF TREATMENT ON OUTCOME

I've stressed that if you or a family member has borderline disorder, you should be hopeful, but I know that this is easier said than done. What you desire are solid reasons to be hopeful. In the medical community, the best tangible reason to believe any claim is to evaluate the results of well-conducted research studies that validly test the claim. The following are three important studies of people with borderline disorder who were evaluated over many years, each of which will give you reason to be hopeful. My main purpose in reviewing these studies of the course of borderline disorder is to provide you with sound reasons for entering and remaining in therapy. These studies show that proper treatment is your best hope of gaining control over your life.

THE MCLEAN STUDY

Mary Zanarini and her colleagues at Harvard's McLean Hospital in Boston reported in 2014 the results of a sixteen-year prospective, follow-up study of 290 patients with borderline disorder initially treated as inpatients. (A prospective study is one designed prior to the study to gather specific information, rather than after the patients have been treated. Such studies increase the accuracy and validity of the results.) All patients were carefully diagnosed with appropriate symptom-rating instruments and met DSM-III diagnostic criteria (the third edition of the *Diagnostic and Statistical Manual of Mental Disorders*, which was in use when the prospective study began). Patients were evaluated at two-year intervals for sixteen years after their initial hospitalizations and entrance into the study. They had remained in various levels of treatment during the course of the study. At the time of follow-up, they received extensive reevaluations of their symptoms and their responses to treatment.

The authors reported three major findings:

1. After two years of treatment, 60 percent of patients were reported to be in recovery from borderline personality disorder. (The study defined "recovery" as symptomatic remission, or no longer meeting DSM's criteria to be diagnosed with BPD, and good social and vocational functioning.)

2. Six factors were found to predict a better possibility of recovery from BPD symptoms. Those positive predictors were no prior psychiatric hospitalizations, higher IQs than those who showed less improvement, a good vocational record during the two years prior to admission, absence of an anxiety cluster personality disorder, high extroversion, and high agreeableness.

3. Some factors were found to have an effect, either direct or inverse, on the amount of time it took for the patient to recover: how much the patient avoided certain personal contacts, their degree of dependency, a cooperative interpersonal style, an absence of adversity in life (whether during childhood or adulthood), and no major additional psychopathology in the patient or in the family.

In a prior study, these researchers had reported that recurrences of borderline disorder were rare in patients who had received intensive treatment and who achieved remission. The researchers concluded that in this intensively treated group of patients with borderline disorder, once the patients felt understood and had learned how to control and adapt more effectively to their symptoms, they made progress toward remission of symptoms—and were able to keep making progress over the course of the study.

Also, these patients experienced significant reductions in symptoms of each of the four dimensions of borderline disorder. However, different dimensions, and symptoms within these dimensions, demonstrated different patterns of improvement over time. On the one hand, emotional disturbances were more persistent and were still present in 60 to 80 percent of patients in six years. On the other hand, some impulsive behaviors, especially self-mutilation, suicidal attempts, substance abuse, and sexual promiscuity, declined dramatically, often down two-thirds of their initial rate of occurrence. Other impulsive behaviors, such as binge eating, verbal outbursts, and spending sprees, decreased only about one-third at the six-year follow-up.

Over time, cognitive and interpersonal symptoms of borderline disorder declined more than emotional symptoms, but less than impulsive symptoms. Psychotic-like thoughts declined from about 50 to 20 percent of the patients at six years, and odd thinking declined from 85 to 50 percent of patients.

Some areas of interpersonal relationships also improved more than others. Over six years, difficulties with therapists declined from 50 to 10 percent of patients. Stormy relationships/manipulation/sadism, and demandingness/entitlement declined from 60–80 percent to 25–50 percent, and reported intolerance of aloneness, abandonment, or dependency concerns decreased from 90 percent of patients with borderline disorder to 60 percent.

The results of this study suggest that borderline disorder is characterized by two distinct types of symptoms. One type represents the more temperamental or enduring aspects of borderline disorder, such as chronic feelings of anger or emptiness, suspicion, difficulty tolerating aloneness, and fear of abandonment. These symptoms seem to resolve more slowly and were still reported by a majority of patients with borderline disorder six years after their initial admission. Other symptoms of the disorder, including self-mutilation, suicide attempts, quasi-psychotic thoughts, treatment regressions, and problems in relationships with the therapist, are manifestations of acute illness. These seem to decline relatively quickly.

The Collaborative Longitudinal Personality Disorder Study

The Collaborative Longitudinal Personality Disorder Study (CLPDS), funded by the National Institute of Mental Health (NIMH) and published in 2003, involved the collaboration of research sites in the departments of psychiatry at Brown, Columbia, Harvard, Texas A&M, Vanderbilt, and Yale Universities. It was designed to study prospectively the outcomes of four personality disorders, including borderline disorder.

This group reported on the possible reasons for sudden "remissions" in the 160 patients with borderline disorder enrolled in the study. Eighteen patients fell to two or fewer criteria during the first six months of the study. Of these 18 patients, only one had suffered a relapse at a two-year follow-up evaluation.

Rapid improvement in ten of the eighteen patients was judged to be due to situational changes resulting in relief from extremely stressful environmental situations—typically, this involved either establishing relationships with new partners or leaving very stressful relationships. Change like this was unusual, reported in less than 6 percent of study patients.

In five other patients, rapid remission from borderline disorder was associated with successful treatment of acute mental disorders that co-occurred with borderline disorder. These included **panic disorder**, substance abuse, major depressive disorder, and bipolar disorder (see Chapter 8 for more information on these disorders).

The important findings from this study are that only 11 percent of a sample of 160 borderline patients experienced a significant remission in six months, yet all but one of these remained in remission for two years. It is likely that if this study were replicated now using more modern medications, psychotherapy, and behavioral changes (e.g., cessation of alcohol intake), these results would be more impressive.

The Links and Heslegrave Study

Paul Links and Ronald Heslegrave of Toronto, Canada, have published a series of reports of prospective studies on the outcomes of eighty-eight patients with borderline disorder. In these studies, patients with the disorder were evaluated at two and seven years after the initial assessment.

Forty-seven percent of the patients were described as having persistent or stable borderline disorder at the seven-year follow-up. This finding is consistent with those of other researchers, who estimate the long-term stability of borderline disorder to lie between 51 percent and 57 percent. These differences in response to treatment and stability of the disorder may be the result of one or several factors.

For example, these researchers were also able to identify factors that were highly predictive of long-term outcome of borderline disorder. The initial level of impulsivity accounted for 25 percent of the differences in outcome at the seven-year follow-up; in other words, a high initial level of impulsivity predicted a greater likelihood of persistent borderline disorder than a low initial level. (This is not surprising given the high degree of heritability of impulsive behavior in patients with borderline disorder.) Patients initially diagnosed with borderline disorder who were also diagnosed with substance abuse disorder were twice as likely to have borderline disorder at follow-up than were those patients without a substance abuse diagnosis. There were two other significant predictors of the course and outcome of borderline disorder found in this study. A severe level of symptoms of borderline disorder and a history of childhood sexual abuse predicted a poorer outcome than less severe symptoms and no childhood sexual abuse.

The authors concluded that individuals with persistent borderline disorder typically demonstrate high levels of impulsivity, and that impulsivity is the engine that appears to perpetuate the disorder over the course of their life. They go on to suggest that modification of impulsive behavior with medications and impulse control–directed therapy, for example, may enable patients with borderline disorder to develop more stable and meaningful relationships.

Taken as a whole, these studies are informative and encouraging about the prognosis of borderline disorder and help dispel the myth that the disorder is always chronic and poorly responsive to treatment. They strongly suggest that with effective treatment and with better control over impulsive behavior, especially substance abuse, you will experience a significant improvement in many of your symptoms. All symptoms do not improve to the same degree, but they all do improve. An overarching factor that determines the rate and degree of your improvement is your remaining in treatment as long as is necessary.

WHAT HAPPENS IF YOU DO NOT RECEIVE TREATMENT OR DROP OUT PREMATURELY?

Unfortunately, for one reason or another, many people with borderline disorder do not seek care, or they leave treatment prematurely. It may be that they fear treatment, or their treatment program is not working as well as they would like. Others may no longer be able to afford the proper care or don't receive badly needed support from their family or spouse. Some are unwilling or unable to give up the alcohol, drugs, and/or other activities and behaviors that prevent them from benefiting from treatment. Regrettably, others are unable to find a psychiatrist and therapist in their community who are skilled in the diagnosis and treatment of borderline disorder and dedicated to working with patients with the disorder. Finally, there are indications that a large percentage of individuals with borderline disorder are in massive denial that there is anything wrong with them, though they have symptoms similar to those who readily enter treatment. This denial persists in many of these individuals and causes a large amount of difficulties with their families, friends, coworkers, and so forth. Because this population of individuals is not seen often by the medical profession, little is known of the critical factors that separate them from those individuals with borderline disorder who seek care.

Not surprisingly, the prognosis is not nearly so positive for those individuals who do not enter treatment, or who drop out early, as it is for those who have been stabilized successfully on medication and who engage and remain in therapy until they have learned to consistently manage their lives more skillfully and effectively.

Therefore, as you get older, if you do not receive effective treatment, it is likely that you will encounter significant and increasing problems in your marriage, occupation, social life, and support systems. Divorces, separations from families of origin, dismissals from work, frequent job changes, and the inability to sustain wholesome friendships and maintain consistent housing are common in individuals who do not receive proper care. The longer treatment is delayed, the greater are the number of irreversible consequences for your life and the more difficult it will be to seek help and make the changes necessary to stop your downward spiral.

Without proper treatment, by the time you reach midlife, it is likely that your socioeconomic status will have declined substantially, and you will become increasingly impoverished both financially and socially. As recently as one generation ago, this fate seemed inevitable to most people who suffered from borderline disorder. This is no longer the case. Help of different types is now available—help that will provide you with the opportunity to salvage your life. I urge you to seek out and take advantage of this help. It is rarely too late to do so.

SIX

Borderline Personality Disorder
in Children

B ORDERLINE DISORDER IS USUALLY FIRST DIAGNOSED IN ADO-
lescence or in early adulthood. Before symptoms become fully
apparent, however, there are indications of behavioral problems observed in children who will ultimately develop the disorder.
Some of these children have symptoms that are similar to those in adolescents and adults with borderline disorder. Others do not. This chapter explores what appear to be the early symptoms and the course of
development of borderline disorder in infants and in children. You will
also find some suggestions on how to ensure that your child is properly
evaluated for borderline or other behavioral disorders, and is effectively
treated if needed. This chapter should be particularly helpful to parents whose children are engaging in frequent temper tantrums; defiant
and disobedient behavior; disrespect of parents, teachers, and others in
authority; lying; stealing; or injuring others maliciously. If you notice
a number of these traits in your child and wish to understand their

origins and what actions you should take, you may find some answers to your questions in this chapter.

DOES BORDERLINE DISORDER AFFECT CHILDREN?

When parents of individuals with borderline disorder are asked at what point they first noticed that something was wrong with their child, they give different answers. Some say that they noticed very little unusual behavior until the child was an adolescent. Some report that they detected problems as early as the first weeks of life. Mothers report that they noticed differences in the temperament of the baby compared to their sisters or brothers at the same age. The affected babies seemed more "colicky," cried more, smiled and laughed less, slept less restfully, were upset more easily by changes in routine, and were more difficult to soothe when upset.

In early childhood, some children who later are diagnosed with borderline disorder are described as having been more demanding and requiring more attention than their brothers and sisters. Some seem to worry more, have more episodes of sadness, are more sensitive to criticism, are more readily upset by changes in routine or plans, and are quicker to anger. They are more easily frustrated, and when frustrated they may have severe temper tantrums. They may have great difficulty separating from home to attend school, and under stress they may demonstrate physical symptoms such as pulling out small strands of their hair, frequent stomach cramps, headaches, problems with eating, and an abnormal sleep pattern.

In spite of such reports from parents, we have little systematically collected information about individuals with borderline disorder as children. Few adults with borderline disorder were seen by psychiatrists when they were children. Some believe that this is because of the three-to-one female-to-male difference in the prevalence of borderline disorder. (This gender difference appears to be decreasing with more rigorously collected information.) Girls are less often seen by psychiatrists and other mental healthcare workers than boys because they are more likely to keep their problems internalized rather than act them out. Further, if girls were seen as children, they may have received some other diagnosis. Boys are more likely to be misdiagnosed with impulse control disorders.

Another reason we're uncertain about any symptoms of children who are later diagnosed with borderline disorder is that the recollections of adolescents and adults with borderline disorder, and those of their parents, are often distorted because of their difficult interactions over time. Such difficulties cloud people's memories and result in information that may not be accurate.

It's not surprising, then, that there are few articles in the medical literature that report systematic studies of the characteristics of borderline disorder in children. Therefore, there is no clear agreement about whether the disorder is present during childhood and what the diagnostic criteria should be.

In fact, some of the most popular academic books about borderline disorder don't even mention the disorder in children. Consequently, if you have a child who's been having significant behavioral problems, I suspect that it has proven difficult to get a clear diagnosis and information about a comprehensive and effective treatment plan.

Before we proceed, I will list the main points to understand about borderline personality disorder in children:

1. **Correctly diagnosing borderline disorder in children is a difficult and uncertain task.** The different criteria for borderline disorder in children do not agree well with one another, and they overlap to some extent with other childhood behavioral disorders. In this chapter I will review the different diagnostic models of borderline disorder in children, and other childhood disorders that resemble borderline disorder. I will also review the course of the illnesses in children that resemble borderline disorder. For example, some, but not all, children who have symptoms of borderline disorder, or another disorder of childhood, appear to continue to suffer from these disorders as adults. The purpose of this review is to underscore for you the difficulty in making a "correct" diagnosis of severe behavioral disturbances in children, and provide you with information on the most likely diagnostic alternatives in your child. In

this section, I will also discuss the importance of making the best possible diagnosis of a significant behavioral illness in your child.

2. **There are consistent findings of biological impairment in children diagnosed with borderline disorder.** This is true in essentially all of the studies that examined this risk factor in children. Although it is a painful realization, it may help you to understand that your child has a bona fide medical problem and is not simply misbehaving and in need of stricter discipline than other children.

3. **The environmental risk factors of borderline disorder found in children appear to be similar to those of adults with the disorder.** Recognition of these risk factors will help you to help your child more effectively.

4. **Timing matters.** I will provide you with guidelines for when to have your child evaluated professionally and how to locate the best help for your child and for you, so that you can learn new strategies that will make a difference.

5. **There is little validated information available about the effectiveness of specific pharmacological and psychotherapeutic treatments of children with the disorder.** However, there are anecdotal reports in the medical literature that the judicious use of medications in children with severe behavioral disturbances resembling borderline disorder benefit these children, and enhance their therapy and your interventions.

DEFINING BORDERLINE DISORDER IN CHILDREN

The early descriptions of borderline disorder in children paralleled the early process in adults described in Chapter 3. For example, there were reports by child psychiatrists, based on their clinical observations, that a group of children had disturbances in the correct perception, and appropriate responses, to many of their daily experiences. These children demonstrated a lack of early pleasurable experiences, hypersensitivity, disintegration under stress, low frustration tolerance, aggression toward parents and other family members, and difficulty in reasoning. Many of these symptoms are similar to criteria of borderline disorder (see Chapter 1). A limited number of similar reports subsequently appeared in the medical literature, broadly describing children with these and other characteristics that resemble borderline disorder in adolescents and adults. While some of these children later developed borderline disorder, other children developed different disorders. This suggests that children with these problems did not necessarily have borderline disorder or that they did have the disorder and a co-occurring disorder as well (see Chapter 8).

RESEARCH ON THE DIAGNOSIS OF BORDERLINE DISORDER IN CHILDREN

In an effort to define valid diagnostic criteria for borderline disorder in children, three different sets of criteria based on empirical research were proposed in the 1980s. In 1982, Jules Bemporad and his colleagues at Harvard University systematically reviewed their experiences with twenty-four hospitalized children who had been selected because their symptoms were similar to those described previously in the medical literature as being consistent with borderline disorder. In general, they found that these children had difficulty functioning in essentially every area, and that no single symptom enabled them to make the diagnosis. The specific symptoms that best described these children were:

- General developmental delay
- Rapid shifts from neurotic to psychotic-like states
- A significant inability to deal effectively with anxiety
- An excessive tendency to move from realistic thinking to fantasy and bizarre thinking
- Significantly disturbed relationships with parents, siblings, other family members, and other children
- Poor self-control marked by difficulty in dealing with frustration and anger, leading to severe temper tantrums and frantic, undirected hyperactivity

- Symptoms of poor social functioning, a noticeable failure to learn from experience, poor self-grooming, difficulty in adapting to change, neurological soft signs (for example, subtle impairments of coordination, perception, and/or intellectual performance), and significant fluctuations between high and low levels of functioning

It was pointed out that, as disabling as the above symptoms were when they occurred, these children could at other times function as well as their peers.

One test of the validity of any set of diagnostic criteria is its ability to define a population of patients who will experience a similar course of illness and outcome. In one of the earliest follow-up studies involving children diagnosed with borderline disorder, Donna Lofgren, Jules Bemporad, and their colleagues followed nineteen children (ages six to ten) who had been hospitalized and who met the Bemporad criteria for the disorder. The major finding in the study was that sixteen of the nineteen children later met diagnostic criteria for a personality disorder, ten to twenty years after they were first evaluated by a mental healthcare specialist. However, only three were diagnosed with borderline disorder as adults (two women and one man), while five were diagnosed with antisocial personality disorder as adults (all men). The authors proposed that borderline disorder in childhood, diagnosed with the Bemporad criteria, appears to be a precursor of a broad array of adult personality disorders. The results of this study suggest that the Bemporad criteria do not clearly distinguish children with borderline disorder from those with other personality disorders.

The results of the second attempt to define borderline disorder in children were published in 1986 by Deborah Greenman, John Gunderson, and their colleagues at the McLean Hospital at Harvard University. They studied eighty-six hospitalized children in order to explore the validity of the term "borderline disorder" in children and its relationship to the disorder in adults. To do so, they developed a modified version of the revised Diagnostic Interview for Borderline (DIB) for use with children. Of the eighty-six children studied, twenty-seven met these criteria.

A number of findings emerged from this study. Two-thirds of the children who met the modified adult criteria for borderline disorder also met the criteria defined by Bemporad. All of the children diagnosed with borderline disorder in this study had disturbances in impulse control, thinking, and interpersonal relationships. Unlike adults, children who met Greenman/Gunderson modified adult criteria for borderline disorder were more likely to be assaultive toward others than to injure themselves. Finally, many of the biological and environmental risk factors for borderline disorder described in adults (see Chapter 4) were found to be present in children with the disorder. The authors concluded that there were enough differences between their criteria for borderline disorder in children and the Bemporad criteria to indicate that a more discriminating set of criteria was needed to identify children with borderline disorder.

At the same time that the Bemporad and Greenman/Gunderson studies were in progress, a different approach was being used by Donald Cohen and his colleagues at Yale University to determine the proper diagnostic classification of children with "borderline syndrome," as they referred to it. In 1983 they suggested that borderline disorder should be included in the broad spectrum of childhood mental disorders associated with the abnormalities resulting from impaired brain development (see Chapter 4). Their proposal was based in part on the common occurrence of physiological disturbances of brain function seen in these children, typically evident by age four.

At this time, they defined a pattern of five areas of developmental impairment in these children. As the result of an extensive study of such children, they elaborated on and published a set of diagnostic criteria in 1993 for the disorder and renamed it multiple complex developmental disorder (MCDD). (MCDD is not listed in DSM-5 as a mental disorder.)

Children with MCDD have impaired regulation of their emotions, including anxiety, beyond that seen in children of the same mental age, which they demonstrate with two of the following symptoms:

1. Intense generalized anxiety, diffuse tension, or irritability
2. Unusual fears and phobias
3. Recurrent panic episodes, terror, or flooding with anxiety

4. Episodes of disorganized behavior lasting from minutes to days with the development of markedly immature, primitive, and/or self-injurious behaviors
4. Significant and wide emotional swings with or without environmental causes
5. A high frequency of idiosyncratic anxiety reactions such as sustained periods of uncontrollable giggling, giddiness, laughter, or "silly" reactions that are not appropriate to the situation

Children with MCDD demonstrate consistent impairments in their social behavior and sensitivity compared with children of the same mental age. They exhibit social disinterest, detachment, avoidance, or withdrawal in spite of being socially competent (at times), particularly with adults. Often their relationships appear friendly and cooperative but are in fact superficial and based primarily on having their material needs met. MCDD causes them to have difficulty in initiating or maintaining relationships with other children and to have disturbed relationships with adults. They often display high degrees of ambivalence, particularly toward their parents and caregivers, which causes them to exhibit clinging, overly controlling, needy behavior, or aggressive, oppositional behavior, including rapidly shifting love-hate behavior toward their parents, teachers, or therapists. They have profound limitations in their capacity to empathize with others, or to read or understand others' moods accurately.

Children with MCDD also have impaired cognitive processing (thinking), which is demonstrated by one of the following:

- Thought disturbances compared with children of the same mental age, including irrationality and sudden interferences of normal thought processes
- Magical thinking
- Making up new words or using nonsense words repeatedly
- Negative thinking
- Blatantly illogical or bizarre ideas
- Confusion between reality and fantasy life
- Perplexity and easy confusability (for example, trouble with understanding social situations and keeping one's thoughts "straight")

- Delusions, including fantasies of personal superiority, paranoid preoccupations, overengagement with fantasy figures, grandiose fantasies of special powers, and referential ideation

The above symptoms must have been present for longer than six months, and the child cannot have the diagnosis of autism.

Adapted with the permission of Lippincott Williams & Wilkins Company from Towbin KE, Dykens EM, Pearson GS, Cohen DJ, Conceptualizing "Borderline syndrome of childhood" and "childhood schizophrenia" as a developmental disorder, *Journal of the American Academy of Child and Adolescent Psychiatry* 1993;32:775–782.

You've probably noticed a significant overlap among these criteria, Bemporad's, and those of adult borderline disorder, with an emphasis on three of the four dimensions of borderline disorder:

1. Poorly regulated emotions
2. Impaired perception and thinking
3. Markedly disturbed relationships

Cohen and his colleagues noted that the ultimate course of the disorder was unknown. They did indicate, however, that reframing the problems of these children from intentionally willful behaviors to inborn developmental disturbances better enabled their parents to accept their children's condition and to learn how to better deal with the disorder. The authors also suggested the potential benefits of medications in children with MCDD, especially low doses of neuroleptics. As I discuss in Chapter 10, this class of medications has proven to be useful in treating borderline disorder in adults. Cohen and his colleagues believe that the conservative use of medications enables children with MCDD to learn more readily and relate more effectively. This conclusion about integrating the use of medications and therapy with children is precisely what is recommended for consideration in the treatment of adolescents and adults (see Chapter 12).

OTHER BEHAVIORAL DISORDERS IN CHILDREN THAT RESEMBLE BORDERLINE DISORDER

There are three other disorders that are listed in DSM-5 that can be confused with the early onset of borderline disorder. They are oppositional defiant disorder, conduct disorder, and attention deficit hyperactivity disorder (ADHD). These are among the childhood disorders most commonly seen by child psychiatrists. A fourth childhood disorder, called Intermittent Explosive Disorder, listed for the first time in DSM-5, also has many of the symptoms of borderline disorder and these other three disorders. It's frequently difficult to distinguish these disorders from one another in children. The correct diagnosis may only become evident in some children as they develop into adolescence. Nonetheless, because the symptoms of these disorders do overlap to some degree with those of borderline disorder, it's important that you have easy access to their diagnostic criteria so you can avoid, when possible, a misdiagnosis and inappropriate treatment.

Oppositional Defiant Disorder

Children with oppositional defiant disorder (ODD) have a pattern of negative, hostile, and defiant behaviors lasting at least six months that are not commonly observed in children of a similar age and level of development. During this period, four or more of the following symptoms are present:

- Frequently loses his or her temper
- Often argues with adults
- Often actively defies or refuses to comply with adults' requests or rules
- Frequently deliberately annoys people
- Often blames others for his or her mistakes or misbehavior
- Is often touchy or easily annoyed by others
- Is frequently angry and resentful
- Is often spiteful or vindictive

In order to be diagnosed with ODD, the behavioral disturbance must cause the child significant problems in social and academic performance, and the child cannot meet the criteria for conduct, mood, or psychotic disorder.

Keep in mind that these children don't demonstrate the disturbances in thinking seen in children with borderline disorder or MCDD, or in attention seen in children with ADHD, nor do they have the impulsive behavior seen in children with these disorders and conduct disorder.

Conduct Disorder

Conduct disorder is a repetitive and persistent pattern of behavior in which the child or adolescent violates the basic rights of others or the norms or rules of society. The diagnosis of this disorder is made by the presence of three or more of the following criteria occurring in the past twelve months, with at least one criterion present in the past six months:

- Children with conduct disorder frequently destroy property by deliberately setting fires with the intention of causing serious damage, or by deliberately destroying property other than with fire.
- These children are deceitful and steal: they have broken into someone else's house, building, or car; often lie to obtain goods or favors or to avoid obligations—that is, they "con" others; or have stolen items of significant value without confronting the victim, for example, by shoplifting or by forgery.
- Children with conduct disorder commit serious violations of rules: they stay out at night despite parental prohibitions, beginning before age thirteen; run away from home overnight at least twice while living with their parents or a parental figure, or once without returning for a lengthy period; and are often truant from school, beginning before age thirteen.

Some children who are diagnosed with borderline disorder in childhood are then diagnosed with conduct disorder in adolescence. It appears that this occurs in boys more frequently than in girls, for unknown reasons. The distinction between conduct disorder and borderline disorder is critical because the methods of treatment are considerably different. For example, medications and psychotherapy don't seem to be especially helpful for children with conduct disorder, while they appear to have some benefit for children with borderline disorder.

Attention Deficit Hyperactivity Disorder (ADHD)

I describe the diagnostic criteria for ADHD in depth in Chapter 8, and the criteria are the same for children. Again, it's essential to differentiate between borderline disorder and ADHD, because the treatments known to be effective for each disorder are so different. However, it's not always possible to make this differentiation, because these two disorders may co-occur. When this is the case, treatment for both disorders is necessary.

Intermittent Explosive Disorder

The fourth and final behavioral disorder of childhood that may resemble borderline disorder is now listed in DSM-5 as Intermittent Explosive Disorder (IED). This diagnosis requires that the following diagnostic criteria be met:

- The person has recurrent behavioral outbursts representing a failure to control aggressive impulses as manifested by either: (1) verbal aggression or physical aggression toward property, animals, or other individuals; or (2) three behavioral outbursts involving damage or destruction of property and/or physical assault involving physical injury against animals or other individuals within a twelve-month period.
- The magnitude of aggressiveness is grossly out of proportion to the provocation or to any psychosocial stressors.
- The recurrent aggressive outbursts are not premeditated; they are impulsive and/or anger based.
- The recurrent aggressive outbursts cause either marked distress in the individual or impairment in occupational or interpersonal functioning, or are associated with financial or legal consequences.
- Chronological age is at least six years.

- The recurrent aggressive outbursts are not better explained by another mental disorder or by another medical condition, or the physiological effects of a substance. For children ages six to eighteen, aggressive behavior that occurs as part of an adjustment disorder should not be considered for this diagnosis.

We don't know to what degree children diagnosed with Intermittent Explosive Disorder meet current criteria for borderline disorder. The symptoms of the disorder appear to be persistent. It seems likely that many of these children continue to have difficulties into adulthood. I suspect that a number of children who meet the criteria for IED suffer from the early onset of borderline disorder, conduct disorder, or a developmental disorder, all of which share symptomatology and risk factors, and that the most appropriate diagnosis may become clear over time.

SHOULD CHILDREN BE DIAGNOSED WITH BORDERLINE DISORDER?

At first, it may seem harmful to label children with any mental disorder early in their lives, especially when we're not certain yet how to validly and reliably diagnose borderline disorder in children. To suggest that doing so will not result in some stigmatic effect is to deny the reality that negative perceptions about mental disorders exist. However, you must weigh the consequences of such attitudes against the harmful short-term and long-term effects on the child and the family of not treating the disorder promptly.

THE IMPORTANCE OF EARLY DETECTION OF BORDERLINE DISORDER IN CHILDREN

In spite of the small amount of definitive information available about borderline disorder in children, it's still crucial to understand what *is* known, for several reasons. First, children with borderline disorder, or those who are at high risk for developing the disorder as teenagers or adults, may be exposed to the environmental traumas I've noted above and in the previous chapter. If children clearly meet criteria from two or three of the research models of borderline disorder noted above, and these signs are identified early, steps can be suggested by experienced psychiatrists to protect them and to help their parents. Second, if the child's symptoms are severe enough, appropriate medications and therapy may help reduce their severity. This will enable your child to benefit from appropriate educational interventions and decrease the short-term and long-term effects of their disorder. Consequently, most experts in the field believe these behaviors should not be left untreated. Finally, the child and their parents can receive therapy and counseling to learn adaptive ways to deal with the symptoms of the disorder.

If you suspect that your child has the symptoms of borderline disorder, or any of the disorders I've mentioned, it's crucial that you seek help immediately to determine the nature of the problem and to begin appropriate treatment if required. Remember, your child may have an illness that would respond to treatment. Your child may not just be headstrong and willful and simply need additional discipline. The sooner you have your child treated, the sooner they will receive relief from their suffering and the less harm will be done to them in the long run. Ask yourself: If my child had symptoms of a significant physical illness, would I wait to have them evaluated? Let's examine, then, the evidence that borderline disorder in children has biological and environmental causes, just as it does in adults.

BIOLOGICAL RISK FACTORS OF BORDERLINE DISORDER IN CHILDREN

As described in Chapter 4, based on repeated quantitative genetic studies, it is now accepted that borderline disorder has a heritability of about 60 percent, one of the highest heritability rates of all mental disorders. Throughout many chapters of this book, I also provide other scientific evidence that indicates there are significant changes in the pathways of the brain that control the behaviors exhibited by individuals with borderline disorder. Medical scientists no longer debate these findings. They are the facts. To continue to believe that, except in mild to moderate cases, the disorder may be treated only by psychotherapy is simply to live in harmful denial and prevent your child from receiving proper care for a serious medical disorder.

ENVIRONMENTAL RISK FACTORS OF BORDERLINE DISORDER IN CHILDREN

A significant number of research studies of children with symptoms that resemble borderline disorder in adults and adolescents have investigated the environmental risk factors of these children. The advantage of these studies over those that depend on recollections of adults with borderline disorder, or those of their parents, is that there is less likelihood of distortions of memory from time or from the effects of traumatic experiences.

In the first study of this type in children, Jaswant Guzder, Joel Paris, and their colleagues at McGill University reviewed the medical records of ninety-eight children admitted to a day treatment program because of severe behavioral problems. Forty-one of these children met the criteria of Greenman/Gunderson for borderline disorder, and the remaining fifty-seven were used as the comparison group. The findings of this study demonstrated that the environmental risk factors of children who meet childhood criteria for borderline disorder are similar to those of adults with borderline disorder. Compared to children who do not meet criteria, those who meet criteria experienced significantly more sexual abuse, physical abuse, and severe neglect. Evidence of persistent abuse and parental neglect was clearly higher in the children who met the Greenman/Gunderson criteria for borderline disorder. However, the findings of this study were limited by the fact that medical record reviews were used, rather than direct evaluations of the children and their parents.

This problem of collecting data in this manner was addressed in a follow-up study at McGill by Phyllis Zelkowitz, Paris, and their colleagues. They directly evaluated eighty-six children in a day treatment program and interviewed at least one of their parents. Thirty-five of the children met Greenman/Gunderson criteria for borderline disorder. The remaining children constituted the control group. Children who had experienced sexual abuse were four times more likely to be diagnosed with borderline disorder than the children in the control group. Witnessing violence was another factor that placed children at risk for borderline pathology.

Since these scientific articles were published, additional information supporting the initial findings have become available and lend credence to the position that borderline disorder is the result of necessary, inherent, biological risk factors that interact with environmental risk factors. Although environmental factors alone do not cause borderline disorder, the evidence is very strong that they increase the likelihood that the disorder will develop more readily in children who have genetic risk factors (see Chapter 4).

WHEN SHOULD YOUR CHILD BE EVALUATED?

Once you've progressed through the difficult task of accepting the possibility that your child may have symptoms of a significant and treatable mental disorder, your next challenge begins. You now need to locate a child psychiatrist who is knowledgeable, experienced, and broadly competent in this area of childhood mental disorders. The principles involved in the overall treatment and care of your child are reasonably similar to those that apply to adolescents and adults. Of course, there are a number of important age-related variations, such as the different levels of communication required with children.

Under certain circumstances, it's not a difficult decision for parents to understand the need to seek help for their child with a behavioral problem. If your child's behaviors are so problematic that they regularly disrupt your normal family routines and special occasions, and seriously interfere with schoolwork as well as the lives and well-being of the child, other family members, and friends, then it's clearly time for help.

But it's not my intent to trivialize this decision; it's just not that easy to take such a step. People have different levels of tolerance for a child's disturbed behavior. Some families will seek help much sooner than others. But is the family's level of tolerance the best guide? Some families may have such a high tolerance level that a child who desperately needs care does not receive it.

Often, the issue is not so much one of tolerance as it is of accepting the possibility that their child may require professional help. I understand how difficult it is for parents to consider the possibility that their child may have a significant mental or physical impairment. We parents have such high hopes for our children that it can be difficult to accept even their minor shortcomings. It's so much more difficult to consider that they may have a serious problem. To do so clashes with our dreams for them and is extraordinarily heart-wrenching.

Nevertheless, effective help is available, and your child does not have to continue to suffer. I hope this knowledge will be a consolation to you. One of our major tasks as parents is to help our children understand their strengths and limitations, and to determine how best to help them to build a good life within these boundaries. This is very difficult work, but as my wife and I have often encouraged and reassured one another, this is one of the ways we earn our pay as parents (we have four children and eight grandchildren—we *do* understand).

So regardless of your level of tolerance and acceptance, I suggest that you consider the following as guidelines for having your child seen for evaluation by a child psychiatrist:

1. There is a significant difference in the behavior of your child from his or her siblings or other children of the same age, or there is a substantial change in behavior. This includes moodiness, anxiety, sadness, anger outbursts, withdrawal from social contacts, and poor school performance.
2. Family members, friends, schoolteachers, church leaders, or others express concern about your child's behavior and performance.
3. You suspect that this may not be just a phase the child is going through, but a consistent pattern of behaviors that is emerging and worsening.
4. You determine that your child has several of the symptoms described as characteristics of borderline disorder, or the symptoms listed as characteristics of similar childhood disorders that I discuss in this chapter.

HOW TO FIND PROFESSIONAL HELP

For most parents, once the decision has been made to seek help, the next two steps are to locate the best help available and then to make the initial appointment.

In midsize to large communities, it's easier to find several sources of skilled professionals in child psychiatry than it is in smaller communities. If you are located reasonably close to a university school of medicine, most departments of psychiatry have a division of child and adolescent psychiatry. If you do not live near a university, large to midsize communities typically have one or more groups of child psychiatrists and other child mental health workers.

Child psychiatrists may also be established in solo practices in both small and large communities, usually working closely with other mental health professionals trained and skilled in the care of children. Another source of help may be provided by the child's school healthcare system.

HOW TO DETERMINE IF THE MENTAL HEALTH PROFESSIONAL YOU CONTACT IS QUALIFIED

Some child psychiatrists and their colleagues have more experience and skills than others in diagnosing and treating children who may be in the early stages of borderline disorder, or another disorder that resembles borderline disorder. It should not take much longer than the initial interview with one of them to determine if the person you have contacted has the level of expertise you are looking for.

First, determine if they evaluate and treat children with the behavioral difficulties demonstrated by your child. Then ask, in their experience, what different diagnoses such children may have. If they list a number of the diagnoses discussed in this chapter, ask if they ever see children with symptoms that resemble borderline disorder. If they haven't, I wouldn't necessarily rule them out, because of the lack of agreement about this issue among mental healthcare professionals. However, if they tell you that they don't believe in making diagnoses in children, or in the diagnosis of adolescents with borderline disorder, ask them how they develop a treatment plan and what the plan includes. The main purpose for attempting to establish the correct diagnosis, or reasonable diagnostic alternatives, is that the diagnosis provides important guides for further evaluation and for treatment planning.

Second, many parents are reluctant to agree that medication be used to treat their child with borderline disorder or other significant behavioral disorders. I understand their concerns. There are still not many controlled studies of the effectiveness and safety of medications in children with these disorders, except for ADHD. Nevertheless, there are some reports that show certain medications can be very helpful for these children. For example, some children with borderline disorder, MCDD, and IED do appear to benefit from medications, especially low doses of second-generation antipsychotic agents (see Chapter 10). I urge you to read Chapter 10 carefully and to keep an open mind about this possible method of treatment. If you are still reluctant, ask yourself the question, Would I deny my child the use of insulin if they had moderate to severe diabetes?

If the child psychiatrist does not use the medications listed in Chapter 10, along with psychotherapy and family counseling, I would be cautious about considering them a viable option. Do be especially careful if they tell you that they don't believe in using any medications for children, and that they focus mainly on intensive inpatient or outpatient psychotherapy as the only viable treatment approach. Also, conversely, be very hesitant if you are told that medications are the primary intervention and that little therapy is required.

Remember that we're not able to determine yet with a high level of assurance an accurate diagnosis and course of illness for many children. So it seems to me most reasonable to find a psychiatrist who knows the relevant medical literature, who has an open mind regarding the different diagnostic possibilities and treatment approaches, and who communicates well with you and with your child. Given our current level of knowledge about borderline disorder in children, it's likely that such a professional will give your child and you the best help available, now and in the future.

PSYCHOTHERAPY

There are a number of different psychotherapeutic approaches that are effective for adolescents and adults with borderline disorder. In addition, there are educational experiences for their parents and families. Understandably, these approaches must be modified if they are to be useful for children. For example, in the case of psychotherapy in children, it is important to understand that the ability to think abstractly does not normally occur until about age twelve, a fact reflected in the significant change in the educational material presented to children in school in the sixth and seventh grades. Difficulty in reasoning is a main symptom of borderline disorder, and impaired processing of auditory information has been reported in children with the disorder. Therefore, therapists and parents of the affected child must focus on developing ways to make compensations in these and other areas.

For example, children in general also have difficulty in accurately describing their feelings. This appears to be true of even adolescents and adults with borderline disorder. Child psychiatrists and psychologists are trained and skilled at gently helping children understand their feelings by using the common techniques of play therapy. Play therapy is used by the therapist to communicate with children because of the child's underdeveloped verbal skills compared to adults and because of their difficulty in conscious, abstract thinking. Essentially, it consists of the therapist using games and other apparatus with the child and asking them to tell stories. Children are often creative storytellers, and the stories they tell typically reveal the concerns, conflicting thoughts, feelings, and problems that they are not otherwise able to put into words.

In addition, your daily responses to your child are a critical part of the treatment process. As part of treatment, you will learn new ways of interpreting your child's communications and helping them understand feelings and behaviors, then channeling these energies in more positive directions. You may also benefit from reading Ross Greene's book *The Explosive Child* (see References for this chapter). He provides a number of helpful strategies to guide you in dealing with your situation.

THE BOTTOM LINE

The scientific literature suggests that borderline disorder may occur as a distinct entity in some children. Still, it's difficult to distinguish the disorder from other mental disorders of childhood that result in similar symptoms. Therefore, a reasonable approach is to enlist the care of a child psychiatrist and treatment team who are knowledgeable about borderline disorder's diagnostic and therapeutic challenges. Ideally, these professionals should be highly skilled and experienced, open and flexible in their approaches to medications and psychotherapy, available to you at times of crisis, and easy for you and your child to communicate with.

SEVEN

Borderline Personality Disorder and the Brain

I T'S IMPORTANT TO FIND OUT AS MUCH AS POSSIBLE ABOUT THE fundamental nature of your symptoms. Only then will you understand in plain language *why* you feel and behave as you do. Learning about the biological basis of borderline disorder can help make it seem less mysterious and even a little more acceptable.

It is a common belief that modern medicine does not know enough about how the brain works to explain any mental disorder at the level at which it occurs in the brain. As one cynic stated, "If the brain were simple enough to understand, we couldn't." Until the past two to three decades, that was largely true for the medical disciplines of both psychiatry and neurology. This was so for at least three reasons. First, as opposed to other body organs, the brain is enclosed securely in the skull. While the skull imparts significant protection for this most important of all organs, it also has limited the access of researchers and clinicians attempting to uncover the brain's mysteries.

Second, as the master organ of the human body, it is by many orders of magnitude more complex than any other organ in its structure, physiological functions, and biochemical processes. The brain's complexity and extraordinary level of activity are clearly demonstrated by the amount of nourishment it requires to function properly. Although the brain consists of only 1 to 1.5 percent of an individual's total body weight, it receives 20 percent of all blood pumped by the heart each minute. This disproportionate share of the body's main source of energy provides a clear appreciation for the importance and magnitude of its tasks. In addition, the brain uses many more of the approximately thirty thousand genes in the human genome than any other structure in the body.

Third, as pointed out by the internationally renowned neuroscientist and neurologist Antonio Damasio, interest in discovering the mechanisms of the brain was discouraged substantially by the concept of a "mind-brain" split proposed centuries ago by the famous philosopher René Descartes. It was Descartes's contention that the functions of the mind had no substantive base in the biological structure and functions of the brain but were inherently metaphysical in nature. Such was the influence of Descartes on thought leaders of his time, and those who followed, that it stifled research in this critical field for many generations.

Fortunately, especially over the past several decades, substantial advances in technology, especially neuroimaging, and the methodologies of quantitative human genetics, combined with other research findings concerning brain function, have produced an exponential increase in our knowledge of the brain and how it directs bodily functions and human behaviors. An in-depth discussion of these rapid advances is beyond the scope of this book, so for our purposes, the bottom line is this: the symptoms of borderline disorder mainly appear to be the result of inherent and acquired disturbances in the biochemical and physiological abnormalities in the neural systems that regulate emotional activity, impulse control, thinking, and relationships. This is true whether these abnormalities have had their origin in genetic, developmental, or environmental factors (as described in Chapter 4).

Prior to examining the neurobiological disturbances identified in individuals with borderline disorder, it is essential that we define the specific behaviors to be examined from a neurobiological perspective. The material in the next section will serve that purpose.

CORE BEHAVIORAL DOMAINS OF BORDERLINE DISORDER

In one of his books on the relationships between behavior and brain function, *The Emotional Brain*, Joseph LeDoux, a prominent neuroscientist at Cornell University, states, "The proper level of analysis of a psychological function is the level at which that function is represented in the brain." In order to understand the brain structures and functions that are believed to be involved in borderline disorder, I will now review briefly the four major domains and behaviors that are affected by the disorder (see Chapter 1) and then describe their neurobiological underpinnings.

DOMAIN I. POORLY REGULATED EMOTIONS

If you have borderline disorder, you may have observed that your emotions are affected in three ways: the *degree* of your emotional response, the *rate of change* in your emotions, and the *rate of return* to your usual levels.

Disproportional Degree of Emotional Responses

In the average person, emotional responses are proportional to the events that cause them. For example, a small negative incident will usually produce a comparably small negative response, whether it is anger, sadness, or anxiety. Likewise, a stronger stimulus will cause a proportionally stronger response. The emotional response is reasonably equivalent to the event that caused it.

If you have borderline disorder, you often experience disproportional responses to situations. You may overreact emotionally to many life events. For example, a minor constructive criticism by your partner may evoke a violently angry response from you, which leads to a major argument. A brief separation from someone important to you may produce an excessive amount of anxiety, sadness, or anger. More serious events, such as the breakup of a close relationship, could cause severe emotional reactions and behavioral consequences, including a variety of damaging and self-injurious actions. Less often, you may underreact emotionally to a disturbing situation, then feel bad later and not know why.

Emotional Lability

In addition to difficulty in controlling the degree of your emotional responses, you may experience rapid changes in your emotions. For example, you may swing from feeling anxious to feeling depressed or angry. As you may recall from Chapter 1, these rapid swings in mood could have resulted in your being inaccurately diagnosed with bipolar disorder.

Delayed Return of Emotions to Their Usual Level

Once in a hyperemotional state, you may have found that it takes your emotions longer to return to their usual level than it does other people. This is another characteristic of emotional dysregulation experienced by people with borderline disorder.

Therefore, it appears that in people with borderline disorder, the mechanisms in the brain that control these three characteristics of emotional response do not function properly. This results in emotional responses that are at times so severe and prolonged that they have been referred to as "emotional storms."

DOMAIN II. IMPULSIVITY

Most people with borderline disorder have difficulty effectively controlling their impulses and behaving in a reasonable and rational manner, especially when they are in a highly emotional state. At such times, you may find it extremely difficult, if not impossible, to calm yourself down, to think the situation through carefully, make a well-balanced decision on how to handle it optimally, and then do so.

Most individuals can recall experiences when emotions have briefly overcome their reason and self-control, and they say or do things impulsively that they later regret. Nonetheless, most of the time, even under stress, they are able to keep their emotions and impulses in check and to behave appropriately. In people with borderline disorder, however, the brain mechanisms that are responsible for regulating impulsive behavior are impaired, making it difficult to develop and carry out well-reasoned and appropriate responses.

DOMAIN III. IMPAIRED PERCEPTION AND REASONING

A number of problems with perception and reasoning occur in people with borderline disorder. These problems are especially evident when you are under stress and your emotions are running high. However, many of them may be present at a more subtle degree most of the time. There is substantial evidence that the brain systems that control cognitive activities do not function properly in people with borderline disorder.

The major symptoms in this domain of the disorder are temporary, stress-related paranoid thinking and dissociative episodes. You may also expect others to be overly critical of you and behave accordingly toward you. You may be uncertain about your core values and beliefs, strengths and weaknesses, and thus not have a well-thought-out and reasonable plan for your future. You may have difficulty in seeing, balancing, and resolving the complex problems of everyday life, but rather perceive and react as if people and situations are either black or white, all good or all bad. Finally, you may have difficulty in reasoning through complex problems, in identifying your alternatives, the advantages and disadvantages of these alternatives, and then choosing the most appropriate response, rather than pursuing a less advantageous action you want to take.

DOMAIN IV. MARKEDLY DISTURBED RELATIONSHIPS

Some experts in the field of borderline disorder consider the impairment in creating and maintaining mature, healthy, and interdependent relationships to be the driving engine of borderline disorder. There are reports from mothers of individuals with borderline disorder that they noticed difficulties in bonding with that child from the time of birth compared to their experiences with their other children. Initially, the baby was more fretful, cried more frequently and readily, and was more easily upset and difficult to soothe than their siblings at a comparable age. As they entered early childhood, they demonstrated attachment behaviors that varied markedly between excessive clinging and dependency and rejections of attempts at closeness.

As preschoolers, these children tolerated separations with above average difficulty, a characteristic that continued as they moved into early school experiences. They also had difficulty interacting with other children in age-appropriate ways, demonstrating sullen, morose, and withdrawn behavior interrupted by episodes of verbal and physical aggression. These characteristics continued through preadolescence, then often increased dramatically in intensity and scope as they passed through puberty and adolescence. Most of these adolescents did not receive professional help. For them, the symptoms of borderline disorder, and especially difficulties in establishing effective relationships, continued to increase through the more challenging years of young adulthood. The ongoing symptoms of borderline disorder became more evident as they continued to fall further behind their peer group socially and in other respects (see Chapter 1).

UNDERSTANDING THE BEHAVIORS OF BORDERLINE DISORDER AT THE BRAIN LEVEL

Why do people with borderline disorder have more difficulty controlling their emotions and impulses and difficulties with thinking, reasoning, and maintaining stable, positive relationships than people without the disorder? To understand the answers to this question requires that you have some understanding of how the brain functions. Again, bear with me here for a while. I believe you may find this a little easier to do and more interesting than you think.

It's estimated that the brain contains approximately a hundred billion neurons. These nerve cells have one primary function: to discharge impulses to other neurons by chemical messengers (to "fire") when they are stimulated to a certain critical level by other neurons. This fact immediately raises a question. If the brain is made up of cells that function simply by firing or not firing, how are the different actions or functions of the brain produced? In other words, how can the firing of these nerve cells produce different sensations such as vision, smell, and touch, as well as physical movements, emotions, motivations, and thoughts? Are the neurons that produce these actions inherently different, or do they use different chemical messengers, called neurotransmitters? To some degree, different types of neurons do have different functions in each neural pathway, but these neurons typically exist in many pathways, and the pathways use essentially the same neurotransmitters. Therefore, differences in cell type and in chemical messenger are not the primary reasons for the different functions of the brain.

THE RELATIONSHIP BETWEEN NEURAL PATHWAYS AND BEHAVIOR

It's not fully understood how the activity of neurons in the brain produces different functions, but it appears that they do so primarily because of their location in the brain and their connections to other, discrete neuronal pathways and specific body organs. For example, the stimulation of neurons that connect the retina of the eye with the part of the brain devoted to processing visual information (the visual cortex) results in visual images. If this pathway is impaired at any point along its course, we will not see well, or at all. Similarly, activity in neurons that connect other regions of the cortex with muscles produces contraction of the muscles, and therefore movement. It is understood that neuronal pathways that control similar body functions are located in specific areas of the brain that are essentially identical in all people and across different species and classes of animals.

These examples are fairly straightforward, but they don't answer the more difficult question of how the activity in neurons in the brain produces emotions, memories, thinking, and impulse control and enables relationships. The answer is only partially known. To a significant degree, activity in specific neural pathways and circuits controls these and other functions. That is, just as occurs in vision and movement, brain activity in certain other pathways results in specific emotions, while activity in yet other pathways results in impulse control, memories, and thoughts. Therefore, the importance of the location of neural pathways is critical in determining their functions.

INTERACTIONS BETWEEN BRAIN PATHWAYS

Although different brain functions are determined by the activity of neurons in different brain pathways, these pathways do not operate in isolation from one another but interact at specific locations in the brain. This enables information in one pathway to be integrated with, and to influence the activity of, other pathways.

For example, activity in specific memory pathways produces specific memories. But it may also have effects on the activity of pathways that produce emotions. Therefore, the memory of a pleasant event may also produce a pleasant feeling. The memory of another event may cause a very unpleasant feeling. The converse is also true. An emotional state may produce memories that are consistent with that emotion. When we are happy, we tend to have pleasant, happy memories and behave pleasantly. When we are sad, we are likely to recall sad and unhappy events in our life, have a sad expression on our face, and behave morosely.

Emotions are very influential in altering our ability to remember certain events. Those events associated with strong emotions are often remembered more vividly and for a longer time than events with little emotional significance. We also know that if an event produces extremely strong and disturbing emotions, accurate memory of that event may be impaired, and significant parts of the event may be forgotten or repressed.

The process of memory includes a number of discrete brain functions, both simple ones and those that are integrated into increasingly complex behaviors. These include odors; discrete images; words and sounds; spatial elements; other people and their dress, behaviors, odors, and so forth; and the emotional content (a single emotion or mixed emotions)—all varying over some period of time. Such complexity necessitates the involvement of numerous, specific, less complicated neural processing systems. The integration of these multiple neural systems in the brain is referred to as "distributed processing." This concept simply indicates that complex brain functions do not occur in a single circuit or region of the brain, but involved the simultaneous integration of information gathered from numerous brain regions.

NEUROTRANSMITTERS AND BRAIN FUNCTION

Neurons cause one another to fire or not fire by releasing neurotransmitters, which interact with their specific receptors on the next neuron. The interaction of these chemical messengers with their receptors ultimately has one of two effects. It either increases or decreases the likelihood that the next neuron will fire. That is, the effect of the neurotransmitter is either stimulatory or inhibitory.

By many orders of magnitude, the two most abundant neurotransmitters produced in the brain are **glutamate**, a stimulatory neurotransmitter, and **gamma aminobutyric acid (GABA)**, an inhibitory neurotransmitter. These two chemical messengers are used by virtually all brain pathways and circuits.

In addition, activity in brain pathways is stimulated or inhibited by other psychoactive chemicals that are called neuromodulators, such as **dopamine**, **serotonin**, **acetylcholine**, and **norepinephrine**. In contrast to the hundreds of millions of neurons in the brain that utilize the neurotransmitters glutamate and GABA, relatively few neurons utilize neuromodulators. It's estimated that the brain contains about a hundred thousand dopamine-producing neurons. Nonetheless, dopamine and other neuromodulators exert a strong influence on brain activity and function. For example, the loss of only a portion of dopamine neurons in one of its pathways results in Parkinson's disease. Alzheimer's disease is associated with the loss of neurons that secrete acetylcholine.

THE NEURAL SYSTEMS INVOLVED IN BORDERLINE DISORDER

Now that you have some understanding of the relationship between the neural pathways of the brain and behavior, you are prepared to consider the specific neural systems and neurotransmitter disturbances that are associated with the symptoms and behaviors of borderline disorder. Data from a number of different research studies support four conclusions. First, the pathways in the brain that process emotional responses appear to be hyperactive in the brains of individuals with borderline disorder. Second, the pathways in the brain that process impulse control appear to be deficient in their levels of the inhibitory neurotransmitter GABA. Third, there is evidence that activity in critical areas of the brain responsible for rational thought, reasoning, and the development of stable relationships is impaired in borderline disorder. Fourth, establishing and maintaining sound interpersonal attachments depends on the normal and well-integrated functioning of many of the above pathways. It is proposed that, collectively, abnormal function in these important and distinct neural systems are responsible for the core behavioral dimensions of borderline disorder. To be more precise, these are the neural circuits that appear to be disturbed in the disorder:

- Emotional dysregulation: **amygdala** system
- Impulsivity: **anterior cingulate cortex** and **orbitomedial prefrontal cortex** systems
- Cognitive-perceptual impairment: **dorsolateral and other prefrontal cortex** systems
- Markedly disturbed relationships: multiple subcortical and cortical distributed processing systems

The Neural Systems of Emotion

Researchers have consistently reported abnormal emotional responses in people with borderline disorder. For example, people with borderline disorder typically demonstrate a greater reaction to pictures of faces that have fearful and angry expressions compared to pictures of faces that have emotionally neutral expressions. This "fear response" is controlled by a structure in the medial (middle) region of the anterior temporal lobe of the brain called the amygdala (see Figure 7.1). The amygdala is the central structure in a neural system that processes emotions, and its main functions are to:

- Determine the emotional significance of new information in light of past experience, and provide this information to other neural circuits for further interpretation and appropriate action
- Rapidly organize and initiate subconsciously both inborn and acquired responses to stimuli
- Provide the essential first step in developing conditioned emotional responses

Information travels through and is processed by the main pathways and structures of the amygdala system as shown in Figure 7.2. Incom-

The Human Brain

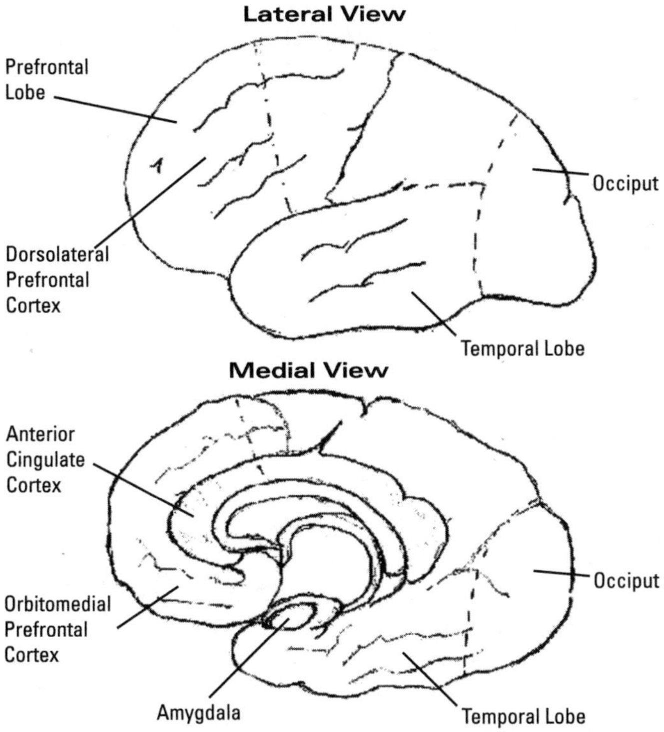

Lateral View

Prefrontal Lobe

Dorsolateral Prefrontal Cortex

Occiput

Temporal Lobe

Medial View

Anterior Cingulate Cortex

Orbitomedial Prefrontal Cortex

Occiput

Amygdala

Temporal Lobe

FIGURE 7.1 Lateral and medial (middle) views of the brain demonstrate regions that are important in the neural systems and pathways that control emotion (amygdala and orbitomedial prefrontal cortex), impulse control (anterior cingulate and orbitomedial prefrontal cortex), and perception-reasoning (dorsolateral prefrontal cortex).

ing sensory information is split at one of the main relay and processing structures in the brain called the **thalamus**. Part of the signal is sent to the amygdala and processed rapidly to determine its emotional significance as a result of past experiences. The amygdala then initiates the appropriate automatic internal and behavioral responses. These include programmed physical, physiological, and hormonal responses that are most adaptive to the situation.

The remaining information processed by the thalamus is directed to prefrontal cortical areas for more precise evaluation and appropriate decision making. This slower system provides more refined decisions

Neural Circuits of Emotion

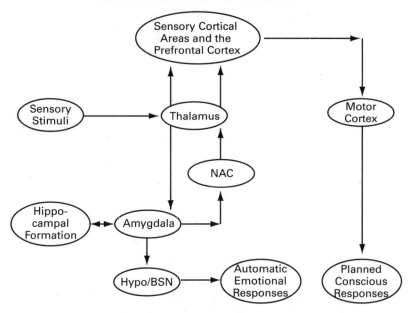

Figure 7.2 Information from sensory stimuli are processed and split at a deep brain structure, the thalamus. Part of the signal is transmitted to the amygdala, where its emotional significance is determined and appropriate automatic responses are initiated. Some of this information from the amygdala is transmitted to the nucleus accumbens (NAC), where it is processed further for the assignment of the appropriate levels of motivation and reward, both positive and negative. Pathways from all of the deep brain structures transmit information to the orbitomedial prefrontal cortex for conscious perceptions of emotional responses that we refer to as feelings.

Finally, part of the original sensory information that was split at the thalamus is transmitted to sensory cortical areas for more precise, conscious evaluation than occurred at the faster, though less precise, subconscious subcortical levels.

(NAC: nucleus accumbens; Hypo: hypothalamus; BSN: brain stem nuclei.)

than those made in the more rapid amygdala system, allowing for some degree of conscious control, which is mediated by structures and pathways related to the anterior cingulate cortex; this system minimizes inappropriate, impulsive behaviors.

The Neurobiology of Conditioned Fear Responses

A specific example may clarify the complex processes described above. One of the best-studied groups of emotion–related behaviors controlled by the amygdala system is conditioned fear responses. These are the automatic and rapid responses we develop when we are exposed to harmful situations. For example, a young child who is being repeatedly, physically abused by a peer on a playground may develop a conditioned fear response that generalizes to all similar sites. Conditioned fear responses typically begin with a brief "freezing" of movement followed by increased blood pressure and heart rate as well as endocrine responses such as increased cortisol and norepinephrine levels. (Endocrines are hormones secreted from endocrine organs into the bloodstream and produce widespread, protective effects throughout the body.)

It's important to understand that these emotional responses are automatic and not under conscious control. In addition, once a moderate to severe conditioned fear response occurs, it appears to be permanently embedded in the brain. It may lessen substantially over time, but it remains in place and may be reactivated by a variety of circumstances and situations that evoke memories of the original situation. It is not surprising, then, that recent research has shown the amygdala is more reactive in response to stressful stimuli in people with borderline disorder than it is in people who do not have the disorder. This hyperreactivity of the amygdala is not specific to individuals with borderline disorder. For example, veterans with posttraumatic stress disorder (PTSD) have vivid experiential memories during which they relive past traumatic combat experiences. Their brain scans demonstrate greater activity of the amygdala when they are exposed to combat pictures than occurs in veterans who have had similar combat experience but who do not have PTSD. It appears that either people with borderline disorder, and the veterans with PTSD in the study, are born with a fear system that is inherently hyperreactive, or their fear system became hyperreactive in response to early, fear-provoking trauma, or both.

People with borderline disorder are more likely to develop PTSD, panic disorder, and chronic anxiety than individuals in the general population.

Motivation/Reward Pathways and Borderline Disorder

The amygdala neural system mediates other emotions as well as fear. For example, the experiences of motivation and reward are tightly linked in the brain to emotion. We are motivated to perform those acts that result in positive rewards and feelings. We avoid situations and actions that produce negative responses and unpleasant feelings. The brain pathway that controls motivation and reward runs through an information processing structure deep in the brain called the **nucleus accumbens**, which is closely associated with the amygdala (see Figure 7.2). Both the nucleus accumbens and the amygdala are subcortical structures essential for determining the emotional significance of an experience and modifying the appropriate response to it.

It appears that the motivation/reward component of the amygdala system does not perform normally in people with borderline disorder. The decreased sense of self-assurance and self-worth that are characteristic of the disorder appear to be related to not feeling a proportionate degree of reward from accomplishments. This blunted response to positive rewards may be due to impaired function in the nucleus accumbens motivation/ reward component of the amygdala system. Ironically and unfortunately, individuals with borderline disorder typically overreact to negative stimuli.

Normal activity of the dopamine neuromodulator in the nucleus accumbens is essential for the motivation/reward system to function properly (Figure 7.5). There is evidence that the activity of this neuromodulator is disturbed in people with borderline disorder. Abnormal dopamine activity in the nucleus accumbens may also account for the high rates of depression and substance abuse associated with borderline disorder. Alcohol and many addictive drugs have been shown to temporarily stimulate dopamine activity in this area of the brain.

Emotion and Memory

As noted previously, memory and emotions are closely related. An important structure in the brain related to memory is the **hippocampal formation**. This is located adjacent to the amygdala and connected to it structurally and functionally by strong neural pathways (Figures 7.1 and 7.2). The close anatomical location of these structures enables low to moderate levels of stress and emotional response to increase memory, while high levels of emotion are known to interfere with memory formation and recall. This relationship between emotional response and memory may explain why some people with borderline disorder have episodes of brief to long lapses of memory when under high stress.

Therefore, it is reasonably well established that the emotional symptoms of borderline disorder, and other disorders that co-occur with borderline disorder (see Chapter 8), are related in part to dysfunctions, particularly hyperactivity, in the amygdala system.

The Neural Systems of Impulse Control

Research studies have shown that people with borderline disorder have a clear decrease in some functions that occur in the prefrontal lobes of the brain (see Figure 7.1). Nerve pathways and circuits in the prefrontal lobes are responsible for thinking, planning, reasoning, and evaluating what to do. Once these processes have occurred, they usually are acted on accordingly. The final step in this multistep process of impulse control is mediated by two other cortical areas, the anterior cingulate cortex (ACC) and the orbitomedial prefrontal cortex (see Figure 7.1), and is often referred to as "top-down control." These circuits perform several functions, including:

- Consciously evaluating the significance of emotionally charged information relayed directly from sensory systems, and indirectly from the amygdala system
- Assessing the potential consequences of behavioral responses to these stimuli
- Integrating and modulating these responses prior to and during action
- Storing this information for future use

It is clear why these functions of the orbitomedial and anterior cingulate prefrontal circuits are crucial in the control of impulsive behavior (Figure 7.3). These circuits exert a conscious, top-down modulation of the automatic activity of structures situated deep in the brain, such as those of the amygdala system. Depending on conclusions and decisions made consciously at the higher cortical level, the automatic, lower-level systems can be either stimulated or inhibited more appropriately. However, this top-down control is not complete. For example, when you're highly anxious, you'll have trouble relaxing, unless you take medication and/or you've developed special skills such as those learned in biofeedback training. Therefore, impairment of these prefrontal cortical circuits appear to result in diminished impulse control because you're less able to make

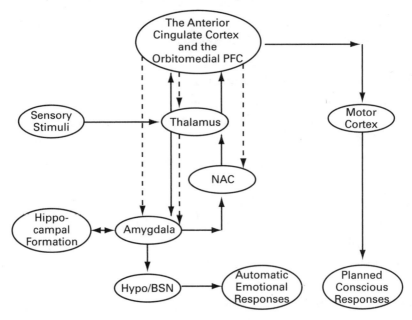

Neural Circuits of Impulse Control

FIGURE 7.3 Once information is processed at the cortical level for factual and emotional content (see Figure 7.2), prefrontal cortical areas, especially the anterior cingulate and orbitomedial prefrontal cortex (PFC), exert "top-down" control through pathways that connect with, and stimulate or inhibit, the subcortical systems (described in Figure 7.2). These pathways are represented by the dashed lines (– – – –) on the diagram.
(NAC: nucleus accumbens; Hypo: hypothalamus; BSN: brain stem nuclei.)

sound decisions and act more appropriately than when you are calm. The top-down process progresses linearly from cortical areas responsible for rational thought to the orbitomedial and anterior cingulate areas of the prefrontal cortex. But is there any evidence of abnormal activity in these areas of the brain in people with borderline disorder?

A recent study utilizing functional magnetic resonance imaging (fMRI) scans (three-dimensional images of the brain that can demonstrate regional levels of activity or function) of people with borderline disorder has revealed important data relevant to this issue. During attempts to inhibit inappropriate actions, subjects with borderline disorder demonstrated significantly less functional connectivity between the anterior cingulate cortex and structures in the medial region of the prefrontal lobes (see Figure 7.1), compared to people without the disorder. The degree of impairment in activity in this area of the brain in people with borderline disorder is associated with the degree of impulsivity that they demonstrate.

The level of impulsivity in people with borderline disorder is related to a decrease in activity of the inhibitory neurotransmitter GABA. This is similar to the findings about the levels of the neuromodulator serotonin in the pathways that control impulsive behavior. Low levels of both GABA and serotonin appear to result in increased impulsivity. Medications that increase serotonin activity in the brain often help people with borderline disorder gain better control over impulsive behavior. Interestingly, such an effect has not been established between impulse control and medications that enhance the activity of GABA in individuals with the disorder.

The Neural Systems of Perception and Reasoning

We know that parts of the lateral (right and left) areas of the prefrontal lobes of the brain are associated with thinking, planning, reasoning, and decision making—also referred to as cognitive behaviors. The dorsolateral prefrontal cortex and related cortical regions and their circuits are especially important in enabling proper cognitive function (see Figures 7.1 and 7.4). These prefrontal brain circuits enable us to:

- Make precise distinctions between similar sensory inputs (e.g., tones, words, shades of color)
- Reason
- Develop strategies for solving complex problems
- Think abstractly
- Facilitate working memory and learning

The dorsolateral prefrontal cortex interacts closely with the medial and orbital prefrontal cortices to enable the full expression of perceptual discrimination, working memory, thinking, reasoning, and so on (see Figure 7.4). This strongly suggests the possibility that some of the symptoms and behaviors of borderline disorder are due to disturbances in pathways that connect these and other structures in the brain. For example, brain imaging studies of people with borderline disorder have demonstrated a significant decrease in neuronal activity in the dorsolateral prefrontal region of the brain.

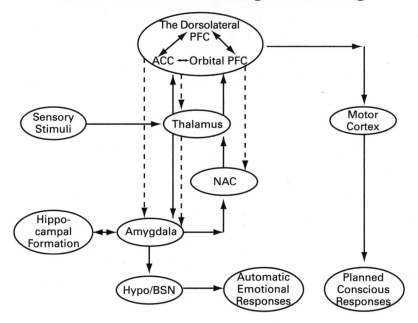

Neural Circuits of Thinking & Reasoning

FIGURE 7.4 Accurate and clear thinking and consciously processing information depend on activity in the dorsolateral prefrontal cortex. This information is integrated with, and processed further by, the anterior cingulate cortex and orbitomedial prefrontal cortex. Pathways from these latter brain regions exert "top-down" control on behaviors generated by the deeper brain structures shown in Figures 7.2 and 7.3.
(PFC: prefrontal cortex; ACC: anterior cingulate cortex; NAC: nucleus accumbens; Hypo: hypothalamus; BSN: brain stem nuclei.)

Certain neuropsychological tests are designed to evaluate cognitive brain functions. These tests consistently show that many people with borderline disorder have impairment of one or more of these functions, compared to individuals who do not have the disorder.

NEUROMODULATOR DYSFUNCTION

Other research findings give us clues about the specific chemical disturbances in the brains of people with borderline disorder, which may account for impaired emotional and impulse control and disturbed thinking and reasoning. There's evidence of abnormal **serotonergic**

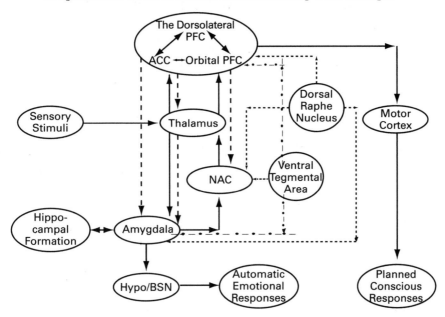

Dopamine & Serotonin Modulatory Pathways

FIGURE 7.5 The pathways diagrammed in Figures 7.2–7.4 utilize the stimulatory and inhibitory neurotransmitters glutamate and GABA, respectively. Activity in these pathways is modulated (stimulated or inhibited) by a number of other neurotransmitters, also referred to as neuromodulators. The neurons of two of these neuromodulators have their origins in the ventral tegmental area (dopamine) and the dorsal raphe nucleus (serotonin), both located in the brain stem. There is evidence that both of these neuromodulator systems do not function properly in people with borderline disorder.

- - - - represent serotonin pathways; – • – • – represent dopamine pathways; – – – –represent top-down control pathways.
(PFC: prefrontal cortex; ACC; anterior cingulate cortex; NAC: nucleus accumbens; Hypo; hypothalamus; BSN: brain stem nuclei.)

and **dopaminergic activity** in certain pathways in the brains of people with borderline disorder. The serotonergic and dopaminergic pathways originate in the brain stem and are distributed widely to many cortical and subcortical structures of the brain. These include the three neural systems involved in borderline disorder (Figure 7.5).

Neuromodulators selectively increase or decrease the level of activity in neural circuits in order to enhance appropriate responses of all types. Abnormal serotonergic and dopaminergic activity may seriously affect the neural pathways controlling the behavioral functions impaired in people with borderline disorder. The evidence that these chemical abnormalities exist in people with borderline disorder provides physicians with the opportunity to develop and use new and more effective pharmacological treatment approaches (see Chapter 10).

IN SUMMARY

Abnormal activity in the amygdala system (emotional dysregulation), along with decreased activity in the orbitomedial and anterior cingulate systems (impulsivity) and the dorsolateral prefrontal system (impaired memory, learning, and reasoning), occurs in varying degrees in people with borderline disorder. There is no reason to believe that everyone with borderline disorder suffers from the same degree of impairment in each of these neural systems. In fact, it's clear that people with the disorder have different levels of impairment in each of the behavioral domains of the disorder controlled by these neural pathways. Some people have more symptoms of emotional dysregulation, while others may have more difficulty in controlling their impulsive behavior. Still others may have the most difficulty in their ability to reason and think clearly and rationally, especially under stress. Indeed, at times of severe stress, they may briefly lose contact with reality to the point where they become very suspicious of people, or feel as if they are having out-of-body experiences or other unusual thoughts and sensations.

The two most important facts to take away from this chapter are:

1. The symptoms of borderline disorder are inherently, or in combination with the effects of deleterious environmental experiences, the result of disturbances in specific neural pathways in the brain, and are *not* the result of intentional or willful behavior.
2. Research continues to provide us with a better understanding of these disturbances, which will result in new and more effective treatments of borderline disorder.

EIGHT

Common Co-Occurring Disorders

I F YOU HAVE BORDERLINE DISORDER, YOU SUFFER FROM A NUMBER of distressing symptoms and behavioral problems described in Chapter 1. Possibly because some of the symptoms of borderline disorder overlap with other mental disorders that are also highly heritable, you may be more prone to develop other mental disorders than people without borderline disorder. These disorders include:

- Substance-related and addictive disorders
- Mood disorders, particularly depressive disorder, dysthymia, and bipolar disorder
- Attention deficit hyperactivity disorder
- Anxiety disorders
- Posttraumatic stress disorder
- Eating disorders, particularly bulimia and anorexia nervosa
- Other personality disorders

These disorders are often correctly diagnosed in people with borderline disorder, but the diagnosis of coexisting borderline disorder is missed. When this occurs, treatment for the other condition is often less successful than it might otherwise be, mainly because the untreated symptoms of borderline disorder are interfering with the effectiveness of other treatment interventions. Also, to effectively treat borderline disorder, your doctor needs to recognize co-occurring disorders if they are present, and prescribe the appropriate additional treatment. As I mentioned in Chapter 5, the early detection and effective treatment of a mental disorder co-occurring with borderline disorder under treatment often results in a rapid reduction of the symptoms of borderline disorder itself. So it's crucial that you and your psychiatrist try to determine the presence of these co-occurring conditions and promptly initiate the appropriate additional treatments if indicated.

In order to provide you with accurate descriptions and definitions of the disorders that commonly co-occur with borderline disorder, throughout this chapter I have used the diagnostic criteria for these disorders described in the *Diagnostic and Statistical Manual of Mental Disorders*, Fifth Edition (DSM-5), published by the American Psychiatric Association and used with its permission. This diagnostic manual is used across most of the world and is considered one of the leading diagnostic standards of mental disorders.

SUBSTANCE-RELATED AND ADDICTIVE DISORDERS

There has been a significant revision in the classification and criteria of mental disorders listed in this category in DSM-5 compared to those in DSM-IV TR. It is beyond the purpose and scope of this book to describe these changes in detail. What is clear is that there is no stronger predictor of a poor outcome for a person with borderline disorder, either untreated or treated, than the abuse of alcohol and/ or addictive drugs.

The careful evaluation of a large group of people with borderline disorder found that a majority of them seriously abused alcohol, street drugs, and/or prescribed drugs. There appear to be a variety of reasons for this. Many people with borderline disorder report that doing so temporarily relieves the severe emotional pain they experience, especially when under stress. Predictably, this relief is short-lived, so the benefit is brief, and the financial, physical, occupational, social, and other costs are great. For example, the use of these substances often drastically decreases already impaired reasoning and increases emotional and impulsive dyscontrol, thus dramatically worsening the symptoms of borderline disorder. It also significantly decreases the effectiveness of medications and psychotherapy on the disorder. These and other reasons are why, unless the person is able to sustain recovery from addiction, substance abuse is a strong predictor of a poor outcome for someone with borderline disorder. There is also evidence that some of the genetic alterations that predispose people to borderline disorder may also be among the group of genes that are risk factors for alcoholism and drug abuse.

Therefore, I strongly advise my patients not to use alcohol or take any street drugs, and to take prescribed medications only as ordered by their physicians. I encourage those patients who have a substance-use disorder to enroll in an alcohol or drug treatment program. I also suggest to some of them that, if appropriate, they may benefit from a trial on the mood-stabilizer topiramate because of its potential to reduce alcohol and drug craving in addicted patients. You should keep in mind that the use of topiramate for the treatment of alcoholism is an off-label use of the drug (meaning it hasn't been approved for this purpose by the Food and Drug Administration), and the potential side effects, such as decreased memory and a lowering of blood bicarbonate levels, should be carefully monitored by you and your physician.

The bottom line is that there is little hope of gaining control over the symptoms of borderline disorder while alcohol and other drugs are being used.

MOOD DISORDERS

Research has shown that the prevalence of major depressive disorder, **dysthymia**, and bipolar disorder are all increased in people with borderline disorder. A major depressive disorder occurs at some time in more than 80 percent of people with borderline disorder, whereas it occurs in 5 to 12 percent of men and 10 to 25 percent of women in the general population. Almost 40 percent of people with borderline disorder will develop dysthymia.

Because major depressive episodes and dysthymia occur so commonly with borderline disorder, it's important that you know their symptoms and immediately alert your physician if they occur.

Major Depressive Disorder

If you develop major depressive disorder, you will experience five or more of the following symptoms for at least two weeks:

- You are depressed most of the day, nearly every day. You feel, or have been observed by others to be, sad, empty, hopeless, or tearful. In children and adolescents, a depressed mood can appear as an irritable mood.
- You've lost interest, or no longer find pleasure, in many or all of the activities that usually bring you enjoyment.
- You've lost or gained more than 5 percent of your body weight in a month, without a change in diet, or you have a decrease or increase in appetite nearly every day.
- Your sleep pattern is disturbed by insomnia or excessive sleep almost every day.
- You notice physical and mental agitation or slowing most of the time, which may be observable to others as well.
- You feel fatigued or have low energy levels nearly every day. This may have resulted in a significant decrease in your usual activities.
- You have inappropriate feelings of worthlessness or excessive guilt. These feelings are not merely self-reproach or guilt about being sick.
- You have a decreased ability to think or concentrate, or you're indecisive, to the point that it interferes with your ability to function normally each day.
- You have recurrent thoughts of death and dying, recurrent thoughts about suicide without a specific plan, or a specific plan for committing suicide or have attempted suicide.

The symptoms of major depressive disorder will most likely cause you significant distress and hinder your ability to function socially, at work, or in other important ways. Before you conclude that you are depressed, it should be clear that the symptoms you're experiencing are not due to the effects of a substance (for example, a street drug or medication), a general medical condition, or the bereavement you feel for the loss of a loved one.

Persistent Depressive Disorder: Dysthymia

The symptoms of dysthymia are similar to major depressive disorder, but there are fewer of them, and they are less severe. If you suffer from dysthymia, you will have been depressed for at least two years. Your depression lasts for most of the day, and for more days than you feel normal.

While depressed, you will have experienced two or more of the following symptoms:

- Poor appetite or overeating
- Insomnia or excessive sleeping
- Low energy or fatigue
- Low self-esteem
- Poor concentration or difficulty making decisions
- Feelings of hopelessness

During this two-year period, you have never been without the above symptoms for more than two months at a time, and the symptoms have caused you significant distress or have interfered with your performance socially, at work, or in other areas of your life. In order to be diagnosed with dysthymia, you cannot have had a manic episode, a mixed episode, a hypomanic episode, or cyclothymic disorder.

It must be clear that your symptoms are not due to the effects of a substance (for example, a street drug or medication), a general medical condition, or bereavement.

Distinguishing Between Borderline Disorder and Major Depressive Disorder or Dysthymia

There's a considerable overlap of symptoms between borderline disorder, major depression, and dysthymia. So at times it may be difficult to determine if you have developed an episode of major depressive disorder or dysthymia, or you're simply experiencing an increase in your symptoms of borderline disorder. But there are some differences between the symptoms of these mood disorders and of borderline disorder that help distinguish one from the other. It is important to distinguish among them because the treatment of each disorder is different.

The sad, depressed, and lonely feelings associated with borderline disorder are frequently triggered by some life event and occur soon afterward. There is also a difference in the *quality* of the depressed mood. When caused by borderline disorder, the depressed mood is often associated with strong feelings of emptiness, loneliness, and fears of abandonment. Differences in the quality and magnitude of dependency on relationships help distinguish between the two disorders. The episodes of depressed mood in borderline disorder typically do not last for two weeks (like major depressive disorder) or two years (like dysthymia), and they can be easily reversed if the situation causing them improves.

People with borderline disorder may have difficulty falling asleep, or they may sleep excessively. However, these episodes of sleep disturbance are usually related to an identifiable, current life stress or crisis and stop when the event is managed successfully. Other examples of borderline disorder situational depressions are those manifested by severe, acute suicidal thoughts and self-injurious behavior that are the direct result of a very stressful situational event (for example, a severe argument with a parent, intimate partner, or boss). These symptoms are usually symptomatic of borderline disorder rather than of mood disorders.

In other words, when you have borderline disorder, you may experience many of the symptoms of major depressive disorder and dysthymia, especially when you are in a highly emotional state and under severe stress. But your symptoms are more likely be the result of poor emotional control, a core feature of borderline disorder, than an indication of a deeply rooted, persistent mood disorder.

Nonetheless, if you think you have the symptoms of either of these disturbances in mood, it's best that you promptly alert your psychiatrist so you can determine what additional treatment is appropriate. Additional treatment for a major depressive disorder or dysthymia frequently involves the use of an antidepressant, or an increase in dosage if one is already being used. Supportive psychotherapy (see Chapter 11) focusing on depression may also prove useful to help identify thought patterns and behaviors that operate as risk factors for mood disorders, and can result in new, more successful behaviors. Often, the appropriate medication change in a severe borderline crisis is the temporary addition of a small dose of an antipsychotic agent and psychotherapy, as noted above.

BIPOLAR DISORDER

Bipolar disorder occurs in about 10 percent of individuals with borderline disorder, whereas it occurs in about 1 percent of the general population. Bipolar disorder is similar in some respects to major depressive disorder but is accompanied by manic and hypomanic episodes. Manic episodes are periods of distinctly elevated, expansive, or irritable moods that last at least one week. These episodes are often associated with severe disturbances in reality testing, such as markedly grandiose ideas or frankly paranoid delusions. Hypomanic episodes consist of at least four days of mild to moderate elevation of mood, improved and positive thinking, and increased energy levels. There are also periods during which symptoms of mania or hypomania occur simultaneously with symptoms of depression. These are referred to as "mixed states." If an individual meets the criteria for both a major depressive episode and a manic episode, they are considered to have **bipolar I disorder**. If the criteria for both a major depressive episode and a hypomanic episode are met, they are diagnosed with **bipolar II disorder.**

Major Bipolar Symptoms
Manic Episodes

Having a manic episode means you experience a distinct, abnormal, and persistent period of elevated, expansive, or irritable mood that lasts at least one week.

In order to be diagnosed as having a manic episode, you must have had three or more of the following symptoms during your period of mood disturbance. They must have been present to a significant degree and have persisted for the entire time.

- An inflated self-esteem or grandiosity
- A decreased need for sleep
- Increased talking or a pressure to keep talking
- A crowding of ideas or the impression that your thoughts are racing
- Excessive distractibility
- An increase in purposeful activity, socially or sexually, or at work or school
- An excessive pursuit of pleasurable activities that often results in harmful consequences such as buying sprees, sexual indiscretions, or ill-advised business investments

These episodes can be quite severe and usually cause obvious problems in your performance at school, at work, and in relationships with others. Sometimes manic episodes require hospitalization to prevent harm to you or to others, or if you experience psychotic symptoms.

As with the other mood disorders I described above, it must be made clear that your symptoms are not due to the effects of a substance (a street drug or medication) or a general medical condition. The symptoms must also be differentiated from those of a mixed episode (see page 145).

Hypomanic Episode

Having a hypomanic episode indicates you experience a distinct, sustained period of elevated, expansive, or irritable mood that lasts at least four days and is clearly different from your normal, everyday mood.

The symptoms may resemble closely those of a manic episode, and you will need to have experienced at least three of them in order to be diagnosed. The symptoms must have been persistent and present to a significant degree for the whole time.

If you have a hypomanic episode, there will be a clear change in your functioning that is not characteristic of you, and the changes are observable by others.

Unlike a manic episode, a hypomanic episode will not hinder your performance at work, socially, or in relationships with others, or require hospitalization to prevent harm to you or others. You will also not experience psychotic symptoms.

Again, it must be clear that your symptoms are not due to the effects of a substance (a street drug or medication) or a general medical condition.

Mixed Episode

A mixed episode or mixed state means that you experience the symptoms and meet the criteria for a manic episode and for a major depressive episode (aside from duration) *at the same time.* Your symptoms must be present almost every day for at least one week.

This type of mood disturbance will hinder your performance at work, socially, and in relationships with others. A mixed episode may also require hospitalization to prevent harm to you or others, or if you experience psychotic symptoms.

As always, you must be clear that your symptoms are not due to the effects of a substance (a street drug or medication) or a general medical condition.

Mixed episodes may be caused by antidepressant treatment, such as medication, electroconvulsive therapy, and light therapy. When that's the case, the episodes should not be considered part of bipolar I disorder.

Because of the significant changes in mood experienced by people with bipolar disorder, this diagnosis is often inappropriately made for people with borderline disorder, which usually means they receive incorrect and ineffective treatment. However, you and your physician should be on the alert for the development of an episode of true bipolar disorder, especially bipolar II disorder, because the hypomanic symptoms can be subtle and easily missed. If bipolar disorder is detected, additional treatment is then needed. Such treatment usually involves the addition of a mood stabilizer such as lithium, divalproex, or lamotrigine, and an antidepressant when one is needed.

ATTENTION DEFICIT HYPERACTIVITY DISORDER

There is sound evidence that attention deficit hyperactivity disorder (ADHD) is—significantly—five times more common in people with borderline disorder than it is in the general population (5 percent versus 25 percent). In addition, it has been demonstrated that there is a genetic overlap between ADHD and borderline disorder. ADHD is characterized by decreased attention span, easy distractibility, and impaired school, work, and social performance. There are three subtypes of ADHD: one is associated with inattention and hyperactivity plus impulsivity, the second predominantly with inattention, and the third predominantly with hyperactivity and impulsivity.

ADHD is more common in boys than in girls. The hyperactive subtype is much more common in boys, while the inattentive subtype (the subtype with normal activity levels) is somewhat more evenly distributed among boys and girls. The disorder is now known to persist into adulthood in about 50 percent of individuals who develop it as children. These adults require the initiation or continuation of treatment. Because ADHD is a heritable disorder, it commonly runs in families.

It's not uncommon for children with borderline disorder to be misdiagnosed with ADHD and treated with stimulants such as **methylphenidate** (Ritalin) or an amphetamine derivative, such as Adderall. Children and adults with borderline disorder treated with these medications typically do not respond well, and may even do worse than without these medications. However, if borderline disorder and ADHD co-occur, there are some anecdotal reports that the combination of a stimulant with a low dose of a neuroleptic or antipsychotic agent for the symptoms of borderline disorder produces a beneficial effect on the symptoms of ADHD without experiencing the deleterious effects of the stimulant. In mild cases, behavioral treatments alone are effective in ADHD.

Inattention

In order to meet the ADHD criteria for inattention, you must have had six or more of the following symptoms of inattention that have persisted for at least six months:

- You frequently fail to give careful attention to details, or you make careless mistakes in schoolwork, work, or other activities.
- You have difficulty maintaining your attention in tasks or recreational activities.
- You consistently fail to follow through on instructions and to finish schoolwork, chores, or tasks at work.
- You have difficulty organizing tasks and activities.
- You frequently avoid tasks that require sustained mental effort.
- You often lose items necessary for tasks or activities, for example, school and work assignments, pencils, books, or tools.
- You are easily distracted by unimportant thoughts or events.
- You are often forgetful during daily activities.

Hyperactivity

In order to meet the ADHD criteria for hyperactivity, you must have had six or more of the following nine symptoms of hyperactivity and impulsivity that have persisted for at least six months:

Hyperactivity

- You frequently fidget with your hands or feet, or squirm in your seat.
- You have difficulty remaining seated in a classroom, at work, or in other situations where doing so is expected.
- Your activity level is excessive in situations in which it is inappropriate, or you often feel restless.
- You have difficulty quietly engaging in leisure activities.
- You often feel driven or compelled to do something.
- You frequently talk excessively.

Impulsivity

- You frequently blurt out answers before others have a chance to complete their questions.
- You have difficulty waiting for your turn.
- You often interrupt or intrude on others, for example, by barging into conversations or other activities.

Whichever symptoms you suffer from, they must have resulted in maladaptive behavior that is inconsistent with your stage of development in order to qualify for an ADHD diagnosis. In addition, some of these hyperactive-impulsive or inattentive symptoms need to have been present before age seven; there must be impairment in social, academic, or occupational performance; and current impairment from the above symptoms occurs in two or more settings, for example, at school, work, or home.

ANXIETY AND PANIC DISORDERS

Anxiety is a common symptom of borderline disorder. You may experience it especially during times of stress—for example, when you have felt personally criticized and rejected—or during periods of separation from people who are very important to you. Moderate to severe anxiety can also lead to other symptoms, like physical pain, headaches, abdominal pain, and irritable bowel syndrome.

Anxiety disorders occur in about 90 percent of people with borderline disorder. A very severe form of anxiety, called panic disorder, occurs in about 50 percent of people with borderline disorder. Panic disorder is characterized by unexpected panic attacks that are followed by at least one month of persistent concern about having another attack and the possible consequences of the attacks, or you have a significant change in behavior that's related to the attacks.

Symptoms can appear unexpectedly and suddenly, for no apparent reason, and disappear either rapidly or slowly. People who suffer from panic attacks may also be fearful of finding themselves in circumstances from which escape may be difficult or embarrassing, such as elevators, shopping malls, and movie theaters. This is referred to as claustrophobia.

Panic Attacks

During panic attacks you experience periods of intense fear accompanied by four or more of the following symptoms that develop suddenly and reach a peak within ten minutes:

- Palpitations
- A pounding heart or an accelerated heart rate

- Sweating
- Trembling or shaking
- Shortness of breath or a sense of smothering
- The feeling that you are choking
- Chest pain or discomfort
- Nausea or abdominal discomfort
- Feeling dizzy, unsteady, lightheaded, or faint
- A feeling of unreality or of being detached from yourself
- The fear of losing control or going crazy
- The fear of dying
- Numbness or tingling sensations
- Chills or hot flushes

If you're experiencing disabling anxiety disorders and panic attacks, you should seek treatment immediately. Treatment must proceed with care, however, because these disorders are commonly treated with certain medications, such as benzodiazepines (like Xanax, Klonopin, or Valium), that have been found to be harmful in some people with borderline disorder because of their addictive potential. Therefore, other approaches may be required, such as a temporary increase in a neuroleptic, atypical antipsychotic, or antidepressant medication if it's already being used. Initiating the use of an antipsychotic agent or an antidepressant may prove effective for moderate to severe anxiety or panic attacks if one is not already prescribed. In addition, a course of cognitive behavioral therapy specifically tailored to target the symptoms of anxiety and panic attacks should be considered as part of the long-term treatment of these problems.

POSTTRAUMATIC STRESS DISORDER

The occurrence of posttraumatic stress disorder (PTSD) in people with borderline disorder ranges from 26 percent in a mixed population of inpatients and outpatients to 57 percent in a totally inpatient population. PTSD significantly complicates the diagnosis and treatment of borderline disorder because of the overlap of some of the symptoms of these disorders. The fact that a history of trauma is present in everyone with PTSD and about 50 percent of those with borderline disorder also complicates the diagnosis in both of these disorders. The high rate of PTSD in people with borderline disorder is not surprising, considering the exposure of many people with the disorder to early and repeated traumas. Although some medical professionals have speculated that borderline disorder is a variation of PTSD, recent research suggests that they are separate disorders.

The term "PTSD" has received considerable public attention and, unfortunately, it's frequently misused. The following definition of PTSD will help you determine whether you suffer from the disorder.

If you have PTSD, you must have been exposed to a traumatic event in which both of the following occurred:

- You experienced or witnessed an event that involved actual or threatened serious injury to yourself or others, the threat of death to yourself or others, or the death of others.
- Your response involved intense fear, a sense of helplessness, or horror.

In addition, you frequently reexperience the traumatic event in one or more of the following ways:

- You have recurrent distressing recollections of the event, including images or thoughts.
- You have distressing dreams, the contents of which are unrecognizable.
- You act or feel as if you are reliving the traumatic event or having flashback episodes.
- You have intense psychological or physical distress when exposed to situations that remind you of the traumatic event.

You avoid situations associated with the trauma and attempt to numb your general level of responsiveness in three or more of the following ways:

- You avoid thoughts, feelings, or conversations about the trauma.
- You make efforts to avoid activities, places, or people that cause you to recall the trauma.

- You are unable to recall an important part of the trauma.
- You have a noticeable decrease in interest, or participation, in important activities.
- You feel detached from other people.
- Your feelings are restricted; for example, you are unable to have loving feelings.
- Your sense of your future has become limited; for example, you do not expect to have a career, marriage, children, or a normal life span.

Finally, you have an increased level of arousal, which is indicated by two or more of the following symptoms:

- You have difficulty falling or staying asleep.
- You are irritable or have outbursts of anger.
- You have difficulty concentrating or you are hypervigilant.
- You have an increased startle response.

Even at mild levels of severity, PTSD causes significant distress or interferes with your life socially, at work, or in other important ways, and has been present for more than one month.

It's important to determine if you have both borderline disorder and PTSD. If you do have both, your treatment plan should be reevaluated by your psychiatrist or primary care clinician (see Chapter 9).

EATING DISORDERS

A recent large study of people with borderline disorder who required hospitalization determined that the rate of eating disorders of all types is over 50 percent among these patients. The rate of the two most common eating disorders, bulimia nervosa and anorexia nervosa, was found to be 26 percent and 21 percent, respectively.

Bulimia Nervosa

Bulimia is characterized by episodes of significant overeating (also known as binging) and purging (self-induced vomiting and excessive use of laxatives), overconcern about body weight and dieting, and dissatisfaction with body size and shape. Bulimia is commonly and effectively treated with antidepressants (especially the selective serotonin reuptake inhibitors [SSRIs]), cognitive behavioral therapy, and other therapies. A trial on topiramate could also be considered because of its effect on appetite stabilization, but keep in mind the cautions described on page 139.

When you have bulimia nervosa, you have repeated episodes of binge eating that involve:

- Eating, in a specific period of time (for example, within two hours), an amount of food that is much larger than most people would eat during this period of time
- Lack of control over eating during the episode

After the binges, in order to prevent weight gain, you attempt to compensate by inducing vomiting; misusing laxatives, diuretics, enemas, or other medications; or resorting to excessive fasting or exercise.

In order to be diagnosed with bulimia, you must have episodes of binge eating and compensatory behaviors, on average, at least twice a week for three months.

Another key symptom is that your self-esteem is inappropriately influenced by your body shape and weight, and that the disturbance does not occur only during episodes of anorexia nervosa (see below).

Anorexia Nervosa

Anorexia nervosa is a very severe, sometimes fatal eating disorder that predominantly affects women. People who suffer from anorexia nervosa have an extreme concern about body weight and a preoccupation with food and calories. They believe they are overweight even when actually underweight, have a tendency to overexercise, and stop menstruating. Antidepressants (SSRIs), cognitive behavioral therapy, and other therapies are commonly used to treat this disorder.

When you have anorexia nervosa, you refuse to maintain your body weight at or above a minimally normal weight for your age. For example, you have weight loss that results in a body weight less than 85 percent of that expected for your age and height, or you fail to gain weight during a period of growth, also leading to a body weight less than 85 percent of normal.

You have a real fear of gaining weight or becoming fat, even though you are seriously underweight. You view your body weight or shape incorrectly, and your self-esteem is unduly influenced by your body weight or shape. If you are a premenopausal woman, you have missed at least three consecutive menstrual cycles. You also strongly deny the seriousness of your precariously low body weight.

OTHER PERSONALITY DISORDERS

Clinicians have observed for many decades that people with borderline disorder also have symptoms of other personality disorders. At times, the number of these symptoms reached the point where a diagnosis could be made for a second and even a third personality disorder. At other times, the number of symptoms of other personality disorders doesn't meet the diagnostic requirements, and the person is said to have "traits" of these disorders.

There are ten personality disorders listed in DSM-5. They are grouped into three clusters based on their most prominent characteristics. The following is a summary of the main features of each of these disorders adapted from DSM-5.

Cluster A (Odd—Eccentric)
Paranoid
Paranoid personality disorder is characterized by a persistent pattern of severe mistrust and suspiciousness of others, associated with an unjustified expectation of malevolent behavior that began by early adulthood. This mistrust is accompanied by a reluctance to confide in others, a strong tendency to bear grudges and counterattack angrily at the slightest perceived provocation, and unjustified suspicions of the fidelity of a spouse or sexual partner.

Schizoid
Schizoid personality disorder involves a pattern of detached social relationships associated with a decreased range of expressed feelings toward

others beginning in early adulthood. The individual with schizoid personality disorder typically:

- Does not seek or enjoy close relationships, even with family
- Chooses solitary activities
- Has little desire for sexual relationships
- Derives little pleasure from any activity
- Lacks close friends
- Seems indifferent to praise or criticism
- Is emotionally cold and detached

Schizotypal

An individual with schizotypal personality disorder has difficulty developing close relationships as a result of odd perceptions, distortions, and eccentric behavior that began in early adulthood. This person has odd beliefs or magical thinking, odd thinking and speech, is suspicious or paranoid, has a decreased range of and inappropriate emotions, exhibits eccentric or peculiar behavior, lacks close friends, and has excessive social anxiety associated with paranoid fears.

Cluster B (Dramatic—Emotional)

Antisocial

People with antisocial personality disorder have a pervasive pattern of disregarding and violating the rights of others. This pattern usually has been present since the age of fifteen, and the diagnosed individual is usually at least eighteen years old. Common behaviors are:

- Repeated illegal acts that are grounds for arrest
- Repeated lies
- Using aliases and "conning" others for personal gain
- Impulsive acts and not planning ahead
- Reckless disregard for personal safety or that of others
- Repeated irresponsibility regarding work, behavior, or financial obligations
- A lack of remorse

Histrionic

Histrionic personality disorder is marked by a pattern of emotional and attention-seeking behavior that begins in early adulthood. This person is uncomfortable unless they are the center of attention and draws attention by using their physical appearance. They have a vague style of speech, and their behaviors are dramatic and can be theatrical, with an exaggerated expression of emotion. This individual is often inappropriately sexually seductive or provocative, has a shallow expression of emotions that shift rapidly, is suggestible, and overestimates the intimacy of relationships.

Narcissistic

A person suffering from narcissistic personality disorder has a pervasive pattern of grandiosity, a need for admiration, and a lack of empathy that began by early adulthood. Typical behaviors and attitudes include:

- An exaggerated sense of importance
- A preoccupation with fantasies of great success, wealth, power, beauty, and perfect love
- A strong sense of being unique and capable of being understood by, or should relate only to, people of high status
- A sense of entitlement
- Exploitation of others
- An unwillingness or inability to identify or understand the needs and feelings of others
- Envious behavior
- Arrogance

Borderline disorder is also included in Cluster B.

Cluster C (Anxious—Fearful)
Avoidant

Avoidant personality disorder involves a pattern of feeling inadequate and being socially inhibited and hypersensitive to criticism that begins by early adulthood. This person avoids work situations that require social contact because of fear of disapproval or rejection, is reluctant to engage with others unless certain of being liked, is restrained in intimate relationships for fear of ridicule, feels inadequate and inferior and is inhibited in new situations because of these feelings, and rarely takes risks or engages in new activities for fear of embarrassment.

Dependent

Dependent personality disorder is characterized by strong feelings of the need for care, resulting in a pervasive pattern of submissive and clinging behaviors and separation fears that begin by early adulthood. This person typically:

- Requires excessive reassurance in making everyday decisions
- Wants others to assume responsibility for most major life situations
- Is fearful of disagreeing because of fear of lack of support
- Fears starting projects because of lack of confidence
- Goes to extremes to gain nurturance and support
- Is uncomfortable when alone because of unrealistic fears of inadequacy
- Urgently seeks another close relationship when one ends
- Is overly preoccupied by the fear of being left to care for themselves

Obsessive-Compulsive

Obsessive-compulsive personality disorder is characterized by a preoccupation with orderliness, perfection, and internal and interpersonal control at the cost of being flexible, open, and efficient, beginning by early adulthood. This person is so preoccupied with organization that the main point of the activity is lost. They are perfectionistic to a degree that interferes with completion of the task; devote excessive time to work at the expense of leisure activities and friendships; are overly conscientious and inflexible about morality, ethics, or values; hoard worthless items of no sentimental value; are reluctant to assign a task or work to others unless the other person will perform it exactly the same way; spend money reluctantly; and are rigid and stubborn.

In a recent study, adolescents with borderline disorder displayed a broader array of symptoms of other personality disorders than did adults, especially schizotypal and passive-aggressive (no longer listed as a personality disorder). In a different study of adults with borderline disorder, antisocial personality disorder co-occurred more commonly than other personality disorders. In a large study of adults, men and women with borderline disorder demonstrated different patterns of co-occurrence. Men were more likely than women to meet criteria for paranoid, passive-aggressive, narcissistic, and antisocial personality disorder.

The high rate of co-occurrence of borderline disorder and other personality disorders can be a major complication in its diagnosis and treatment. The significant overlap of symptoms between personality disorders is a major reason why a diagnostic approach to personality disorders based on symptom *dimensions,* such as emotional dysregulation and impulsivity, is thought to be more accurate and useful than the current approach of defining distinct *categories* of personality disorders.

WHY IS THE ISSUE OF CO-OCCURRENCE IMPORTANT?

It's a very real possibility that some of your symptoms are caused by a co-occurring disorder, not borderline disorder. This should be considered if some of your symptoms don't match up with those of borderline disorder. It's essential to keep this in mind, because these symptoms may be readily treated and improve your condition significantly. Many people simply assume that these symptoms are the result of their borderline disorder and then think that their treatment plan is failing. This in turn causes a number of individuals to drop out of treatment, which is the worst choice they can make.

These co-occurring disorders *can* be treated, and there's evidence that their successful treatment may also significantly reduce the severity of the symptoms of borderline disorder, which of course would be a great relief.

NINE

The Key Elements of Treatment

PROPER TREATMENT OF BORDERLINE DISORDER INVOLVES THE following components: locating a **primary clinician**, determining the most appropriate level of care for you, evaluating your need for medication, and selecting the type of psychotherapy that will be most effective for you. This chapter will provide information on the first two steps of this process, so you can make more informed decisions about your care. I will also describe in detail the role your primary clinician plays in the treatment, and the process you both use to determine your proper level of care at any time. The following two chapters will cover the topics of medication and psychotherapy.

BORDERLINE DISORDER TREATMENT COMPONENTS

The most important step in obtaining proper treatment for borderline disorder is selecting a psychiatrist or other mental health professional skilled in the diagnosis and treatment of the disorder. This person will serve as your primary clinician. Together, you will determine the level of care that is the least restrictive and provides you with optimal safety and support at any given time during treatment. Once this is determined, you may need to try a number of medications before you find the one medication or the combination of medications that yields the best results with the fewest side effects. Although there is no medical magic bullet for borderline disorder, medications often help lessen the severity of the symptoms and also set the stage for the best possible results from psychotherapy.

Abstaining from alcohol and street drugs is essential if you are to make any progress in your treatment. It's also essential that psychotherapy be part of your total treatment plan. Therefore, the most appropriate psychotherapeutic approaches need to be determined. Individual psychotherapy provides the optimal long-term therapeutic experience for patients with borderline disorder.

In addition, working in group therapy and participating in support groups with other people with borderline disorder can be helpful. Realizing that others also suffer from this disorder and learning ways to deal with emotional crises, better control impulsive behaviors, and improve your reasoning skills will benefit you. For example, you will be more likely to develop and sustain successful relationships. Group therapy may facilitate the work you accomplish in individual psychotherapy and shorten the process. It's also helpful to work with parents, spouse, and other family members to build and strengthen these critical relationships. But this work can't occur without your strong commitment and effort, and those of involved family members.

In order to be effective, all forms of psychotherapy require changes in old behavioral habits that do not work well. Habits are difficult to break, especially when they need to be replaced by new behaviors that at first feel strange and frightening.

Many of my patients initially find the process of getting started in treatment a bit overwhelming, but I try to reassure them that they are not alone in their struggle to gain control over their lives. In addition to my help, a team of skilled professionals and an extensive range of strategies have been proven over time to be extremely helpful. Gradually increasing the number and intensity of treatment approaches is an effective way to help you gain a better understanding of your illness and control over it, and to learn new skills at a reasonable and tolerable pace.

TAKING RESPONSIBILITY

The successful journey to a more stable, happy, productive, and satisfying life for people suffering from borderline disorder depends on a number of factors, but it's essential that you understand clearly and believe deeply that you, more than anyone or anything else, have the ability and responsibility to gain control over your own life.

You need to seek out the best clinicians to help you understand more about the characteristics and nature of your disorder, the specific ways it affects your life, and what you can do to minimize its effects. You must learn to exert the self-discipline required to do what needs to be done. It is important that you encourage and allow your family to learn how to best help you. In other words, you have to take responsibility for building the foundation for your own recovery. Patience and persistence are crucial to your success, and these virtues are usually not strong points of people with borderline disorder. However, they *can* be developed, especially with the proper help, and as you achieve small and large successes, failures become less common.

FINDING A PRIMARY CLINICIAN

Finding the right clinician to help you is critical. Given the number and complexity of issues, mental health providers, and decisions involved in the proper treatment of borderline disorder, you need a single clinician to assume a central role in helping you. This person is referred to as your "primary clinician." In his book *Borderline Personality Disorder: A Clinical Guide*, John Gunderson describes the responsibilities of the primary clinician:

- To educate the patient about the nature and causes of borderline disorder
- To ensure that all appropriate evaluations are performed in order to determine the patient's specific needs

- To develop with the patient a comprehensive treatment plan that best meets these needs
- To ensure that the plan is implemented
- To routinely determine the patient's safety and progress in treatment
- To implement changes in the treatment plan when indicated
- To ensure communication among other therapists, if any, who are involved in the patient's treatment

There is some controversy, even among experts, as to the qualifications and skills required to serve most effectively as the primary clinician for people with borderline disorder. My experience has led me to side with those who believe that the optimal choice for the role is a psychiatrist who is well trained and experienced in this area. Because of psychiatrists' training in the discipline of medicine, they are best able to understand and explain to patients with borderline disorder the biological, as well as the environmental, bases of the disorder. As physicians, psychiatrists are accustomed to making judgments about the safety of patients and taking prompt action when indicated. Also, psychiatrists are trained in most aspects of treatment, have unique knowledge about the appropriate use of medications, and, if trained properly, are familiar with most of the psychotherapies effective in treating borderline disorder. Finally, as is the case for all physicians, psychiatrists are traditionally trained and generally expected to serve as the leader of multidisciplinary treatment teams and to make the final clinical decisions.

Having stated this, I know that in many communities there are no psychiatrists who have sufficient training and experience with borderline disorder to fill the role of primary clinician. Under these circumstances, you should go with the clinician who is best trained and most experienced in borderline disorder. He or she is preferable to a physician of lesser training and experience, and may serve you effectively as your primary clinician.

Once you locate and engage with a primary clinician, a treatment plan should be developed. There are several components of a successful treatment plan for borderline disorder that need to be considered. These include the determination of the proper level of care (e.g., hospital, residential, intensive outpatient, or regular outpatient), and the selection of the appropriate combination of medications, psychotherapy, group therapy, and participation in support groups.

LEVELS OF CARE

A careful evaluation by a psychiatrist or other skilled physician will lead to the determination of your most appropriate level of care. If the risk is high for self-harm or harm to others, you may require hospitalization and close supervision. If this is not the case, but your symptoms are severe and can't be managed effectively on an outpatient basis, you may require a partial hospitalization program or residential care. But most often, intensive or regular outpatient care will be the most appropriate setting for your treatment. Intensive outpatient care includes a weekly or biweekly meeting with your psychiatrist, two or more psychotherapy sessions with your therapist each week, and life coaches who work with you two or more days a week and are available when you need them.

At times, making the best decision on the appropriate level of care can be difficult for you, your physician, and your family, especially early in the treatment process when your knowledge of one another is limited. Changing your level of care may be necessary at any time during the treatment process. After you have been in treatment for a while, the decision to change the level of care is easier than early in treatment, because of the degree of knowledge and trust that has been built among you, your physician, and your family. Under most circumstances, whenever a change in the level of care is considered, everyone should engage in a thorough discussion of the alternatives and the relative benefits and risks in order to make the best decision. Once the proper level of care for you has been determined, it's time to make important decisions about medications and psychotherapy. The following two chapters will provide you with information about these two critical areas of your treatment and their smooth integration.

ten

Medications

THERE ARE TWO REASONS WHY MEDICATIONS ARE USED IN THE treatment of borderline disorder. First, they've been shown to be very helpful in stabilizing emotional disturbances, reducing impulsivity, enhancing thinking and reasoning abilities, and improving relationships. This improvement in symptoms significantly reduces the level of your discomfort and enables you to benefit more from psychotherapy. Second, medications are also effective in treating certain symptoms of other mental disorders that are frequently associated with borderline disorder, such as depression, panic attacks, ADHD, and physical disorders like migraine headaches.

It's difficult for people with borderline disorder to learn about themselves and their disorder, to deal effectively with their problems, and to make real progress in psychotherapy when they are not able to adequately control their emotional reactions and impulsivity, to perceive subtle communications accurately, to think rationally and clearly, and to interact more effectively with others. Many people with borderline disorder feel as if they are fighting a losing battle because they know they shouldn't allow their emotions and behaviors to get out of control, but they can't seem to stop it from happening. They feel continually frustrated because they're unable to exert adequate control over their feelings and impulses, and unable to reason and act the way they would like to under stress.

For example, it's important that you become increasingly aware of your feelings and internal conflicts. Try not to escape from them when attempting to respond effectively to a particularly difficult issue, such as separations, and the sorrow, fear, anger, and other painful feelings that accompany them. These are the times when you're most likely to lose track of what you've learned in therapy and to act in self-destructive ways, such as excessive drinking, drug use, or self-injury. The situation is additionally frustrating because other people do not understand why you lose control from time to time. They often consider such behavior to be entirely willful and self-centered, and you know that this is not so.

I believe that you and your family will be pleasantly surprised and considerably relieved to learn that medications can help reduce some of the most troublesome of your symptoms of borderline disorder to a more tolerable level. Then you will be better able to remain engaged in difficult situations, and to learn to handle conflicts and other problems more effectively than you have in the past. Remember that Mrs. Davis (Chapter 2), the first patient with borderline disorder I treated with psychotherapy, did not benefit much from therapy until she agreed to take a small dose of medication to help her.

THE MEDICATIONS USED TO TREAT BORDERLINE DISORDER

The American Psychiatric Association in 2001 published a supplement to their journal, the *American Journal of Psychiatry*, titled "Practice Guideline for the Treatment of Patients with Borderline Personality Disorder." In this guideline, neuroleptics, and more recently developed antipsychotic agents, are recommended for people with borderline disorder who have symptoms of disturbed thinking, such as paranoia, as well as depressed mood, impulsivity, and self-destructive behaviors.

More recent studies of both the original, first-generation and then the second-generation antipsychotic agents (FGAs and SGAs) have supported the beneficial effects of a number of these agents in the reduction of specific symptoms of borderline disorder. These symptoms include emotional dysregulation, impulsive aggressiveness, and cognitive disturbances such as suspiciousness, acute episodes of paranoid thinking, difficulty integrating emotions, and thoughts that result in irrational and unreasonable behaviors.

The 2001 guideline recommended a class of antidepressants referred to as selective serotonin reuptake inhibitors as the initial pharmacological treatment for people with borderline disorder who are suffering from the emotional symptoms and impulsivity associated with the disorder. However, additional studies have not supported the use of SSRIs for the treatment of any symptoms of borderline disorder. The use of SSRIs in the treatment of individuals with the disorder is now primarily for the relief of symptoms of major depressive episodes that may co-occur with the disorder (see Chapter 8).

Another class of medications, referred to as mood stabilizers, have been studied to evaluate their effects on the core symptoms of borderline disorder. The results support the use of these medications, especially topiramate (Topamax), lamotrigine (Lamictal), and valproate (Depakote). These studies demonstrate benefits in the stabilization of the symptoms of mood dysfunctions and the harmful impulsivity observed in borderline disorder, but these medications have not been shown to be effective for the treatment of cognitive disturbances such as suspiciousness, paranoia, and difficulty in reasoning.

THE NEUROSCIENCE-BASED NOMENCLATURE (NbN) FOR PSYCHIATRIC MEDICATIONS

It has become increasingly apparent that the current system used for naming classes of psychopharmacological medications can be significantly misleading to the patient and clinician. This can make patients resistant to taking medications for a disorder when it is indicated. For example, it has been well known for over fifty years that some patients with moderate to severe depressions do not respond to antidepressants alone, but require the addition of an antipsychotic agent to augment the activity of the antidepressant, even in the absence of any psychotic symptoms. Understandably, some patients are reluctant to take a medication that is indicated for schizophrenia and bipolar disorder when they are not suffering from either disorder and are not psychotic.

Therefore, the six major psychopharmacological societies in the world have proposed and passed a neuroscience-based nomenclature (NbN) for psychiatric medications. The NbN has gained the support of the Food and Drug Administration (FDA) and many clinical and academic programs from across the world. The primary purpose of my mentioning the NbN is to familiarize you with the name and the reasons for this new nomenclature. However, until the NbN becomes more prevalently used and familiar, in this book I will refer most often to the current system of classification of psychopharmacological agents. I will also generally use the common trade names for drugs because it is more likely you will recognize them than the generic names, which I will still use on occasion.

NEUROLEPTICS AND ATYPICAL ANTIPSYCHOTIC AGENTS

The classes of medications that have been studied most for the treatment of borderline disorder are neuroleptics, now referred to as first-generation antipsychotics (FGAs), and atypical antipsychotic agents, also referred to as second-generation antipsychotics (SGAs; see Table 10.1). The FGAs were the first medications found to be effective in the treatment of psychotic disorders such as schizophrenia and bipolar disorder. They include chlorpromazine (Thorazine), trifluoperazine (Stelazine), haloperidol (Haldol), thiothixene (Navane), perphenazine (Trilafon), and other less commonly used medications in this class. FGAs work by blocking a specific brain dopamine D2 receptor; this mechanism of action appears to produce both their therapeutic effects and a number of their side effects.

Because FGAs have a tendency to produce movement disorders (such as acute dyskinesias and **tardive dyskinesia**—see page 170) and other problematic side effects, the SGAs were developed. The SGAs include the first drug discovered in this class, clozapine (Clozaril), and olanzapine (Zyprexa), risperidone (Risperdal), quetiapine (Seroquel), ziprasidone (Geodon), aripiprazole (Abilify), lurasidone (Latuda), brexpiprazole (Rexulti), and others. As a class, the SGAs appear to be more effective than the FGAs, and appear to be less likely to cause dyskinesias and other side effects. SGAs block both the specific brain dopamine D2 receptor and the serotonin 5-HT2A receptor, which appears to account for the differences in SGAs' therapeutic effects and their side effects.

The five SGAs that appear to be used most frequently in patients with borderline disorder in the United States are aripiprazole (Abilify), olanzapine (Zyprexa), risperidone (Risperdal), quetiapine (Seroquel), and lurasidone (Latuda; see Table 10.1). Zyprexa has been studied the most extensively in placebo-controlled trials, and the two largest trials were conducted to obtain an FDA indication of borderline disorder for this medication. One of these two trials met FDA criteria, but the second failed to do so by a small margin. Therefore, the FDA did not approve borderline disorder as an indication for the use of Zyprexa. Nonetheless, because of the strong data supporting its efficacy, Zyprexa remains in use as a medication for borderline disorder. In meta-analyses of antipsychotic agents in individuals with the disorder, Abilify, Haldol, and Zyprexa appear to reduce symptoms of emotional dysregulation, impulsivity, and cognitive-perceptual impairment.

In addition, a 2014 study by Donald Black, MD, and colleagues suggests that quetiapine (Seroquel) at 150 milligrams and 300 milligrams per day is superior to placebo in the treatment of subjects with borderline disorder. Interestingly, the effect seems greater at the lower dose.

The major side effects of most SGAs are weight gain, elevation of blood lipids and prolactin levels, and a reduction in glucose tolerance, which may interfere with the control of diabetes. Also, these side effects may enhance your risk of developing type 2 diabetes. Since its approval by the FDA, I have also used Latuda with increasing frequency, in spite of the lack of any published studies on its effects on borderline disorder, mainly because of its lower side-effect profile compared to the other SGAs. I have found Latuda to be as effective in all areas as other SGAs, but significantly less likely to produce weight gain, hyperlipidemia, and glucose intolerance than the other SGAs with the exception of ziprasidone (Geodon).

Geodon, unfortunately, has been reported so far to be ineffective in the treatment of borderline disorder when administered orally, even at moderate doses. However, in people in acute borderline crises who present to the emergency room, it has been reported that ten-milligram intramuscular doses of Geodon appear to provide prompt and significant reduction in aggressive and psychotic symptoms of the disorder. I have experienced similar results in my patients with borderline disorder who are treated with Geodon. The mechanism of action behind the uncoupling of the therapeutic effects of oral and intramuscular Geodon has not been clarified in the research literature.

As is the case with most medications, many patients with borderline disorder will respond well to one SGA but not to one or more other medications in this class, or they will respond to an FGA. Your psychiatrist may need to try you on two or even more medications before one is determined to be optimally effective for and tolerable to you.

I usually begin this search for the best fit between an SGA or FGA and the patient's inherent biology with Latuda (because of its preferable side-effect profile) or Abilify (because of the evidence from meta-analyses of consistently beneficial therapeutic effects). If neither one proves sufficiently useful, I move on to a third medication. Using this systematic approach to the selection of a medication for my patients with borderline disorder, I am rarely unable to determine an SGA or an FGA that is both significantly effective and well tolerated.

As I mentioned earlier, some patients who are started on an antipsychotic agent are concerned about taking a medication that is typically used for people with more severe mental disorders. In the practice of medicine, physicians are permitted to and often use medications for problems other than the FDA indications (this is referred to as "off-label"), mainly because there is evidence that they also work well for these other problems. Nonetheless, despite the research that supports the effectiveness of this class of medications for people with borderline disorder, some physicians are reluctant to prescribe, and some patients are reluctant to take, an antipsychotic agent for the disorder because of a specific side effect that these medications may produce: tardive dyskinesia (TD). This is an abnormal, involuntary movement disorder that typically occurs in patients receiving average to large doses of neuroleptics.

I can find no evidence in the medical literature linking the use of antipsychotic agents in patients with borderline disorder to tardive dyskinesia. Nonetheless, you, your family, and your psychiatrist should consistently evaluate the early signs of TD, which are typically subtle, spontaneous movements of the tongue and the mouth, and other side effects of these and other medications.

Case Example

If you have borderline disorder that is not improving with therapy alone, and are reluctant to take these or other medications, I hope that the following case example will encourage you to do so. One of my patients with borderline disorder, a woman in her mid-twenties, initially came to see me because of increasing bouts of depression and the rapid deterioration of her marriage. After two years of marriage her husband was ready to leave her because of her extreme jealousy, her continual demands for attention and reassurance, their frequent arguments, and her severe outbursts of temper. He stated that because of her jealousy and continual need of reassurance, she called him at work several times a day. He often found it impossible to discuss problems with her in a thoughtful way, because at these times her reasoning just did not make sense. Prior attempts to treat her depression with antidepressants were only mildly and briefly effective.

After I made the diagnosis of borderline disorder and discussed the nature of the disorder with both the patient and her husband, they concurred with the diagnosis. A treatment plan was then developed. We continued using the antidepressant because I did not want to confuse the effects of tapering this medication with the effects of a low dose of an FGA that I added every night. Two weeks later, both she and her husband reported a noticeable improvement in her temper, jealousy, and oversensitivity to criticism. She was sleeping more restfully, and her nightmares had stopped. Also, there was a noticeable improvement in their ability to discuss and work out their problems. Finally, she was able to sustain this level of improvement over time and to engage in meaningful psychotherapy.

This example may seem overly simplistic, and it certainly does rank as one of my less demanding treatment experiences of borderline disorder.

Obviously, this woman suffered from a mild to moderate level of severity of the disorder. However, I do see responses of this type reasonably often in previously undiagnosed and untreated individuals.

THE SPECIAL ROLE OF CLOZAPINE IN THE TREATMENT OF BORDERLINE DISORDER

If a patient's borderline disorder symptoms are moderately to markedly severe and disabling, and have proven to be medication-resistant in rigorous therapeutic trials on both SGAs and FGAs, I will discuss with the patient and their family the possible use of clozapine. Clozapine is the original medication in the SGA class and is still considered the gold standard of SGAs. Very unfortunately, it has a tendency to inhibit the production of a specific white blood cell that reduces the amount of these cells in the circulating blood. In a very small percentage of individuals who take clozapine, this reaction may cause serious and sometimes fatal results if not monitored properly. Therefore, many psychiatrists, especially in the United States, are reluctant to use this effective medication to treat the patients with mental illnesses for which it has appropriate indications (e.g., schizophrenia). In an effort to increase the appropriate and safe use of clozapine in the United States, a Clozapine Risk Evaluation and Mitigation Strategy (REMS) Program was approved recently by the FDA. The Clozapine REMS Program initiative has significant implications for the pharmacological treatment of borderline disorder.

The importance of the Clozapine REMS Program to patients with a moderate to severe, treatment-resistant borderline disorder is that, in early trials, a significant majority of these patients *have* demonstrated therapeutic and safe responses to clozapine. Charles Schulz and I have written a section on this issue in a book on the neurobiology of personality disorders to be published in 2018 by Oxford University Press. We have concluded that, based on the studies already published, there is a real need for further, careful evaluation of the efficacy and safety of clozapine in medication-resistant patients with borderline disorder. I have personally treated three patients with clozapine who met the above criteria. All three responded exceptionally well, and continue to do well in follow-up, with no serious decrease in their white blood cell count.

MOOD STABILIZERS

Antiepileptics

There are two classes of mood stabilizers that have shown usefulness in the treatment of borderline disorder (see Table 10.1). One includes the antiepileptics topiramate (Topamax), lamotrigine (Lamictal), and divalproate (Depakote). The second, in a class by itself, is lithium. The antiepileptics were initially used for people suffering from a complex partial seizure disorder. Complex partial seizure disorder originates in the medial temporal lobes of the brain. This brain region has also been determined to be malfunctional in borderline disorder. Specifically, this region contains the amygdala and the anterior cingulate cortex, two brain structures important in the generation and control of emotions and impulsivity (see Chapter 7). The amygdala is known to be hyper-reactive, and the anterior cingulate cortex hyporeactive, in a number of mental disorders, including borderline disorder.

Antiepileptics can calm down seizure activity in this region of the brain, which is involved in producing emotional dysfunction and impulsivity. People with bipolar disorder often display impulsive behavior and abnormalities of emotional control—sustained episodes of euphoria and depression, irritability, and anger outbursts—and antiepileptics have been found to be effective in treating these symptoms. It seems reasonable that if these medications are useful in the treatment of bipolar disorder, they may also be able to reduce the emotional turmoil and related behaviors in people with borderline disorder. Research trials with valproate, topiramate, and lamotrigine in patients with borderline disorder are still limited in number. However, meta-analyses of these studies suggest that they do significantly reduce emotional dysfunction and impulsivity in the disorder (see Table 10.1).

Over the past decade, the antiepileptic class of mood stabilizers has been studied more thoroughly and is now considered the second class of medications effective in the treatment of symptoms of borderline disorder.

Antiepileptics are important here for three reasons. First, antiepileptic drugs appear to exert their therapeutic effects by altering different neurotransmitter pathways than those affected by FGAs and SGAs. The FGA class of medications primarily effects the activity of dopamine D2 receptors, and the SGA class effects both dopamine D2 and serotonin 5-HT2A receptors in the brain (see Chapter 7, page 125). The medication effects of FGAs and SGAs are thought to result in the improvement of symptoms of borderline disorder in the domains of emotional instability, impulsivity, and cognitive disturbances. By contrast, the antiepileptics appear to work by affecting the activity of GABA and glutamate pathways in the central nervous system. These medications effect mainly symptoms in the domain of emotional instability and impulsivity, but not cognitive disturbances.

Glutamate is the major excitatory neurotransmitter in the brain, and GABA is the major inhibitory neurotransmitter (see Chapter 7, page 125). There is evidence of abnormal GABA activity and abnormal brain levels of GABA in individuals with borderline disorder, and these differences correlate with the mechanisms of action of effective medications. Normal activity of the brain is dependent on the interactive balance of glutamate and GABA. It seems reasonable to consider that abnormalities in the activity of either or both of these neurotransmitters are risk factors for borderline disorder. Therefore, antiepileptics provide physicians with another class of medications that operate through brain mechanisms involved in borderline disorder, and these medications are complementary to antipsychotic agents. The complementary functions of antipsychotic agents and mood stabilizers increase the likelihood of achieving therapeutic benefits for those individuals with borderline disorder that arises from different chemical abnormalities.

Second, because of their different mechanisms of action, the psychiatrist may add an antiepileptic to augment the effects of the antipsychotic agent in patients who are partial responders to the antipsychotic.

Third, the three antiepileptic drugs Topamax, Lamictal, and Depakote appear to have somewhat different therapeutic effects and side effects from one another, as well as from those of the antipsychotics. For example, Lamictal has antidepressant effects that are superior to those of Topamax and Depakote. Therefore, Lamictal may be more useful for those individuals who have frequent, brief, borderline-related depressive episodes that are not well controlled by classic antidepressants.

In addition to its effects on some of the symptoms of borderline disorder, topiramate seems effective in reducing food, alcohol, and drug cravings. At least 50 percent of patients with borderline disorder are dependent on alcohol and street drugs and/or have eating disorders. Finally, while divalproate may cause significant weight gain, lamotrigine appears to be weight-neutral, and, as noted, topiramate may reduce weight.

These antiepileptics are not approved by the FDA for the treatment of borderline disorder. Because treating borderline disorder with them is off-label use, you should review their benefits and risks carefully with your psychiatrist before using any of them for the treatment of symptoms of borderline disorder. Of course, that's true for any medication that is prescribed for you.

Lithium

Lithium is another mood-stabilizing medication that can be helpful in treating borderline disorder. This medication is most commonly used to treat people with bipolar disorder. There are similarities in a number of the symptoms of depression and other mood disturbances in bipolar disorder and the symptoms of borderline disorder. These similarities suggest that lithium could also be useful for people with borderline disorder. In **open-label** clinical research trials (in which the patient and the physician know that lithium is being administered), lithium does appear to be effective in some patients with borderline disorder (see Table 10.1). It's less commonly used in treating borderline disorder than the three mood stabilizers I've mentioned above, because lithium can be toxic at blood levels that are not much higher than those that are therapeutic. This use of lithium requires close monitoring of lithium blood levels when treatment is initiated, and at least once or twice a year when levels have stabilized. Even at therapeutic levels, lithium may decrease thyroid and kidney function. Nonetheless, if other mood stabilizers fail to help, and this medication appears to be required by the symptoms of a patient with borderline disorder, the risk-benefit ratio of using lithium may suggest in some cases that it is a reasonable alternative.

ANTIANXIETY AGENTS AND SEDATIVES

Anxiety and poor sleep are common symptoms of borderline disorder. The class of medications most frequently used for these symptoms is benzodiazepines, such as diazepam (Valium), alprazolam (Xanax), temazepam (Restoril), flurazepam (Dalmane), and triazolam (Halcion). Research studies and clinical experience indicate that these medications should be used with caution in people with borderline disorder, because of their high addictive potential and a reported capacity to increase impulsive behavior.

Some patients also experience adverse responses to the nonbenzodiazepine sedative zolpidem (Ambien), such as aggressiveness, extroversion, agitation, hallucinations, and depersonalization. If this medication is prescribed for you, be aware of these possible problems.

NUTRACEUTICAL AGENTS

Mary Zanarini and Frances Frankenburg at Harvard's McLean Hospital were the first to report the results of a creative therapeutic approach to the treatment of borderline disorder. Cross-national studies had shown that higher rates of seafood consumption were associated with lower rates of bipolar disorder and depression. Also, in placebo-controlled trials, people with depression and bipolar disorder had benefited from mixtures of certain fatty acids found in fish oil. Extending these discoveries, Mary Zanarini and Frances Frankenburg conducted a placebo-controlled study of the effects of omega-3 fatty acids in women with borderline disorder. Their results showed a significant reduction in aggression and depression in women treated with this nutraceutical (nutritional supplement) agent compared to the control group. This finding has been replicated in two additional studies and suggests the therapeutic effect is valid. Also, few side effects were reported in the studies. Finally, the mechanism of action of omega-3 fatty acids on borderline disorder, though unknown, may well be different from that of the other classes of medicines effective in the treatment of symptoms of the disorder, and lead to a better understanding of the nature of borderline disorder. This may lead to other, innovative treatment approaches.

HOW MEDICATIONS ARE SELECTED FOR TREATING YOUR SYMPTOMS OF BORDERLINE DISORDER

You will notice that in Table 10.1 (page 183), the classes of medications used to treat borderline disorder produce partially overlapping but not identical results. This raises two questions:

Why are different classes of medications effective for some of the same symptoms of borderline disorder but not for other symptoms?

How does your doctor decide which medications, or combination of medications, will be most helpful for you?

The Scientific Rationale

You'll remember from Chapter 7 that the neural systems in the brain that regulate emotional control, impulsivity, cognitive functions (such as memory, reasoning, and planning), and interpersonal relationships (e.g., bonding) appear to be impaired in people with borderline disorder. To function properly, each of these neural systems uses the stimulatory neurotransmitter glutamate and the inhibitory neurotransmitter GABA. The actions of these two neurotransmitters are modified by other neurotransmitters, such as serotonin and dopamine, also called neuromodulators. The different classes of medicines described in Table 10.1 each have different sites of action and different effects on the activity of the glutamate and GABA pathways from the sites of action and biochemical effects of neuromodulators such as dopamine and serotonin. Therefore, the same behaviors can be affected by the activities of different medications at their specific chemical sites of action, in each of the specific neural systems controlling these behaviors.

It now seems likely that the symptoms of borderline disorder result from the interaction of genetic, developmental, and environmental risk factors (see Chapter 4). As is true for many medical disorders, including mental disorders, *multiple* genetic mutations are probably necessary for borderline disorder to develop. These genetic abnormalities would impair some of the neural systems involved in the disorder at multiple sites in their neural pathways. In doing so, they would affect the functions of several neurotransmitter mechanisms that produce specific symptoms. Because it is unlikely that every person with borderline disorder carries the identical genetic mutations in the pathways affected in borderline disorder, patients with the disorder present with different variations and ranges of severity of each symptom.

These multiple points of neurotransmitter dysfunction along critical neural pathways then become the chemical targets of the different classes of medications used in the treatment of borderline disorder. Because there may well be many sites and types of disturbances, as just noted, often more than one medication may be required to achieve the desired therapeutic effects. In other words, if the neural pathways are "broken" at several chemical sites of action, different medications may be necessary to help restore these pathways to a more normal level of function to reduce or eliminate specific symptoms. This requires your psychiatrist to determine the medications that best fit your particular set of symptoms and their chemical causes.

The Sequential Selection of Medications

The most appropriate selection of medications for you will depend on at least four factors: your specific symptoms of borderline disorder, the proven effectiveness of a medication for one or more of the symptoms, your tolerance of the medication, and cost.

First, the main symptoms that affect you suggest which medication class may be most helpful. For example, let us assume that you, like most patients with borderline disorder, experience symptoms of anger, anxiety, depression, and impulsivity; one or more cognitive disturbances; and difficulty with interpersonal relationships. Under these circumstances, you will most likely benefit from a broad-spectrum medication such as an SGA.

However, if you do not have significant self-destructive or outwardly aggressive behaviors, suspicious or paranoid thoughts, split thinking, dissociative episodes, or difficulty in reasoning, a mood stabilizer, such as Topamax, may be a more appropriate first choice.

If medications from both classes are tried separately and prove only partially beneficial, you may require a medication from each class in order to adequately control your symptoms, for the reasons discussed in the preceding section.

The second factor determining the appropriate selection of medications is your ability to tolerate a specific medicine or class of medicines. All medicines can cause side effects, and some people experience more side effects of a specific medicine or class of medicines than others. The ultimate goal of medication treatment is to achieve the optimal level of therapeutic effect and the smallest number and least severity of side effects. This often requires some trial and error before the best medications and doses for you are determined.

The final factor in the selection of an appropriate medication is cost. For example, although the atypical antipsychotic agents (SGAs) appear to be effective in treating some symptoms of borderline disorder, and may have a lower risk of tardive dyskinesia than traditional neuroleptics, you may find them too expensive. That is less true now than it was a decade ago because a number of these medications are now available in generic form. If financial considerations are still a problem, it's worth discussing with your doctor the relative risks and benefits of using the even less expensive FGAs, as opposed to SGAs.

Remember that brain function does not depend on how much you paid for medicine. It is only affected by the fit between the medicine you take and the specific biochemistry of your brain. For example, before SGAs were available, I treated a number of patients with FGAs, many of whom had a very satisfactory response. However, after the SGAs became available, and after we had discussed the relative merits of both classes, some of my patients reasonably decided to switch to an SGA. Several attempts were made with different medications in this class. Nonetheless, it seemed clear that for some of these patients, their original medication was more effective than any of the SGAs we tried. They then returned successfully to the original medication.

A PERSONAL NOTE ON THE USE OF ANTIPSYCHOTIC AGENTS IN THE TREATMENT OF BORDERLINE DISORDER

My clinical and research interests in the use of antipsychotic agents in borderline disorder date back to my first year of training as a resident in psychiatry at Duke University Medical Center in 1967. These interests were initially sparked by a gentleman who came under my care on the psychiatric inpatient service.

This patient was a dentist and an unmarried man who was frequently admitted to the hospital with anxiety attacks that were totally disabling. When these attacks occurred, he couldn't work, and he became so paralyzed by fear that he was not able to care for himself. He would then simply stay in bed for days. He had been treated with the new class of antianxiety agents available at that time, the benzodiazepines diazepam (Valium) and chlordiazepoxide (Librium), but they were of only minimal help. The recently discovered tricyclic antidepressants mainly caused side effects or made his symptoms worse. This patient had been in psychotherapy for years. The only treatment that seemed to help temporarily was a week or two of the psychiatric inpatient service. With around-the-clock care and nurturing, his symptoms would gradually decrease to the point that he was able to take care of himself again and return to work. A few months later, he would relapse and be readmitted to the hospital.

This man's diagnosis was severe anxiety neurosis. The patient had never demonstrated any symptoms of overt psychosis. However, he was extremely dependent on a few close relatives and on his psychiatrist. When he became symptomatic, he would become so frantic that he would punch himself. He did not have temper outbursts or complain of severe depression, just a deep sense of loneliness. He had never been able to develop a mature relationship of any kind, frequently driving people away with the demands associated with his clinging dependency.

The formal diagnosis of borderline disorder did not exist when I was a first-year resident, so he was not evaluated for that possibility. Even if he had been, few psychiatrists then were skilled in its treatment. I don't recall the presence or absence of other symptoms of borderline disorder in this man's history, but I suspect that he would now meet criteria for the disorder. It was clear that neither the medications nor the psychotherapy that had been used were having any beneficial effect for him. After reading through his medical records, I realized that he had never been tried on a major tranquilizer, which is what we called the new class of medicines that we now refer to as first-generation antipsychotics. I suggested to the faculty member supervising me that we try using a very low dose of one of these medications on this patient. At first, the faculty member was skeptical, but the dose I proposed was so small, one to two milligrams per day as opposed to the usual dose of ten to twenty milligrams per day, that the physician gave his approval. The patient readily agreed when I discussed the idea with him.

To our mutual surprise and pleasure, the patient's symptoms diminished in severity. We finally determined that the optimal therapeutic range of the medication for this patient was one to three milligrams per day, depending on his level of stress. I recall that the nursing staff, who had come to know this patient quite well over many hospitalizations, were initially doubtful about this idea. They had become accustomed to the faculty and the other residents using this class of medication at much higher doses.

Although we all thought the observed improvement might be a placebo effect, no other medication in the other classes we tried had resulted in this improvement. The ultimate test was his long-term response. I remained on the inpatient service for another three months and never saw him readmitted. Later that year, I confirmed with his psychiatrist that he continued to do better than he had in the past. He was able to work regularly and was now rarely readmitted to the hospital.

The following year, when I was assigned to outpatient service, I recalled my experience with this patient when my treatment with psychotherapy of a patient with a very likely diagnosis of borderline disorder, Mrs. Davis, wasn't working (see Chapter 2). Her positive response to a different medication with an FGA prompted me to continue to use this approach with other patients with borderline disorder. Many, but certainly not all, improved on low doses of this class of medications.

In 1974, I left my faculty position at Duke and accepted an appointment as director of the division of psychopharmacology in the Department of Psychiatry at the University of Washington School of Medicine in Seattle. After I arrived, two other faculty psychiatrists and I spent some time discussing our mutual experiences in treating patients with borderline disorder. We quickly discovered that we had observed essentially the same therapeutic results from low-dose FGA treatment of patients with the disorder.

By then, John Gunderson and Margaret Singer had published their seminal article on the diagnosis of borderline disorder. This article greatly expanded interest in this population of patients. My colleagues John Brinkley and Bernard Beitman and I determined that there was no report of the positive therapeutic effect of low-dose FGA treatment for patients with borderline disorder in the medical literature. In fact, the body of literature on the topic generally discouraged the use of any medications for the treatment of borderline disorder. Therefore, we wrote a review of this literature to challenge the prevailing position on medications. We added to this review five cases from our personal clinical experiences of patients with borderline disorder who had responded well to FGAs. The article was published in 1979.

The two main reasons we wrote this article were to alert other psychiatrists to the potential benefit of the use of low-dose FGA treatment in patients with borderline disorder and to suggest that placebo-controlled clinical trials were needed to test our hypothesis. In 1986, my team of researchers at the Medical College of Virginia and Paul Soloff's team at the University of Pittsburgh published simultaneously two such studies in the same scientific journal, the *Archives of General Psychiatry*. Together these studies suggested improvement in some of the symptoms of borderline disorder in response to low-dose FGA therapy. Since then, additional controlled studies have been published utilizing FGAs and mainly SGAs in the treatment of borderline disorder. All but one of these studies have demonstrated significant advantages of treatment with the medications used compared to placebo in patients with the disorder.

CONCLUDING THOUGHTS ON THE USE OF MEDICATIONS IN THE TREATMENT OF BORDERLINE DISORDER

It's my expectation and hope that borderline disorder will soon be an approved indication by the FDA for one or more medications, most likely one of the antipsychotic agents. This will be an important step in the process of firmly establishing the use of this and other classes of medications for people with borderline disorder. I believe this step will substantially increase their use in, and benefit to, those with the disorder.

Although this goal has not yet been achieved, Mary Zanarini and Charles Schulz recently came extraordinarily close to doing so with olanzapine (Zyprexa). I remain confident that borderline disorder will be an indication not only for multiple antipsychotic agents but also for one or more of the antiepileptic mood stabilizers and possibly omega–3 fatty acids.

TABLE 10.1 Medications Studied and Used in the Treatment of Borderline Disorder

DRUG CLASS	MEDICATION	SYMPTOMS IMPROVED BY ONE OR MORE MEDICATIONS IN THE CLASS
Antipsychotics		
Neuroleptics (FGAs)	thiothixene (Navane)* haloperidol (Haldol)* trifluoperazine (Stelazine)* flupenthixol*	anxiety, obsessive-compulsivity, depression, suicide attempts, hostility, self-injury/assaultiveness, illusions, paranoid thinking, psychoticism, poor general functioning
Atypical Anti-Psychotics (SGAs)	olanzapine (Zyprexa)* aripiprazole (Abilify)* risperidone (Risperdal)+ quetiapine (Seroquel)* lurasidone (Latuda)- clozapine (Clozaril)*	severity, anxiety, anger/hostility, depression, self-injury, impulsive aggression, suspiciousness, paranoid thinking, split thinking, interpersonal sensitivity, interpersonal problems, and positive, negative, and general symptoms
Mood Stabilizers		
Antiepileptics	topiramate (Topamax)* lamotrigine (Lamictal)* divalproate (Depakote)*	unstable mood, anger, irritability, anxiety, depression, impulsivity, interpersonal problems
Lithium	lithium salts	poor general functioning
Nutraceutical Agents	omega-3 fatty acids	severity, anger, depression, aggression
Other Miscellaneous Agents	oxytocin	inconsistent results

Placebo-controlled studies; + open-label studies; – no published studies

ELEVEN

The Psychotherapies

APPROXIMATELY 60 PERCENT OF THE RISK OF DEVELOPING symptoms of borderline disorder are genetic factors that produce imbalances in brain chemistry and function. A significant amount of risk factors—about 40 percent—appear to be environmental in nature and also produce impairments in behavior and brain function.

Environmental factors and behavioral symptoms also ultimately cause disruptions in the normal development of effective patterns of behavior and of sound relationships. Therefore, it's critical that you have a safe, supportive, and effective relationship with a person who is able to help you learn about your illness, how it affects your life, and how to make those changes that will enable you to gain the best possible control over your emotions, impulsive behaviors, thought patterns, and the turbulent relationships that are characteristic of borderline disorder. A competent therapist fulfills these needs and serves in other important roles as well. Psychotherapy is essential if you are to gain optimal control over your symptoms and your life. There has been, and there remains, a shortage of therapists who are well trained and experienced in the treatment

185

of borderline disorder. But there have been recent sea changes in the approach to the use of psychotherapy for borderline disorder. These developments promise to make therapy more available and increase its effectiveness for borderline and other personality disorders. It is most encouraging that an increasing number of therapists are learning the psychotherapy skills required to help patients with borderline disorder and developing the necessary experience to use these skills effectively.

Psychotherapy can be rewarding, interesting, and even enjoyable. Many people initially view psychotherapy as a mysterious and somewhat frightening experience. They are afraid that the main issues raised in therapy will be negative. You may be pleasantly surprised to learn in therapy that you have a number of positive attributes and skills, and how you can use these strengths to your advantage.

This chapter gives a brief overview of types of psychotherapy that have been proven effective in people with borderline disorder. You can discuss these types with prospective therapists to determine the most appropriate way for you to proceed, because different forms of therapy appear to work more effectively for patients with specific symptom profiles.

PHARMACOTHERAPY AND PSYCHOTHERAPY: A DUAL APPROACH

Before we move to the psychotherapies for borderline disorder, I would like to highlight why it is so important and beneficial to pursue both medication and psychotherapy for treatment. As noted in the previous chapter, the primary uses of medications in treatment are for the reduction and relief of disturbing, and oftentimes chronic, symptoms of the disorder that cannot be addressed through psychotherapy. The often rapid improvement of such disturbing symptoms of borderline and co-occurring disorders that you experience from these medications will bring welcome relief and help you to initiate sound and trusting therapeutic alliances with your psychiatrist and therapist. Pharmacotherapy is often just the initial phase of optimal treatment of the disorder. Psychotherapy enables your treatment to advance much more. This is why I recommend both medication and therapy in effective treatment of borderline disorder.

Medications, of course, cannot impart information about borderline disorder to you. But by significantly reducing the severity of your symptoms, they do enable you to acquire, take in, and appropriately apply new information you will learn in therapy. In order to become a well-rounded person with balanced attitudes, sound relationships, and effective approaches to life, you must be able to perceive subtle emotions in yourself and others, to discern between those emotions and thoughts that are accurate and those that are not, and to be able to discriminate between opportunities that bring you lasting pleasure and satisfaction and those that are initially exciting but cause long-term harm. To achieve the second level of treatment successfully, a skillful therapist is often necessary to help you gain a greater understanding and appreciation of your strengths and deficiencies in the important, increasingly complex interactions of your emotions, knowledge, and wisdom, especially as they apply to your relationships. These attributes become more accessible with the aid of proper medications, but no medication itself contains such information. It is mainly through the work of psychotherapy that one is able to achieve this critical knowledge.

BORDERLINE DISORDER–SPECIFIC PSYCHOTHERAPIES

To understand the origins, rationale, and key components of the current forms of therapy, it is helpful to understand how psychotherapy was historically used to address borderline disorder.

Until the past twenty-five years, the rationale for psychotherapies for borderline disorder was essentially philosophical and experiential rather than evidence-based. There was little rigorous research used to test either the underlying theories or the results of most forms of therapy. The limitations of psychotherapy for borderline disorder during this period were clearly described in a seminal and prescient article on the disorder published by the American psychoanalyst Adolph Stern in 1938. Stern stated then that conventional psychoanalysis was rarely effective in achieving significant improvement in patients with borderline disorder, and suggested modifications that he found useful in his clinical experience. A number of these modifications are employed in the borderline-specific psychotherapies now used.

Because psychoanalysis and other traditional, Generation I forms of psychotherapy proved to be relatively ineffective for many individuals with borderline disorder, over the past twenty-five years a number of borderline-specific psychotherapies have been developed. Of these, seven have research evidence supporting their efficacy:

1. Dialectical behavior therapy (DBT)
2. Mentalization-based treatment (MBT)
3. Transference Focused Psychotherapy (TFP)
4. Schema-focused therapy (SFT)
5. Good Psychiatric Management (GPM)
6. Systems Training for Emotional Predictability and Problem Solving (STEPPS)
7. Interpersonal group psychotherapy (IGP)

Note that none of the borderline-specific therapies listed were tested rigorously in the absence of medications. In addition, the types and dosages of medications were not reported. This is an important uncontrolled variable that confounds the results of these studies. Because of this omission, many therapists concluded that the therapy alone was responsible for any improvements seen in the study sample. Until recently, it had been assumed and frequently stated that medications are of little benefit in the treatment of borderline disorder and were supplemental to therapy at best. It is increasingly accepted that the proper medications do provide a significant reduction in certain symptoms of borderline disorder, and thereby enable and enhance the efficacy of therapy. The major takeaway here is that you should be skeptical of any therapist who opposes the use of medications out of hand in the treatment of borderline disorder, unless your symptoms are no more severe than mild to moderate. Under these circumstances, a *trial* on psychotherapy in the absence of medications is a reasonable alternative.

Dialectical Behavior Therapy (DBT)

Dialectical behavior therapy has been tested in more controlled studies than any other therapy for borderline disorder and is widely used.

Marsha Linehan, a psychologist from the University of Washington in Seattle, developed DBT specifically for people with borderline disorder, especially those who engage in frequent self-destructive and self-injurious behaviors and who require frequent, brief hospitalizations for these behaviors. DBT is based on the theory that symptoms of borderline disorder result from biological impairments in the brain mechanisms that regulate emotional responses. The early behavioral effects of this impairment are magnified when a child with this heritable risk factor interacts with people who don't understand, don't validate their emotional pain, and don't help them learn effective coping skills to reduce their suffering.

DBT has gained considerable favor in the treatment of borderline disorder because of the results it has achieved in multiple research studies, especially in reducing suicidality, self-injurious behaviors, and the frequency of hospitalizations, and in improving social adjustment. DBT can be taught to and be used by many mental health therapists. While there are workshops available for clinicians to learn more about DBT, a fully trained therapist must have attended a ten-day intensive course of training. Each year, more therapists are receiving this gold standard of DBT training, but there is no official certification of DBT therapists.

The objectives of DBT overlap to some extent with those of individual supportive psychotherapy, especially those using cognitive behavioral techniques, but the treatment approach is based on a different theoretical concept and employs a number of different therapeutic strategies. DBT seeks to validate your feelings of emotional dysregulation and its resulting problems, but it balances this acceptance by gently encouraging you to make productive changes. DBT therapy also focuses on the development of specific skills to address the opposing, or dialectical, tensions or conflicts that arise in the lives of people with borderline disorder, such as the patient's perceived need for a high level of dependence on the therapist and others, and the fear and guilt aroused by such dependency.

There are other differences that distinguish DBT from other forms of borderline-specific psychotherapy. DBT consists of the combination of once a week individual psychotherapy by a DBT-trained therapist, twice a week two-and-a-half-hour DBT skills training sessions conducted in a group setting, and a weekly team meeting of the therapists involved in your care. In DBT you are usually discouraged from using the hospital or medications as means of controlling your emotional tension, because the goal of treatment is to learn to manage current conflicts and emotional crises in more effective ways than were used previously. It is noteworthy that in one study the combination of DBT and an antipsychotic agent (but not the SSRI antidepressant fluoxetine [Prozac]) were more effective than DBT or the antipsychotic medication alone. Trained and skilled DBT therapists are available in many communities. However, as noted below, there is no evidence that DBT is more effective than any other borderline disorder–focused form of psychotherapy.

Mentalization-Based Treatment (MBT)

Mentalization-based treatment was developed by Anthony Bateman and Peter Fonagy. As opposed to the theory underlying DBT, which assumes that borderline disorder is the result of the interaction of inherent emotional dysregulation combined with an invalidating environment, Bateman and Fonagy propose that borderline disorder is based on the interaction of inherited and acquired disturbances in the following brain processes:

1. Affectivity, or the range, intensity, lability, and appropriateness of emotional responses
2. Impulse control
3. Interpersonal functioning
4. Cognition, or the implicit and explicit perception and interpretation of oneself, other people, and events, and their coherent integration

These are the central foci of MBT and are referred to collectively as "mentalization."

In other words, Bateman and Fonagy contend that individuals with borderline disorder have inherent, primary difficulties in mentalizing the cognitive functions noted above. This results in secondary disturbances in their emotional responses, impulse control, and interpersonal functioning because they cannot be integrated into a coherent whole. As a result of these primary difficulties, and of great importance to the development of positive and skilled relationships, changes in therapy are mediated mainly by the interactive work of the therapist and the patient.

The clinical application of MBT has four key features. First, the therapist focuses on the patient's existing thoughts, feelings, wishes, and desires. Second, discussions are avoided that are not concerned with subjectively felt reality. Third, a therapeutic climate is created that encourages the open discussions of thoughts and feelings. Fourth, the clear understanding of the thoughts and feelings under discussion should be clarified before they are acted on. In summary, the primary change mechanism in MBT is enhanced mentalization in the context of the attachment of the patient's relationship with the therapist.

Much like DBT and other theoretically based therapies, a major limitation of MBT is that its conceptual base and its use are too limited and inflexible to accommodate the great variability within the multiple domains of borderline disorder. (This issue will be addressed in greater detail below.)

Transference Focused Psychotherapy (TFP)

Transference Focused Psychotherapy is another specialized form of therapy developed specifically for patients with borderline disorder. It is strongly based in psychodynamic principles. In contrast to many other forms of therapy for borderline disorder, it is proposed that psychological disturbances in the basic form or structure of personality underlie the specific symptoms of the disorder. The disturbances that divide an individual's perceptions into extremes of bad and good are particularly important in TFP. This results in a serious inconsistency in both thoughts and feelings that determines the patient's way of experiencing themselves and others. In brief, it determines their experiences and interpretations of reality.

Treatment in TFP focuses initially on the therapist establishing with the patient a behavioral agreement that recognizes that threats to their relationship are very likely to occur during treatment and that they must be resolved properly. Therapy then moves on to modify primary psychological disturbances and reduce symptoms, mainly by examining, understanding, and improving the patient's interactions with the therapist.

The fundamental goal in TFP is the integration of polarized representations of self and others, or the reduction of split thinking. The treatment approach is clearly contracted and structured. This gives the patient the opportunity to integrate perceptions, thoughts, and emotions that were previously split and disorganized. The therapist provides an emotional and cognitive "holding" environment and expects the patient to have a thoughtful and disciplined approach to cognitive and emotional states and behaviors. The therapist uses clarification, confrontation, and interpretations of the therapeutic relationship in the here and now (referred to as "transference") that lead the patient to reexamine disparate information.

A significant limitation of TFP is that psychodynamic psychotherapy of this type is not appropriate for all patients with borderline disorder. Some patients may not have the ego strength (the resilience) to tolerate the interpersonal emotions raised in this form of therapy. They may not be in sufficient control of their impulsive behaviors or have the time or finances to devote to the treatment process. Also, not all psychotherapists have the training, experience, and skill to provide this type of therapy for patients with borderline disorder. As is true with all forms of psychotherapy for the disorder, these issues should be determined and considered before TFP is undertaken.

Schema-Focused Therapy (SFT)

Schema-focused therapy offers a structured integration of the techniques of psychodynamic, supportive, and cognitive behavioral therapies. SFT is based on the premise that people with borderline disorder have a more rigid personality structure, chronic psychological problems, and deeply held but inaccurate belief systems.

Among the most difficult challenges in the treatment of borderline disorder are the very rapid switches in mood and thoughts, especially from love to hate, and the breadth and severity of all symptoms experienced by the patient. In an attempt to deal with these significant threats to therapy, SFT groups the behaviors of patients into five personas, or schemas, that the borderline patient "flips" through to attempt to cope with their difficulties. These five schemas are: (1) the abandoned and confused child, (2) the angry and impulsive child, (3) the detached protector, (4) the punitive parent, and (5) the healthy adult.

The four mechanisms of healing and change underlying treatment of borderline disorder with SFT are (1) "limited reparenting" by the therapist; (2) emotion-focused work, principally using imagery and dialogues; (3) cognitive restructuring and education; and (4) the breaking and rebuilding of ineffective and harmful patterns of behavior.

Because of the different conceptual approaches employed, a significant problem with SFT is that there is no single theory or integrated group of theories that clearly guide the therapist and the patient through the treatment process. As with all forms of psychotherapy for borderline disorder, not all individuals with the disorder are suitable candidates for SFT, and the number of therapists specifically trained in SFT is limited.

Good Psychiatric Management (GPM)

Good Psychiatric Management integrates different modalities in the treatment of borderline disorder. These include psychodynamic psychotherapy, case management, and pharmacotherapy. Psychotherapy used in GPM uses cognitive, behavioral, and psychodynamic interventions and focuses especially on the relational aspects of the disorder, which result in disturbed attachment patterns, and the effective regulation of emotion in relationships.

Pharmacotherapy in GPM is symptom-targeted and prioritizes treating mood lability, impulsivity, and aggressiveness. This adheres to the 2001 APA Practice Guideline for the Treatment of Patients with Borderline Personality Disorder. The pharmacological component of this guideline is now seriously out-of-date as a result of more recent research findings (see Chapter 10). Even so, there is evidence that GPM is as effective as DBT when used by psychiatrists and other therapists who understand the principles and processes of GPM and have an enthusiastic interest in the treatment of individuals with borderline disorder.

Patients' symptom improvement with GPM appears to last for at least two years after one year of treatment. When researchers tested GPM, the psychotherapeutic approach was described in a written manual, but the manual has not yet been published, so it can't be broadly used.

The evidence supporting this form of psychotherapy for borderline disorder is limited. Nonetheless, it should not be discounted. GPM was developed by John Gunderson with Paul Links. Gunderson has extensive experience in treating patients, conducting research, and publishing scientific articles about borderline disorder, and he is highly respected in this field. In addition, there's a great need for more psychiatrists and other mental health professionals to become engaged in the care of patients with borderline disorder, and Gunderson's recently published handbook on GPM serves as a clear and concise explanation of the rationale and clinical application of the processes used in GPM.

Systems Training for Emotional Predictability and Problem Solving (STEPPS)

STEPPS is a group outpatient educational program developed by Nancee Blum, MSW, and her colleagues to supplement, but not replace, individual psychotherapy and medications for patients with borderline disorder. For this reason, the developers call it "value-added." The program's stated goals are to educate patients and those in their support system about borderline disorder, to teach emotion regulation and behavioral management skills, and to bolster the effectiveness of their ongoing support system (significant others, family members, and treatment providers). The program has accumulated a large evidence base showing that it effectively reduces depression, symptoms of borderline disorder, and healthcare service utilization. STEPPS has been tested and used in the United States and in the Netherlands.

In STEPPS, borderline disorder is viewed as a disorder of emotional and behavioral regulation, including perceptual and cognitive disturbances such as all-or-nothing thinking (splitting). It was developed to address the major symptoms of the disorder and to avoid the limitations of DBT and MBT. DBT requires a significant time commitment and specifies that individual therapy and skills training be administered only by qualified DBT therapists. STEPPS consists of a two-hour weekly classroom session conducted over twenty weeks, plus individual treatment with the patient's current therapist. Importantly, in some cases, the requirement that both individual therapy and skills training be administered by those trained in DBT separates patients from their current therapists. Finally, the developers of STEPPS point out that DBT and MBT are not readily accessible, are labor intensive and time consuming, and require substantial therapist training.

Interpersonal Group Psychotherapy (IGP)

It is now well established that significant disturbances in relationships are one of the four major domains of the specific symptoms of borderline disorder. A number of individuals with the disorder demonstrate improvement in group settings, especially improvement in relationship skills. Group therapy settings can also help to improve emotional dyscontrol, impulsivity, and specific disturbances in perception, reasoning, and problem solving.

Individuals with borderline disorder create specific disturbances in families. Furthermore, as we have seen, borderline disorder is heritable—it commonly exists in other members of the family (as can disorders like depression, substance abuse, and others). The interplay of these genetic and environmental risk factors increases the risk of developing borderline disorder and the degree of its severity. So it has proven effective to develop educational and therapeutic programs for members of the family, especially parents and partners, to help them understand how to improve their interactions with their family member with borderline disorder. Family programs offer information about borderline disorder, teach families coping skills for their own well-being, and provide an opportunity to develop a support network.

Although it may be helpful, you should approach participation in such groups with caution. Considerable harm can be done if one or more individuals in the group act in an angry, manipulative, malicious, or otherwise inappropriate and destructive way toward another group member or the group as a whole. Without a trained leader or facilitator present to step in to handle the situation promptly and properly, a member of the group, and even the group itself, may be exposed to significant harm.

Prior to joining a support group, you should seek recommendations about local groups from mental health professionals who work with people with borderline disorder. In addition, it may be helpful to request information from members of such groups before joining.

LOOKING AHEAD: THE FUTURE OF BORDERLINE DISORDER–SPECIFIC PSYCHOTHERAPIES

A number of experts have concluded that all existing therapies have significant limitations, and we need to make major changes in our therapeutic approach.

The most prolific and creative of these experts has been W. John Livesley, MD, PhD, professor emeritus in the Department of Psychiatry at the University of British Columbia in Canada. Livesley has summarized his thinking and integrated the thoughts of other experts in the field in a recent book to encourage the development of a new therapeutic model for personality disorders. This model of therapy is called integrated modular treatment (IMT).

Livesley and his colleagues propose that the current approaches to treatment imply that therapy must be limited to just one of the therapies I discussed above. Additionally, none of these approaches address the vast differences in personality disorder symptoms, especially borderline disorder, either conceptually or in practice. In other words, the main limitation of current psychotherapeutic models is that they are too narrow in scope and depth. Each patient's individual, inherent, and acquired limits of resilience will keep that patient from achieving the optimal benefits that integrating another type of therapy might provide.

The developers of IMT wanted to overcome these limitations. The approach combines a number of treatment principles, strategies, and methods derived from all effective treatments and applies them to treat specific impairments. In this way, IMT improves on those models that assume a single impairment and apply a limited number of narrow treatment methods.

A "treatment module" in IMT is defined as "an interconnected series of therapist interventions that have a specific dysfunctional target." Some modules are derived from therapeutic interventions that have been tested in empirical research trials. Others are recommended by therapists experienced and highly skilled in the treatment of specific domains of personality disorder psychopathology. IMT provides guidance for matching these domains of psychopathology with the appropriate treatment modules. IMT treatment modules are grouped into general or common modules that are present in all therapies, and specific modules designed to treat specific impairments that are not present in all patients. Both sets of modules are chosen from all current treatment models. The five phases of common and specific treatment modules in IMT are (1) safety, (2) containment, (3) regulation and modulation, (4) exploration and change, and (5) integration and synthesis. IMT has an eclectic structure and can be confusing. By understanding and progressing through these five phases, the therapist can limit this confusion.

All effective therapies for personality disorders focus on establishing a well-integrated, coherent sense of the patient's self-identity and on the patient's chronic impairment of interpersonal relationships. Thus, the common treatment modules in IMT include a structured agreement on the rules of treatment; a treatment alliance between the patient and the therapist; the therapist consistently holding to the therapeutic framework; the therapist's validation of the content and legitimacy of the patient's experiences; the patient's motivation to change; and the patient learning processes to acquire a clear understanding of self and others along with the ability to carefully reflect on the mental states of both. The initial targets of therapy are embedded in the phases of safety, containment, and regulation and modulation. Progress through these basic phases of treatment varies according to how severe a patient's disorder is and how resilient they are.

As the treatment targets of the common modules are addressed and their associated goals are achieved, the patient and therapist progress to the specific treatment modules that best meet the individual needs of the patient. These phases of treatment typically are the latter ones of regulation and modulation, exploration and change, and integration and synthesis. Specific modules are tailored to each patient according to their level of resilience and their idiosyncratic symptoms. This pragmatic approach of IMT provides the flexibility, scope, and depth of treatment lacking in current treatment models.

Treatment modules are not discrete or linear, but overlap and progress or regress simultaneously and independently. Therefore, the conceptual framework provided by these five phases of treatment help the therapist and patient to identify where they are in therapy and remain effectively focused on the work at hand.

Another important strategy of IMT is the integration of the concepts and approaches that guide current therapies. Livesley and his colleagues state that more research and knowledge are needed before this will be feasible. Because the description of IMT has just been published, few therapists have significant knowledge about it or experience in using it to treat borderline disorder. Nevertheless, many of the thought leaders in this field have expressed support for this method. I believe IMT will become more commonly used and available in the near future. Until then, proceed with the therapy that is available to you and is the best fit for you.

STRATEGIES FOR LOCATING A THERAPIST

If you suspect that you, or a member of your family, has borderline disorder, you'll likely have a number of questions on how to find optimal care. You may use the following guidelines to seek out a therapist in your area.

First, determine if any therapist in your community has the skills and experience required to treat borderline disorder effectively.

Second, find out if they support the use of medications in the treatment of the disorder. If they are a psychiatrist, ask which medications they typically use and for what purposes. Compare their responses to the information provided in Chapter 10.

Third, inquire about which psychotherapeutic approach the therapist uses, and compare it to your symptoms and the therapies described in this chapter to see if there is a good fit.

Fourth, determine if the therapist, with your written permission, confers with close family members and the treating psychopharmacologist (psychiatrist) when needed during evaluation and treatment.

The first task, finding a therapist who regularly treats patients with borderline disorder, is often the most difficult. Many communities in the

United States still do not have therapists who have the skills, experience, and commitment required to provide the level of care now judged to be the accepted standard. If you are unable to locate a therapist, contact the Borderline Personality Disorder Resource Center through its website (bpdresourcecenter.org) or by phone (888-694-2273). The center has developed the most comprehensive list of clinicians in the United States who are dedicated to treating patients with borderline disorder.

tWELVE

The Integrated Use of
Medications and Psychotherapy

UR UNDERSTANDING OF THE NATURE AND TREATMENT OF borderline disorder has increased exponentially in the past twenty years. Until recently, many experts in the field stated that, at best, medications played a minor role in the treatment of borderline disorder and should be discontinued after only short-term use. Others strongly advocated that psychotherapy was the *only* legitimate treatment of patients with borderline disorder and that medications had no role in the treatment of this disorder other than for coexisting disorders such as depression and anxiety. Indeed, even some prestigious, professional organizations still contend that medications should not be used for the treatment of the disorder.

Much of the negativity about the use of medication under appropriate conditions in the treatment of borderline disorder has now been reversed by experts in the field. The scientific evidence supporting its use is much stronger today than it was fifteen years ago. The question of how best to integrate the use of medications and psychotherapy is addressed in W. John Livesley and colleagues' recent, seminal book on an integrated, modular, psychotherapeutic approach to personality disorders (see Chapter 11). In one of the opening chapters of this book, the editors give priority to safety, building the alliance between patient and therapist, and patient motivation, and they argue that medications are effective in treating the psychotherapeutic-resistant symptoms of moderate to severe impulsivity, affective lability, and cognitive dysregulation. It is now rare to see in consultation a patient with properly diagnosed borderline disorder who is not being treated with medications, albeit in some cases less than optimally.

The central task now for the psychiatrist treating a patient with borderline disorder is to decide, if necessary, how best to use medications combined with psychotherapy to achieve optimal results. Dr. Ken Silk and I addressed this question in a chapter of Livesley's book, which was written for clinicians and psychiatrists; below is a summary of our main points.

THE CLINICAL TREATMENT TEAM

Some psychiatrists continue to provide all modalities of the care of patients with borderline disorder and their families. That means they provide crisis intervention, medication management, individual and group psychotherapy, and family therapy. However, most psychiatrists who treat this disorder have discontinued practicing in this manner—their time is limited, the right medications produce rapid responses in patients, and patients have a strong tendency to "split" close relationships (this is one manifestation of the split thinking common in borderline disorder). It is simply not practical for the same psychiatrist to serve all these functions.

The treatment model that involves two or more clinicians appears to have become the most popular and effective form of care. That is to say, it's now common for a prescribing psychiatrist and one or more therapists to collaborate on treatment for individuals with borderline disorder and their families. The boundary conditions of this collaboration are complex and must be clearly understood, agreed on, and consistently practiced by all parties involved if this model of care is to succeed. Because of the nature of borderline disorder, a patient will present with varying levels of severity of the disorder over time, and their clinical condition will often fluctuate rapidly. Members of the treatment team must understand their roles and be prepared to provide rapid and appropriate therapeutic responses, whether the patient is in a borderline crisis, is at stable but varying levels of severity and resilience, or is in partial remission. All members of the treatment team, as well as the patient and family, must understand which medications and form of psychotherapy are being used, for what purposes, and what outcomes to anticipate. Simply put, the team must work together—coherent and coordinated therapeutic efforts are essential.

BUILDING A COLLABORATIVE RELATIONSHIP AMONG PROVIDERS

To get the most benefit from therapy, you will want to clarify with your psychiatrist, or with your therapists and psychiatrist, the following information before you begin treatment. Whether you are working with one clinician or with a psychiatrist and therapist team, you should carefully review the specific terms of treatment with everyone involved in your care. In addition, many clinicians find it advantageous to include, when needed, important family members in the evaluation and therapeutic phases of treatment. Depending on your situation, these family members could be a spouse or partner, parents, and sometimes siblings and children. (As I mentioned in the previous chapter, involving family in the treatment process helps the patient in building a support network and provides their family and loved ones with important knowledge and coping mechanisms.) Both your attitude and those of the psychiatrist and therapist about involving family members in treatment are important to discuss and resolve before beginning therapy. Finally, learn the name of any medication that is prescribed, its specific purposes and expected results, its timeframe of action, its therapeutic limits, and its potential short-term and long-term side effects.

The following issues are well worth reviewing carefully with a prospective psychiatrist or a combination of providers.

Individual Psychiatrist

1. Clarify if any of the medications prescribed may be used on an "as needed" (PRN) basis and, if so, the conditions for doing so.
2. Ask the psychiatrist to explain how medications and psychotherapy work in combination in your overall treatment plan.
3. Define with the psychiatrist the limits of the effectiveness of medications and psychotherapy in your case.
4. Define clearly when and under what conditions it is appropriate for you to contact them between appointments.

Combination of Treatment Providers

1. Determine that the psychopharmacologist (psychiatrist) and the therapists believe that borderline disorder is a medical condition that often requires that you take medications *and* engage in psychotherapy to achieve improved emotional self-awareness, emotional and behavioral self-control, thinking, reasoning, and integration of thoughts and feelings that enhance your life skills. If there is dissent among the group about the nature and severity of your borderline disorder and the environmental factors that influence you, you might consider continuing your search for treatment providers.
2. Determine that the psychiatrist and therapists clearly understand their own roles on the collaborative team as well as the other team members' roles, and that they respect and support the work of their colleagues. No member of the team should be even subtly disdainful of the importance of the work of the other members.
3. Agree on when and under what conditions you should contact each member of the team (aside from regular appointments). Which team member should you contact in crisis and other situations that cannot be delayed until the next scheduled meeting? As treatment progresses, the need for these contacts will become infrequent.
4. Understand that the therapists may inquire about your compliance with medications and ask about their efficacy and side

effects, and that the psychiatrist may inquire about the central themes currently being worked on in therapy. Sharing this information is essential to each clinician so that your care is coordinated properly.

AN INTEGRATED TREATMENT CASE EXAMPLE: MS. P.

The following case example illustrates the use of medications integrated into the psychotherapeutic treatment of Ms. P., a twenty-two-year-old single woman diagnosed with borderline disorder. Her therapist referred her to me for psychiatric treatment because her emotional dysregulation, poor behavioral control, and impaired thought processes were interfering significantly with her relationships and her work in therapy.

When I met Ms. P., my first impression was of a well-groomed young woman in no acute distress. Her speech was spontaneous, relevant, and coherent. There was no evidence of psychomotor abnormalities. As she told it, her predominant moods were irritability and a chronic, low level of hopelessness. Ms. P. had entered therapy several months previously, with a psychotherapist extensively trained and skilled in the therapeutic treatment (specifically, dialectical behavior therapy, or DBT) of individuals with borderline disorder. But in spite of a weekly single, individual psychotherapy session and two one-and-a-half-hour skills training group sessions per week, she had not made any significant gains in treatment. Her therapist referred her for further evaluation to find out if a trial on medications might be useful. The terms of this suggestion were made clear: Ms. P. would continue with her work in psychotherapy, and the therapist would be in contact with me as required. Medications would not in any way be a substitute for therapy but were intended to complement it by reducing some of the disturbing symptoms of borderline disorder that she manifested. These included her severe outbursts of temper both in and out of therapy, her self-injurious and harmful behaviors (some of which required frequent visits to the emergency room), her suspiciousness of her therapists, and her brief dissociative episodes under stress. At first, Ms. P. had refused this suggestion, even though her therapist had told her about this possibility before they started work together. But eventually she was frustrated that she wasn't making any progress, so she agreed to consider this option and meet with me.

During the opening ten or so minutes of the initial evaluation, Ms. P. was quite guarded in her responses. I paused and commented that she seemed reluctant to fully answer many of my questions. I asked her directly why this was the case. Eventually, she confessed that she was afraid if she gave honest answers to some of my questions, I might judge her to be too seriously impaired to continue working with her current therapist. I reassured her that that the purpose of the evaluation was to determine if medications could reduce the severity of some of her symptoms to the point where psychotherapy would be more effective than it had been so far. I added that in my initial conversation with the therapist, she had been eager to continue her work with Ms. P.; I hoped that I could make her work with her therapist more beneficial. Ms. P. appeared to relax somewhat, and I continued the evaluation.

She reported no symptoms or history of major depressive episodes, hypomania, ADHD, anxiety or panic attacks, obsessive-compulsive disorder, or eating disorders. She had no history of serious medical illnesses or surgery and was not taking any medication.

Ms. P. reported that depression and anxiety seemed to run in her immediate and extended family, but she had no knowledge of a family history of substance use disorders, eating disorders, or ADHD. Ms. P. denied any history of physical, emotional, or sexual abuse by her family or others. In general, she thought the family did very well except for her; she saw herself as the black sheep. All members of her immediate family had graduated from college, but it had been hard for her to get her degree. She trained to become a teacher, but she had difficulty controlling her temper with her superiors and some of her fellow teachers, which resulted in her being dismissed on one occasion.

Ms. P. reported that she had suffered from anxiety and depression from childhood and that they had increased gradually until she entered middle school. At that time, both symptoms increased substantially, and her anger progressed dramatically. She engaged in frequent verbal and physical fights with her siblings, and occasionally with her parents. During the first year of this rapidly increasing turmoil at home, she began to cut and scratch herself on her forearms when she was especially angry. Ms. P. recalled that the idea to do so simply occurred to her one day, so she tried it. She said it had helped her to calm down and gain better control over her emotions for at least several hours. However, when her parents discovered this behavior after a particularly severe episode of cutting and bleeding, they took her to the emergency room. There she was given what she believed was a small dose of a mild tranquilizer and then discharged. After this, similar episodes would occur several times a month and were sometimes severe enough to result in a trip to the emergency room. Ms. P. reported she had never entertained thoughts of suicidal behavior or been hospitalized. She denied any excessive use of alcohol or legal difficulties, but admitted to brief trials of marijuana and cocaine, and casual and unprotected sexual encounters.

When I asked about the nature of her depressive episodes, Ms. P. replied that they occurred after she experienced a serious disappointment, typically a breakup with her boyfriend or another friend, and guilt over these fights or some other misbehaviors. They tended to gradually subside over the course of several days.

Ms. P. had always felt that others were hypercritical of her and tended to think poorly of her. There were times when, under stress, she believed that family and acquaintances were making plans to harm her in some way. During some episodes of extreme stress she would "zone out" of the situation for up to fifteen minutes or more and could not recall events and discussions that occurred during this interval. In addition, she noted that on important issues and in close relationships she had difficulty in balancing her thinking and feelings but tended to see things as all or nothing.

Finally, making and sustaining close relationships had been difficult for her since childhood, even with her parents, her siblings, and other members of her extended family. Outside of the family, she had few close friends she trusted, and these relationships typically ended with her feeling betrayed by and disappointed in the other person. When she did have a boyfriend, she often argued with him because she thought he wasn't paying enough attention to her and ultimately believed he was cheating on her. She then dissolved the relationship.

When I asked about her experiences in therapy, she admitted that although she liked her therapists, she made little progress as the result of therapy. "Probably because I am not trying hard enough. Also, I don't seem to be able to understand everything they teach in therapy, and when I do understand, my anger and depression are so overwhelming, I can't attempt the new behaviors or even think of them when I need to," Ms. P. said.

After the evaluation, I asked Ms. P. if she would like to hear my thoughts on the likely source of her difficulties, how it affected her life, and the possible usefulness of medications in helping her in and out of therapy. She did, so I laid out my assessment. I agreed with her therapist's belief she suffered from a moderately severe level of borderline disorder. Her depressive episodes were those typically associated with BPD and not one of the major depressive disorders. I reviewed with her how borderline disorder manifested itself in her case and gave her several examples of the effects it had on her life. (For example, on occasion she exhibited a moderate degree of dichotomous or split thinking, especially when discussing her feelings toward and thoughts about her family, boyfriends, and friends.) I then discussed with Ms. P. the biological and environmental factors that place individuals at risk of developing borderline disorder. Very few of the usual environmental factors appeared to have occurred in her life. This suggested that genetic factors were predominantly at work in her case, and we discussed the implications of that conclusion. Most notably, the brain pathways that were "misbehaving" for Ms. P. could be helped with the use of one or two medications. I emphasized that her difficulties in benefiting from therapy were most likely due to disturbances in these pathways and not to her lack of trying.

Ms. P. was initially concerned. The SSRI medications that she had been prescribed in the past had caused side effects, especially weight gain, a decrease in her interest in sex, and a flattening of most of her emotions. She also was worried that medications would change her from the person she really was. I noted that the side effects could be markedly reduced by the careful selection and dosing of medications, and changes in medication if required. Also, I commented that the impaired function of several pathways in her brain prevented her, or anyone, from fully knowing her true self and real capabilities and that they prevented her from living her life optimally. We finished our session with a discussion of what would come next: I would discuss my findings and recommendations with her therapist and suggested that Ms. P. talk over with her therapist the relative benefits and risks of adding a medication to her treatment regimen. About four weeks later, I received a phone call from Ms. P. After careful consideration and speaking with her therapist, she wanted to start a trial on medication.

At the beginning of our second meeting, Ms. P. and I reviewed the major issues we had discussed previously. I then asked her what symptoms were the most troubling to her and that she would like significantly reduced by a medication if possible. She quickly brought up excessive anger; self-injurious, verbal, and physically aggressive behaviors; suspiciousness; "zoning out" episodes; and her difficulties with relationships.

Some of these symptoms were likelier than others to respond to medication, I told her. We discussed the two major classes of medications that are the usual starting points in treatment, the second-generation antipsychotic agents and the mood stabilizers. I told her that because of her symptoms of split thinking, dissociative episodes, and suspiciousness, the antipsychotic class of medications seemed preferable. I suggested that we begin with a trial of lurasidone (Latuda); in my experience, it demonstrated significant effectiveness for many of the symptoms she noted. We also discussed possible side effects.

Armed with all the information on medications that I could give her, Ms. P. agreed to a trial of Latuda at twenty milligrams every day at bedtime. She would return in one week for a medication evaluation. I also provided her with my mobile and home phone numbers with instructions to call if she developed significant side effects in the meantime. At the follow-up appointment, the early signs were encouraging. She told me that she wasn't experiencing episodes of anger and other mood instability as frequently. She began to feel a calmness she had not previously experienced, and she noticed a decrease in her suspicious thoughts and urges to inflict self-harm. Her initial responses to this medicine were promising, but it was too soon to determine the full benefit of this dose on all of her symptoms. She continued taking the same twenty-milligram dose of Latuda for another three weeks. Then she and I reevaluated her status. During that interval, she had experienced a gradual improvement in most of her symptoms, including a mild to moderate decrease in suspiciousness and split thinking and no episodes of dissociation. One month later, Ms. P reported no significant improvement from the prior visit, so we increased her dose to forty milligrams a day.

Over the next three months, we saw that this dose seemed optimal for Ms. P.'s symptoms, and she wasn't experiencing notable side effects. Her therapist agreed that her symptoms and her ability to work in and out of therapy had significantly improved, and there didn't seem to be any reason to change or increase the medication she was taking.

This is a case example of a patient who presents with the clear diagnosis of borderline disorder and without any co-occurring disorders. In my practice, such a patient is a rarity. Most patients with borderline disorder present with one or more co-occurring disorders, usually major depressive episodes, ADHD, and/or a substance use disorder. Each of these disorders complicates treatment. This case example is primarily meant to illustrate how important it is to integrate the use of medications and psychotherapy in the treatment of patients with borderline disorder. It also demonstrates the collaborative work of the psychiatrist prescribing medications and the therapists providing psychotherapeutic interventions.

When other disorders co-occur with borderline disorder, the use of medications for them, if any are indicated, are determined by the nature of the co-occurring disorder and the stage of treatment with medications of the borderline disorder. For example, if ADHD is a co-occurring disorder, it is necessary in most cases, especially if cognitive disturbances are present, to initiate and stabilize your other symptoms with an SGA such as Latuda or Abilify before starting treatment with either a methylphenidate-based or an amphetamine-based medication. This will significantly reduce the possibility of stimulating a number of your symptoms of borderline disorder. If a major depressive episode is the co-occurring disorder and is at a mild to severe level, it is often appropriate to start treatment with an SGA and an appropriate antidepressant simultaneously.

ᵗHIᴿᵗEEN

When a Loved One Has
Borderline Personality Disorder

I F YOU HAVE A SPOUSE, SIBLING, PARENT, CHILD, OR FRIEND WITH
borderline disorder, then you know firsthand the difficulties they
have with relationships, especially with the people who are closest to them. Episodes of angry outbursts, moodiness, and unreasonable,
impulsive, and erratic behaviors, which often appear unprovoked, can
cause considerable harm to their important relationships. Any attempt
to work out reasonable solutions to problems frequently turns into a
highly emotional battle. If you cannot have effective discussions of differences, it's difficult to maintain and improve relationships.

Family and friends usually end up feeling anxious and frustrated.
They attempt to placate the person with borderline disorder, and then
become angry with them when the limits of normal patience have been
exceeded. Most families and friends of people with the disorder are
relieved to learn that effective treatment is available and that there are
ways they can help as well. Two of the most significant advances in the
area of borderline disorder have been the research on the effectiveness

of different educational and therapeutic experiences for families, and the development of consumer-led organizations focused on the disorder.

BORDERLINE DISORDER FROM THE INSIDE

In order to be helpful to a family member with borderline disorder, and to minimize the negative effects on the rest of the family, it's important to understand as much as possible about the disorder and how it affects the people who have it. Much of this book is devoted to describing what is currently known about borderline disorder from a clinical perspective. But for the families and others looking at the disorder from the outside, it's also important to understand how your loved one feels and thinks of themselves so you can do your best to support them and validate their difficulties.

The Sharon Glick Miller Study

In 1994, Sharon Glick Miller, a psychologist in the Department of Psychiatry at the University of Florida, published a study of ten patients (eight women and two men) with borderline disorder from whom she obtained life-history narratives in a series of ninety-minute interviews over a one-year period. After careful analysis of the data, she concluded that the self-reports of these patients were highly consistent with one another, but they differed in certain important respects from typical clinical descriptions.

She found that while clinicians described these patients as having an identity problem, the patients seemed to have a sense of *themselves* as being impaired. They reported that the strategies they used, such as changes in appearance, might seem like a problem with identity, but they were mainly attempts to feel better about themselves. They also indicated that they did not reveal themselves easily to therapists or to others because they anticipated disapproval and would rather appear to be lacking in identity than have confirmation of their perceptions of themselves as flawed.

They did not see themselves as having an illness but as leading a life in which they constantly struggled against feelings of despair. This was a central theme of how they perceived their fate in the world.

Most of the patients reported feeling alone and inadequate, regardless of their achievements. These feelings began in some patients as children and in others as adolescents. For the most part, they did not know the origins of these feelings, though two identified family problems and another the discrimination she experienced because of obesity. The sense of emotional pain and despair they reported was overwhelming. They all expressed the wish not to be alive.

COPING STRATEGIES

These patients each developed a number of coping strategies to lessen their deep sense of pain and despair, always with the hope that, just once, something would help. The main coping strategy was to block out or dissociate themselves from these feelings as best they could. If that was not successful, many turned to alcohol and drugs. They viewed their bedrooms or apartments as safe havens, except when they felt depressed and desperate. At these times, some realized that it was dangerous to be alone because of the strong impulse to hurt themselves.

Social situations typically provoked in them intense anxiety and feelings of inadequacy. These feelings resulted in strategies either to push through the event, which exacted a high toll on their energy, or to escape from the situation.

One potential coping strategy that was notably absent was the use of social support. Patients consistently reported that they did not openly share their feelings with family, friends, and even their therapists because of fears of rejection and of being viewed as a burden. However, not sharing their struggles resulted in the worsening of their sense of isolation.

They also felt conflicted about sharing negative feelings with their therapist. To not do so could be perceived as not working in therapy, but doing so could reveal a lack of progress that might result in increased pressure to perform, or in hospitalization. They viewed hospitalization as a respite from the constant struggles with despair and from the desire not to be in this world. Once the crisis was over, they then wished to be discharged. They learned they could not refer often to their constant thoughts of self-harm, as this might result in an undesired hospitalization.

THE IMPORTANCE OF SELF-DISCLOSURE

An important finding from this study was that patients with borderline disorder felt more comfortable revealing information in the research setting than elsewhere because no challenges were being made to their presentations. This led them to believe that the researchers understood them better than their families, friends, and even some of their therapists. They perceived themselves to be collaborating with the researchers because they were the experts about themselves, which helped reduce their conflicts over dependency issues.

I hope this patients' perspective helps you better understand and deal with the many issues that you confront with your family member with borderline disorder. Of course, there is no single view of borderline disorder that adequately captures the entirety of their experiences. But it's clear that it's helpful for you to stay involved with and listen carefully to your family member with the disorder. Understanding their feelings and perspective is an important early step in the process. Your best response may be nothing more than, "I understand that it must be very painful to feel that way," but validating their suffering is considerably more helpful than ignoring or dismissing it. Remember that letting them know that you understand how they think or feel does not mean that you agree with their reasons for such thoughts or feelings.

THE FAMILY'S VIEW

There is growing evidence that continued family involvement with a family member with borderline disorder is extremely beneficial. However, there is little clearly sampled information available on the perceptions and experiences of the family—in other words, what it is like to have a family member with borderline disorder.

As you know, I was raised in a family with a sister who suffered from borderline disorder. I have tried to report accurately some of my perceptions and experiences, and a few of those of my mother and of my other sister without the disorder. However, anecdotal accounts of this type have only limited value. How accurate is my memory? How much of what I recall is colored by my many emotional experiences with Denise over the years and my grief over her loss? Also, not all people with borderline disorder suffer from the same symptoms and from symptoms of the same severity. This means that the families of different people with the disorder will have different experiences.

I think it's worthwhile, then, to review some of the few research studies that exist that address the effects and perceptions of borderline disorder in families.

The Gunderson/Lyoo Study

In 1997, John Gunderson and Kyoon Lyoo, at Harvard's McLean Hospital, published a study comparing the perceptions that twenty-one young women with borderline disorder had of their families to the perceptions of their parents. There were two main findings from this study.

First, the women viewed their family environment and their relationships in the family as more negative than their parents did. Specifically, they perceived less cohesiveness, more conflict, less organization, less expressiveness, and less support of independent behavior in the family than did their parents.

The fathers usually perceived their families as healthier, less conflicted, and more supportive of independence than did their daughters. In spite of these perceptions, their daughters were more negative of their fathers than of their mothers, seeing their relationships with their fathers as weak. In addition, daughters felt that their fathers' values, such as honesty, and their norms, such as dressing neatly for meals, were inconsistent with, and often different from, their behavior.

Both parents viewed their relationship with their daughter with borderline disorder as weak, especially in the areas of expressing emotion, accomplishing tasks, and clear communication. Parents always agreed with one another more than they did with their daughter. Interestingly, the daughter rated both parents as weak on emotional involvement.

Gunderson and Lyoo concluded that when evaluating the quality of parenting a person with borderline disorder, it's important to get the parents' and siblings' perspectives. "We believe that clinicians need to be wary of BPD patients' vilification of their parents and to take active measures to hear and consider parental viewpoints as well."

The Effects on Children of a Mother with Borderline Disorder

The effect that parents with borderline disorder have on their children is another critical aspect of this discussion. Child psychiatrist Margaret Weiss and her colleagues at McGill University in Montreal published a study in 1996 of twenty-one children of mothers with borderline disorder, compared to twenty-three children of mothers with a different personality disorder. Here's some background information: There is a 15 percent risk of mental disorders in the first-degree relatives of people with borderline disorder. Depression and alcoholism are the most common diagnoses in this group. Also, about 10 percent of people with borderline disorder have a mother with the disorder. In this study, only 24 percent of women in the original sample with borderline disorder had children. This is consistent with other studies indicating that fewer women with borderline disorder have children than is the norm.

This study revealed a significantly higher number of mental disorders in the children of mothers with borderline disorder (the borderline group) than children of mothers with a different personality disorder (the control group). The diagnoses found to be more common in the borderline group included borderline disorder, attention deficit hyperactivity disorder, and disruptive behavior disorders.

A surprising finding was that a higher frequency of trauma did not contribute to the increased occurrence of psychiatric disorders in children of mothers with borderline disorder. (It would be important to determine if this finding was replicable in studies with proper sampling and methods of measurement of the major outcome understudy.) Finally and not surprisingly, the borderline families were found to be less stable and less cohesive and organized than the control families.

The authors conclude that the children and mothers in the borderline group have shared biological (genetic) vulnerabilities and a faulty family structure. This is consistent with most other research findings regarding the biological and environmental risk factors of borderline disorder (see Chapter 4).

There continues to be insufficient solid information on the spectrum of experiences of parents, children, and spouses of people with borderline disorder, possibly because there are so many variables that are difficult to control. Such information is badly needed in order to determine the true toll that borderline disorder takes on all people involved. Nevertheless, it is reasonable to conclude from anecdotal reports that the toll on families is quite high and should be considered an important component of the process of treatment of patients with borderline disorder.

Other Perspectives of the Effects of Borderline Disorder on the Family and Partners

In 1998, Paul Mason and Randi Kreger first published *Stop Walking on Eggshells*; a revised edition was released in 2010. Mason is a certified professional counselor who has clinical experience treating patients with borderline disorder, as well as related teaching experience, and has published a research article on the disorder. Kreger is a professional writer and businesswoman who had a personal relationship with someone with borderline disorder. In their introduction, Kreger notes that "most studies [of the family environment of people with borderline disorder] looked at behavior directed toward the person with BPD rather than the behavior of that person toward others."

Kreger established contact with numerous people related to someone with borderline disorder by e-mail, through her website, and by postal mail. As a result of the information she gathered, Kreger and Mason developed a perception of the most common ways people with borderline disorder affect others. For example, if you are related to someone with borderline disorder, you may suffer a grief reaction and experience Elisabeth Kübler-Ross's five stages of grief: (1) denial, (2) anger, (3) bargaining, (4) depression, and (5) acceptance.

Other common responses you may have are bewilderment, loss of self-esteem, feeling trapped and helpless, withdrawal, guilt and shame, adapting unhealthy habits, isolation, hypervigilance and physical illness, adoption of borderline-like thoughts and feelings, and codependence. Even this long list of problems described by people related to someone with borderline disorder may not capture the true depth of your suffering. People with borderline disorder experience different symptoms and levels of severity, and respond uniquely to their symptoms. Some are more angry and vindictive than others. Some are less willing to seek help for their problems and blame these problems on their relatives or partners. Therefore, your experiences with a person with borderline disorder are most likely both similar to and quite different from those of someone else.

The second part of *Stop Walking on Eggshells* offers a number of coping strategies, including for when the person with borderline disorder does not take appropriate responsibility and seek help but continues to blame their problems on others.

As one of a few sources of information of this type, it's not surprising that this book has prompted a significant response from people who are affected by someone with borderline disorder. It seems to strike a particularly responsive chord in people related to someone with the disorder who lacks insight into their problem and is unwilling to seek help.

Although parents, siblings, and spouses suffer deeply, it's the children of a person with borderline disorder who appear to suffer the most, aside from those with borderline disorder themselves. Experience over the years has taught me that the most useful advice I can offer you to reduce your suffering is to try to convince your loved one that they need treatment, to learn as much as you can about the disorder and how to respond to its symptoms, to find and join an appropriate support group (see the Resources section starting on page 263), and to be kind to yourself and as supportive as possible of everyone else involved.

TEN GUIDELINES FOR FAMILIES

Clearly, it's difficult to be related to someone with borderline disorder. Many family members and partners have strong reactions of anger and resentment that conflict with their feelings of empathy and their desire to help. Here are ten specific actions that you can take to help the person in your life with borderline disorder gain better control over their life. These actions will also be a help to you in the process.

1. Gain knowledge. It truly provides you with an edge. It's essential for you to understand that your loved one with borderline disorder is suffering from an illness that is as real as diabetes, heart disease, or hypertension. Because it's a disorder that affects specific pathways in the brain that control emotions and behavior, you can only see the behavioral symptoms, though physical symptoms may be present as well (see Chapter 1 for more information). For most people, physical symptoms are easier to accept as indications of disease than behavioral symptoms. But if you think about it, there's no reason to assume that a complex organ such as the brain is less susceptible to diseases that affect behavior than are other bodily organs that result in physical symptoms. Recently developed medical technologies that demonstrate abnormal brain structure and function in people with borderline disorder confirm this conclusion (see Chapter 7).

It's also helpful to realize that people with borderline disorder didn't acquire their problem mainly through actions of their own, nor do they enjoy having the disorder. Imagine what it must be like to feel that you are at the mercy of forces within you, over which you have little control, and that cause you extreme emotional pain and significant life problems.

A critical first step in the process of helping them and yourself is to learn as much as you can about the symptoms and nature of borderline disorder, and the specific causes of severe episodes in your loved one.

2. Remain calm. Try to remain calm but involved when episodes do occur. Reacting angrily will usually just add to the problem. Acknowledge that it must be difficult to experience the feelings they express, even if they seem out of proportion to the situation. This doesn't mean that you agree with these feelings, or that you think the actions resulting from them are justified. It's reassuring to them if you listen to their feelings, the pain they are experiencing, and the difficulty they are having in dealing with this pain. Remember that you do not have to defend yourself if attacked, or develop solutions for them yourself, even for their thoughts of self-harm.

Allow and encourage them to try to bring their response levels in line with the situation at hand. You may need to give them a little time alone to collect themselves. Then it may be possible to more calmly and reasonably discuss the relevant issues.

In addition, don't hesitate to express your feelings freely and openly, but with moderation. Recent research suggests that caring involvement with your family member with borderline disorder is associated with better outcomes than a cool, disinterested approach. Please stay involved.

3. Get professional help. If your family member has not sought professional help, strongly urge them to do so. You can facilitate the process of finding the best help by using the strategies in Chapter 9. It may be necessary that you do the initial work necessary to set up the first appointment. It's also helpful if you agree to go with them, especially if they say you are a major cause of their problems, but don't insist on it.

Some people with borderline disorder initially refuse to seek professional help. Give them a copy of this book, and ask them to read the Introduction and the first two chapters. This may help them understand their potential problems well enough to agree to an initial appointment with a psychiatrist.

Other people with borderline disorder are steadfast in their refusal of help. This, of course, is a major problem. I have asked Dr. Perry Hoffman, the founding president of the National Education Alliance for Borderline Personality Disorder (NEA-BPD) for some advice here. The NEA-BPD is an advocacy group for families of people with borderline disorder, and those with the disorder (see the Foreword by Jim and Diane Hall). She says:

> The best way to approach this problem from my perspective is to accept that you cannot get someone into treatment. Timing is important as to when someone might be open to hearing the idea. But the bottom line is to free families of feeling guilty, and to understand that they are not so powerful to affect that goal. Along that line, relatives need to get help and support for themselves as they watch their loved one in the throes of the illness.

4. Stick with the program. Once in treatment, encourage your family member to regularly attend therapy sessions; to take medicine as prescribed; to eat, exercise, and rest appropriately; and to take part in healthful recreational activities. If alcohol or other drugs are a problem, strongly support their efforts to abstain completely from these substances, and encourage regular attendance in treatment programs or self-help groups, such as Alcoholics Anonymous. There is little hope of improvement of the symptoms of borderline disorder if they abuse alcohol and drugs. Remain persistent in your efforts to do everything possible to help reduce the risk of this behavior and not enable it.

5. Plan ahead for destructive behaviors. Develop a clear understanding (it may even be written) of the realistic consequences of recurring, problematic, destructive behaviors such as episodes of alcohol and drug abuse, physically self-damaging acts, and excessive spending and gambling. Also, agree beforehand on how best to respond to threats of self-harm.

These behaviors are often triggered by stressful events that need to be identified, and a clear plan needs to be developed for handling these situations more appropriately and effectively in the future. Such a plan is best developed with the help of your family member's therapist. Encourage and support consistent follow-through with the plan.

Experience has shown that if you respond positively to your loved one's appropriate behaviors, it encourages them to adopt new and more successful ways of handling stressful situations. It also reduces the rate of inappropriate behaviors that then cause additional problems. Issuing ultimatums should be used only when all else fails.

6. Be positive and optimistic. Remain positive and optimistic about the ultimate results of treatment, especially when your loved one has a setback. The usual course of borderline disorder under treatment is one of increasing periods of time when symptoms are absent or minimal, interrupted by episodes when the symptoms flare up. As time goes by, the specific causes of these relapses can be identified—for example, separations, family get-togethers, and periods of change. Once you know what are precipitating events, you can anticipate them. Then you can take steps to develop alternative, more adaptive and effective responses. Occasional family meetings with the therapist may help clarify the causes of relapses and identify new ways of preventing them.

7. Remember that information is your edge. If educational experiences about borderline disorder, such as DBT family groups (see Resources for more information), are offered in your community, participate in them. It's important that you learn as much as possible about borderline disorder and your role in the treatment process. Your participation in such groups will benefit both you and the family member with the disorder.

If an appropriate borderline disorder family support group is active in your community, I encourage you to join it. The problems and challenges of family members of people with borderline disorder are understandably different from those with the disorder itself. Listening to others who have stories and problems similar to yours, learning skills to retain and enhance your own sense of well-being, and developing a support network will be of great help to you. Attending such a group will also validate your own feelings and concerns, and you will discover new approaches to handling your own specific challenges. Working with others who are in similar situations is a productive way to learn more about borderline disorder, and it may bring you significant relief. Finally, once you become reasonably comfortable in doing so, sharing your thoughts, feelings, and problems with other people who truly understand the situation can be a helpful and strengthening experience.

8. Join a lay advocacy organization. If there is a local chapter of a borderline personality lay advocacy organization in your community, seriously consider joining it. You will then have available to you a large amount of new information about borderline disorder, what you can do to help the member of your family with the disorder and yourself, and compassionate and understanding support in your efforts. If there is not a group in your area, consider starting one with other family members you have met. Also think about joining one of the national advocacy groups for borderline disorder. For information on lay advocacy groups, you can find one or more listed on the web: for example, the NEA-BPD and the Treatment and Research Advancements National Association for Personality Disorders (TARA). For more information, see the Resources section on page 263.

9. Encourage responsibility and growth. Remember that it's the responsibility of the person with borderline disorder to take charge of their behavior and their life. Although difficult at times, it's important for you to provide the opportunity for them to take reasonable risks in order to try new behaviors. It's also important that you help them to be accountable for the consequences of old, destructive behaviors.

Excessive dependency on family and friends is not helpful in the long run. Beware of the tendency of people with borderline disorder to act at the extremes. The proper alternative to excessive dependency is not immediate, total independence. During episodes of great stress you may be tempted to propose, or accept the proposal, that they separate from the family. Typically, if they do so, at some point they will return for help, and the cycle of involvement and no involvement will then just repeat itself without benefit. It's far better for you to remain engaged with your loved one and gradually help them move to a more mature relationship level of mutual interdependency.

10. Take good care of yourself. Finally, always remember that you cannot save your loved one with borderline disorder on your own. Based on my personal experience with my sister Denise (see Chapter 2), I can assure you that to try your best, given the information you have, is all you can do. Take time for yourself to meet your own needs. Then, when your loved one needs your help the most, you'll be able to provide it.

FOURTEEN

Research:
The Ultimate Reason for Hope

W
E HAVE MUCH MORE TO LEARN ABOUT THE PREVALENCE,
causes, nature, treatments, and prognosis of borderline disorder. It is also clear that we won't learn what we need
to know without a substantial increase in the amount of high-quality
research in each of these areas. Research offers us the best reason to remain hopeful about living more comfortable and productive lives with
the disorder. This chapter outlines some of the main issues in current
borderline disorder research and the areas of research that hold the most
promise for progress. I also review the available sources of funds for
research on borderline disorder, the inadequate level of funding for research in this area, and how you can help the overall endeavor.

WHERE DOES RESEARCH INFORMATION COME FROM?

There are two main sources of research information. The first source is
anecdotal reports, and the second is empirically derived research data.

Anecdotal reports arise from the personal experiences of clinicians and researchers as they see patients or perform their research. Some of these clinicians publish their more unusual and provocative findings in scientific journals. This information may then pass quickly to other practicing clinicians whose patients may benefit readily from these findings. Anecdotal information typically does not represent a random sample of patients seen, is not systematically collected, does not include a control group, and is usually more qualitative than it is quantitative. In other words, it is not considered research in the true sense of the term, though it may inspire research studies.

Empirical research employs a more rigorous research design that includes the selection of a representative sample of subjects whose characteristics are precisely defined and who are randomly assigned to an experimental or a control group, the use of well-designed and controlled interventions and instruments to measure results, and statistical analysis of the data. Most medical experts consider such empirical research to be the gold standard in drawing conclusions about the validity of research results and making decisions on the clinical application of the information. In this book I have tried to identify the manner in which information is collected, as it has a bearing on the level of credibility you place on the conclusions drawn from the information.

The Value of Anecdotal Information

The value of anecdotal reports should not be trivialized. The clinical observations made and reported in the medical literature often provide influential ideas that become the conceptual basis for rigorous research studies. For example, Adolph Stern's anecdotal observations in 1938 of the clinical symptoms, psychological limitations, and responses to treatment of his "border line group" of patients (see Chapter 3) were very important to shaping the thinking of clinicians at that time and the later formulation of empirical research endeavors.

Anecdotal reports also provide us with useful information that helps us do our best to care for patients before empirically derived research findings are published. I wouldn't be able to help my patients as much without these anecdotal reports from other clinicians. I also believe that those anecdotal reports I have submitted for publication, such as the one with John Brinkley and Bernard Beitman on the use of low-dose neuroleptic therapy for patients with borderline disorder (see Chapter 10), have been of some value to other physicians, patients, and researchers before the ideas were tested by controlled studies.

The Need for Empirical Research

Anecdotal reports alone cannot advance our knowledge to the extent that we need. We must rigorously test those ideas that have generated a consistent and credible body of anecdotal reports with empirical research studies. Much of the knowledge we now possess about borderline disorder comes from such research, and it's crucial for several reasons.

In clinical studies, the most valid research results depend on using random assignments of research subjects to determine those who will receive the tested intervention and those who will serve as control subjects. In addition, if both groups of subjects are selected randomly from the appropriate sample of members of the general population, the results are less subject to inadvertent sampling biases.

In most empirical studies, in order to minimize any biases of researchers or subjects, a control group and the double-blind method are used. The double-blind method means that neither the subject nor the investigators know if the subject is in the experimental or the control group.

Sound research requires the use of instruments that accurately define the research group used, and outcome measures that validly evaluate the critical results in question. Researchers obtain careful statistical analysis of the results and provide doctors with the knowledge upon which to act.

Animal studies also enable researchers to better understand the brain systems associated with the behaviors that are disrupted in borderline disorder. It's not intuitively obvious that animal research could provide us with important information relevant to a clinical problem as human and as complex as borderline disorder. Nevertheless, the brain mechanisms that control many behaviors of animals have been preserved in the human brain from many evolutionary ancestors of humans. This allows researchers to study the anatomical, physiological, and biochemical processes of behaviors related to borderline disorder in ways that otherwise would not be available.

This animal research is critical in determining the fundamental biological processes that should be evaluated in humans with borderline disorder, using minimally invasive and noninvasive techniques such as brain imaging studies. Animal research also enables researchers to evaluate the effectiveness and safety of new pharmacological treatments for borderline disorder before they are tested in humans.

What We Have Learned from Research

Throughout this book, I have relied on, and attempted to clarify for you, a considerable amount of information about borderline disorder from both anecdotal and empirical studies. I've included information about the prevalence of borderline disorder in the general population, the most valid and reliable criteria available for diagnosing the disorder, the current state of our understanding of the occurrence and treatment of borderline disorder in children, the biological basis of the disorder as we now understand it, the genetic and environmental risk factors that result in borderline disorder, and the typical course of the illness and its prognosis. Because of their importance, I discussed at length the recent changes in treatments and the best-tested pharmacological and psychotherapeutic treatments for borderline disorder.

Very little of this information would be available without research studies conducted by investigators dedicated to better understanding borderline disorder. As you have learned, there are many gaps in our knowledge that need to be filled. Unfortunately, there are more questions that need answers than there are qualified researchers and research funds available to answer them. We need at least a three-pronged strategy to help us move forward. First, we must focus the resources currently available on those questions about borderline disorder that are most pressing and that have the greatest likelihood of significant payoff. Second, we need to increase the number of high-quality researchers in the field of borderline disorder. Third, we need to increase the amount of research funds available to adequately support their research efforts.

The Most Promising Areas of Research

There are numerous promising areas of research in the field of borderline disorder. The following is a list of eight that I find particularly noteworthy:

1. Development of techniques to increase awareness among people with the disorder and their families
2. More specific determination of the degree of heritability of the fundamental symptoms (endophenotypes—symptoms linked to stable, measurable brain functions that have a clear genetic connection) of the disorder, such as increased and blunted emotional sensitivity
3. More specific determination of the efficacy of pharmacological and psychotherapeutic interventions, and their combinations, on specific, fundamental symptoms of the disorder
4. More precise identification of the exact neural pathways, circuits, and networks that underlie the endophenotypes involved in the disorder
5. Improved tests that more accurately define the disorder and are more replicable than those in current use
6. The development of a diagnostic classification of borderline disorder that will be more useful in developing and testing the fundamental nature of the disorder and its treatment
7. Descriptions of the course of the illness under different treatment circumstances
8. Further clarification of genetic, epigenetic, and environmental risk factors

The following is a selective sample of these topics to give you some idea of what the future may hold.

Prevalence

Until recently, the best information available suggested that the prevalence of borderline disorder in the general population was about

2 percent, with a three-to-one female-to-male ratio. These estimates were based on a limited number of research studies using methodologies that varied significantly from study to study and many that do not meet current standards. More extensive, recent studies that use more current research methods suggest that the prevalence of borderline disorder in the general population is approximately 6 percent and that a gender difference may not exist. It is likely that the 6 percent prevalence for borderline disorder obtained from the most recent population survey of mental disorders is still inaccurate. One of the major problems confronted by researchers engaged in large population surveys is that there is an unknown but suspected high number of individuals included who suffer from borderline disorder but who are in great denial of this fact. To the degree that this is so, the prevalence figures now available underestimate the true number of individuals with the disorder.

Accurate prevalence data provide a rationale for allocating an amount of clinical care, training, and research funds to borderline disorder that is warranted by the amount of suffering and the other costs of this disorder to our society. As you'll see later in this chapter, there appears to be a disproportionately small amount of research funds committed to borderline disorder compared to other illnesses of comparable severity and prevalence in the general population.

Diagnostic Strategies

Another important area of research involves developing a new conceptual model for classifying personality disorders. It seems clear that we are moving toward diagnostic strategies based on the genetic, developmental, and environmental causes and the pathophysiology of these disorders. Such diagnostic approaches are used for the great majority of medical disorders. In the case of borderline disorder, these behavioral domains include emotional control, impulse regulation, perception, reasoning, and bonding. Our current categorical diagnostic approach has served us well for almost forty years. But there is growing evidence that the proper domain-based approach will increase diagnostic sensitivity and accuracy, and it will stimulate more effective and focused treatment and research. This is generally considered to be one of the most fertile and necessary areas of research on borderline disorder, and it is the topic of significant discussion in Section III of the DSM-5.

The Course of the Illness

Additional studies are needed to determine more precisely the various courses borderline disorder takes from infancy to old age. These will not be the same in all individuals with the disorder because the illness depends on the specific biological and environmental risk factors operating in each person's life. It will be an arduous task to tease out subpopulations of people with similar risk factors in order to determine their most likely courses of illness. This work is necessary if we're to offer some concrete answers to one of the questions you and your family most likely have: What is my future going to be?

Genetic Strategies

Genetic approaches to the study of borderline disorder can help identify individual differences in the biological and environmental risk factors of the disorder, and the degree of risk conferred by each of these factors. Separating these individual differences is important if we are to estimate accurately the severity of the specific behavioral domains of borderline disorder experienced by an individual, and determine the most specific and effective forms of treatment for that person versus for another person with a different complex of symptoms of the disorder.

You now know that borderline disorder appears to be the result of a number of necessary genetic risk factors. Only some of the genetic risk factors need be present from a larger genetic pool of risk factors for borderline disorder in order for the disorder to occur. Therefore, we see a wide variation in the type and severity of symptoms from person to person. It's likely that they carry different genetic patterns that place them at risk for the disorder.

Ultimately we need to identify the total pool of genetic risk factors for borderline disorder and the level of risk each factor confers. We need to understand how the different combinations of these factors operate and interact with environmental risk factors.

Environmental Risk Factors

We know that exposing children who have a biological predisposition to borderline disorder to specific environmental factors increases the likelihood that they will develop the disorder (see Chapter 4). However, a number of important questions about the effects of environmental factors on the development of borderline disorder require further study. For example, are some environmental risk factors more serious than others? Specifically, which environmental factors are more likely to produce epigenetic effects that enhance or reduce the risk of developing the clinical characteristics of the disorder?

How Environmental Risk Factors Affect Brain Function

We are beginning to understand how environmental factors alter brain circuits through epigenetic processes (see Chapter 4). More specific and advanced studies will provide us with information of which environmental risk factors are most likely to have deleterious effects on specific symptoms and endophenotypes of borderline disorder. It's also important to know if there are critical developmental periods when children with genetic predispositions to borderline disorder are most susceptible to negative environmental influences as the result of epigenetic activity levels.

The Neurobiological Basis of Borderline Disorder

Defining the precise behaviors in each core domain of borderline disorder opens up a large new spectrum of research studies. These studies include investigating the anatomical, physiological, and biochemical brain mechanisms and processes that ultimately control each behavior associated with the disorder. Recent advances in neuroscience and modern biomedical technology, such as brain imaging techniques, have already resulted in great progress in this area. For example, a variety of brain neuroimaging techniques have shown alterations in structure and function in specific brain regions of people with borderline disorder and have related these brain changes to specific behavioral domains, such as emotional dysregulation and impulsivity. We need to know more about the brain circuits that are associated with each specific symptom of borderline disorder. Further research using the knowledge and methodological advances already made will greatly facilitate future research in this area.

Treatments

As knowledge expands in the above areas of research, considerably more specific and effective treatments for borderline disorder will be discovered than are now available. For example, we will understand more accurate indications for the use of medications in the treatment of borderline disorder and which specific classes of medicines are likely to be most effective in each person's case (see Chapter 10). We may then more promptly initiate the most appropriate pharmacological approach for each specific patient's symptom profile. This will require many more controlled and methodologically creative studies of the different classes of medications available to us that show promise on the basis of anecdotal reports and controlled trials.

A number of different psychotherapeutic approaches are now being used for people with borderline disorder, but we have little hard data on the specific indications and effectiveness of these techniques (see Chapter 11). It's essential that we have these data if we are to develop the most effective and comprehensive treatment plans possible for people with the disorder. The most promising approach to advancing the effectiveness of psychotherapeutic interventions for individuals with borderline disorder is integrated modular treatment, which has recently been proposed by W. John Livesley, Giancarlo Dimaggio, and John F. Clarkin (see Chapter 11). However, before IMT is able to replace existing therapeutic approaches, much developmental research is required.

The message I would like you to take away from this section is that there are a large number of important areas of research on borderline disorder that could yield vital information that would make your life better. The question is, why isn't more of this research being done?

What Determines How Much Research Is Performed for Borderline Disorder?

Understandably, most people don't understand the processes that enable medical research to proceed in the United States. Those who do understand the system are either researchers themselves, suffer from a medical disorder, or are closely related to someone with a disorder.

Actually, the system is fairly straightforward. The amount of medical research performed in any area depends on these factors:

1. **The relative importance of the disease**. There is more research performed on heart disease and cancer than there is on diseases that affect fewer people and are less life-threatening and devastating. However, some medical disorders receive research funding that is greater or less than you would predict based on their prevalence, severity, and importance to society. This means other factors are also important.

2. **The total amount of research funds available in the area from all sources**. No matter how important an area of research is, academic researchers cannot devote their time and talents to an area if there is inadequate funding.

3. **The amount of grassroots support** from people and families affected by the disorder, either acting individually or as members of lay advocacy groups. Advocacy is a constitutional right of every citizen and has proven to be an enormously effective instrument in enhancing research funds and the attention of the academic medical community to areas of need. For example, consider the impact of advocacy groups on the amount of funding devoted to AIDS research in this country.

4. **The perception that the illness has an identifiable biological basis and therefore is a "real" disease**. It was not until such evidence was available in the areas of schizophrenia and affective disorders that the stigma associated with these illnesses declined and research funding and support services increased. The leaders and members of two advocacy groups, NEA-BPD and TARA (see Resources), have been effective in helping secure the funding of a number of research grants on borderline disorder from the National Institute of Mental Health (NIMH) and private sources.

5. **The availability of well-trained researchers at academic institutions**. No university or department of psychiatry is so

well funded that it is able to support all worthwhile areas of academic work. Therefore, the leadership focuses its limited resources on those areas that match their strengths and that have the greatest need and greatest potential for research funding. If there are too few high-quality research grant applications in borderline disorder, then one reason is there have been too few funds to attract departmental chairs and bright young investigators to the field.

CURRENT FUNDING OF RESEARCH ON BORDERLINE DISORDER

As noted above, funding for research on borderline disorder in this country comes from two major sources. Most financial support is provided by the NIMH, a federal agency that is part of the National Institutes of Health. The NIMH provides most of the research funds available for clinical and basic research in mental disorders.

Additional funding is provided by private organizations such as the National Alliance for Research on Schizophrenia and Affective Disorders (NARSAD). Also, a new organization named the Black Sheep Project has been created to increase awareness of and raises research funds for BPD (see below for more information and page 267 for contact information).

NIMH

In 2001, three important review articles describing the future of research on borderline disorder were published in the scientific journal *Biological Psychiatry*. These articles were discussed in an editorial, "A New Beginning for Research on Borderline Personality Disorder," by Stephen Hyman, former director of the NIMH. In his editorial, Hyman, a psychiatrist and now provost of Harvard University, addressed the issue that in 2001 borderline disorder received only 0.3 percent of the NIMH research budget, in spite of its prevalence and its clinical significance. He stated that these low levels of NIMH funding were not the result of priority-setting by the NIMH but due to the small number of high-quality grant applications and well-trained researchers in the field of borderline disorder. In his editorial, Hyman speculated that one reason qualified researchers may avoid the area of borderline disorder is the controversy over the current diagnostic approach to personality disorders in general. He suggested that young researchers might be wary of devoting their academic careers to an area of controversy.

Although this may have been one of the problems at that time, it is less of a problem than it was fifteen years ago. It's also well known that researchers will gravitate to those areas that are interesting, challenging, clinically important, ready to yield important results, and well funded. I have had more than forty years of experience in academic psychiatry, many of them as the chair of departments of psychiatry, with the responsibility for guiding the research careers of young faculty members. It's been my experience that these factors are more important in the selection of a research career pathway than is the lack of controversy in the area. Actually, many of the best researchers are attracted to areas of controversy because academic controversy typically identifies areas of great opportunity. Therefore, I believe that the major determinative factor in borderline disorder research is adequate funding.

According to recent reports, the NIMH has committed about $5 million per year to research for borderline disorder over the past decade. In December 2016, Congress passed the 21st Century Cures Act, which added $6.3 billion in funding for medical disorders, mostly to the NIH budget. Some of these funds were then distributed to the NIMH. About $400 million of those funds were ultimately dedicated to research on serious mental illnesses. Unfortunately, the NIH failed to designate borderline disorder as a serious mental illness, a decision that prevented researchers in the area of borderline disorder from competing for the designated funding. At this time, there is action in Congress to petition the NIMH to confer on borderline disorder the designation of a serious mental illness, which would enable competition for the allocated $400 million fund. Considering the early onset, the degree of disability, and the impact of the disorder on the individual, their family, and society, such a designation seems long overdue and well warranted.

To clarify the importance of this change it is necessary to understand how NIH funds are distributed. NIH research funds are typically divided between researchers who work at the NIH in the intramural program and those who work across the country, usually at academic medical centers, referred to as the extramural program. The decisions on who receives research funds from the NIH are made by panels of experts in a large number of research areas, such as the ones I discussed earlier. This is called the peer review system, and it is designed to fund the most promising research grant applications.

Private Research Foundations

The Brain & Behavior Research Foundation (formerly NARSAD) and the Black Sheep Project are two private research foundations that provide researchers interested in borderline disorder with access to additional sources of research funds. The Black Sheep Project is a foundation created to support research on borderline disorder in seven core areas, including the reliability and validity of the diagnosis of the disorder, investigations on genetic and environmental risk factors for the disorder, epidemiology, neurobiology, and pharmacological and psychotherapeutic treatments. (I serve as the chief medical consultant to the Black Sheep Project, a position that includes responsibility for oversight of seven committees of experts that recommend the allocation of its research funds.)

The Brain & Behavior Research Foundation is a well-established foundation that has predominantly supported research in the areas of schizophrenia and affective disorders. About fifteen years ago, its leaders signaled their interest in also supporting research on borderline disorder.

The acknowledgment that additional federal and private funding for research on borderline disorder is needed is a promising sign and the result of three factors. First, it is now more widely accepted that borderline disorder is a prevalent medical disease that causes much human suffering and that it has a clearly demonstrated biological basis. Second, significant advances have been made in the development of specific, effective pharmacological and psychotherapeutic treatments for borderline disorder. Third, the recent emergence of lay advocacy groups has enhanced awareness and knowledge of borderline disorder by the public and by federal, private-sector, and academic leaders. These are the same factors that came together thirty-five years ago in the areas of schizophrenia and affective disorders, which resulted in a significant increase in funding of and research on these two groups of illnesses.

HOW YOU CAN HELP ADVANCE RESEARCH ON BORDERLINE DISORDER

I have noted above, a disproportionately small amount of funds and qualified researchers are available for research on borderline disorder. You may wonder if there is anything you can do to help increase research on the disorder, and thereby help yourself or a loved one. Our experience in the areas of schizophrenia and mood disorders noted above has indicated that you personally have much more influence on this than you probably imagined. I believe in the sentiment that extraordinary achievements are accomplished by ordinary people with an extraordinary passion.

In addition to all of the suggestions I have made in this book, I add the following:

1. Join a borderline disorder lay advocacy group such as the Black Sheep Project, the NEA–BPD, or NAMI. These and others are listed in the Resources section of this book.

2. If you have the personal funds, make a contribution to these organizations and to private research foundations that solely support research on borderline disorder, such as NAMI, the Black Sheep Project, and the BPDRF. If you make a contribution to NAMI or the Brain & Behavioral Research Foundation, ask that the money be targeted for research on borderline disorder.

3. If you have ample personal funds, consider supporting at a school of medicine an endowed chair, professorship, or departmental fund directed solely at enhancing clinical care, research, and training in borderline disorder. Departments of psychiatry at these schools need such resources in order to commit faculty time to the care and research that will benefit individuals with borderline disorder and their loved ones. Simply put, more funds are needed for the education and training of medical students and residents in the area and, of course, for research.

4. Write letters and make visits to your member of Congress and senators. Letters to the NIMH and to the research office of the American Psychiatric Association (see Resources) are also appropriate and effective.

You might think that it would be more effective if these requests for increased support for borderline disorder came from psychiatrists and other mental health professionals, especially those in academic institutions. Having spent most of my professional career at a number of academic medical centers, I have come to understand that advocacy by professionals is only partly successful. While academicians are able to report the latest scientific advances and other relevant information, our pleas for help do not have the heartfelt immediacy of people directly affected by the disorder. Please don't underestimate your capacity to make a difference in this area. It is enormous.

A Final Word

MUCH PROGRESS HAS BEEN MADE IN OUR UNDERSTANDING of the symptoms, course of illness, biological basis, causes, and treatments of borderline disorder. Ignorance and pessimism are being replaced with knowledge and optimism. I find it particularly encouraging that physicians and other mental health professionals are continuing to learn more about borderline disorder. Physicians now more often make the proper diagnosis when people with this disorder develop emotional and physical symptoms that are otherwise difficult to diagnose and treat. Once the diagnosis of borderline disorder is determined, referrals are now made more frequently to psychiatrists and other mental health professionals who specialize and are skilled in treating this complex disorder. Lay advocacy groups and private, resource, and research funding organizations are focused specifically on borderline disorder; they are growing in size, influence, and capacity to offer information and support to people with the disorder and their families and to make more research funds available.

Not all psychiatrists and other mental health clinicians are equally experienced and proficient in diagnosing and treating people with borderline disorder. However, there are now usually one or more psychiatrists, other physicians, or mental health clinicians in most communities who possess the training, experience, and commitment to be of significant help, and to even serve as the primary clinician, for those with the disorder. It generally doesn't take more than some online research or a few phone calls to the offices of local psychiatrists to find the best place to start locating these professionals. For example, the Borderline Personality Disorder Resource Center and the Black Sheep Project provide valuable referrals and information.

It's also encouraging that more medical scientists across the world are becoming involved in serious research on the many different aspects of borderline disorder. Studies are being conducted on the prevalence, causes, and natural course of the illness. Advanced research technologies, including structural and functional brain imaging, genetic studies, biochemical assays, sophisticated neuropsychological tests, and treatment trials, are underway at a number of leading academic medical centers across the world. Although these research efforts are in their preliminary phases, they are already yielding the types of knowledge that I've described in this book.

If you have borderline disorder, or if someone in your family or a close friend suffers from this illness, you should feel hopeful about the present and optimistic about the future. We now know enough about borderline disorder to provide quick and significant relief for many of your most disturbing symptoms and to help bring about continued, incremental improvement in the remaining symptoms and associated problems. Ongoing research will result in additional knowledge and more effective treatments, and someday prevention and cure.

I urge you to continue to make the effort to learn as much as you can about borderline disorder. I am confident that you will not regret it.

Robert O. Friedel, MD

Glossary

Acetylcholine: a neurotransmitter that stimulates or inhibits the activity of neurons in the brain.

Amphetamine: a stimulant of the central nervous system used to treat ADHD in children or adults.

Amygdala: an almond-shaped cluster of neurons located in the middle portion of the temporal lobes of the brain. It is the central structure in the brain system that processes emotion information.

Anterior cingulate cortex: a strip of cortex located in the middle portion of the frontal lobes of the brain that monitors and modulates behavior.

Antipsychotic agent: a member of a class of drugs used to treat the symptoms of psychotic disorders such as schizophrenia. In low doses, some of these agents also appear to be effective for some patients with borderline disorder.

Antisocial personality disorder: a disorder characterized by a pervasive pattern of disregard and violation of the rights of others present since the age of fifteen in an individual at least eighteen years old.

Attention deficit hyperactivity disorder (ADHD): a disorder characterized by decreased attention span, easy distractibility, and impaired school, work, and social performance. There are three subtypes of ADHD: one is associated with inattention and hyperactivity plus impulsivity, the second predominantly with inattention, and the third predominantly with hyperactivity and impulsivity.

Bipolar I disorder: similar to major depressive disorder but accompanied by manic episodes. An individual will be diagnosed with bipolar I if they meet the criteria for both a major depressive episode and a manic episode.

Bipolar II disorder: similar to major depressive disorder but accompanied by hypomanic episodes. An individual will be diagnosed with bipolar II if they meet the criteria for both a major depressive episode and a hypomanic episode.

Dissociative episode: periods of time when thinking, behavior, and memory occur outside of a person's awareness.

Dopamine: a neurotransmitter that stimulates or inhibits the activity of neurons in the brain.

Dopaminergic activity: activity related to the neurotransmitter activity of dopamine.

Dorsolateral prefrontal cortex: areas of the cortex located on the lateral portion of the frontal lobes of the brain that are involved with the processes of thinking and reasoning.

Dysthymia: a disorder that is similar to major depressive disorder, but with fewer and less severe symptoms. Also known as persistent depressive disorder.

Ego functions: those psychological processes that regulate our thoughts, feelings, and responses to external reality.

Ego psychology: a division of psychology that focuses on the mental processes that enable us to deal effectively with our thoughts, feelings, and responses to external reality.

Emotional lability: unusually rapid fluctuations of mood that are not proportional to the experiences that elicit them.

Empirical research: carefully designed and controlled research studies that lead to quantifiable results.

Etiology: the causes or origins of a medical disorder.

Factitious illness: characterized by physical or psychological symptoms that are intentionally produced or feigned.

Gamma aminobutyric acid (GABA): the brain's primary inhibitory neurotransmitter.

Glutamate: the brain's primary stimulatory neurotransmitter.

Hallucination: a false sensory experience that has no external stimulus.

Hippocampal formation: brain structures that are located on the middle portion of the temporal lobes near the amygdala. They are critically involved with the processes of memory development.

Histrionic personality disorder: a disorder characterized by a pervasive pattern of emotional and attention-seeking behavior beginning by early adulthood.

Hyperreactive: having or showing abnormally high sensitivity to stimuli.

Latent schizophrenia: a term previously used to describe people who had some of the symptoms of borderline personality disorder.

Magical thinking: the conviction that thinking is the equivalent of action. It is present in the dreams of children and in patients with a variety of conditions, and it is characterized by an unrealistic relationship between cause and effect.

Major depressive disorder: a mental disorder associated with a severe and sustained decrease in mood; decreased ability to experience pleasure; changes in sleep, appetite, and weight; inappropriate guilt; impaired thinking, concentration, and decision making; and suicidality.

Methylphenidate: a stimulant of the central nervous system used to treat narcolepsy and ADHD in children and adults.

Multigenic disorders: disorders that require a number of genetic mutations before the disorder manifests itself.

Narcissistic personality disorder: a disorder characterized by a pervasive pattern of grandiosity, the need for admiration, and a lack of empathy beginning by early adulthood.

Neural: pertaining to one or more nerve cells.

Neuroleptics: the original class of drugs used to treat patients with psychotic disorders, such as schizophrenia. In low doses, some of these drugs also appear to be useful in some patients with borderline disorder.

Neuromodulators: neurotransmitters that regulate the activity of neural pathways and circuits, e.g., dopamine, serotonin, acetylcholine, and norepinephrine.

Neurotic: a term originally used to describe mental disorders that do not have psychotic symptoms.

Neurotransmitters: chemical messengers secreted by neurons that stimulate or inhibit other neurons.

Norepinephrine: a neurotransmitter that stimulates or inhibits the activity of neurons in the brain.

Nucleus accumbens: a cluster of subcortical neurons in the frontal lobes of the brain that are associated with the processes of motivation and reward.

Open-label trials: research studies in which the medicine used is known to the patient and to the research team.

Orbitomedial circuit: the cortical–subcortical pathway of neurons associated with the orbitomedial cortex.

Orbitomedial prefrontal cortex: a portion of cortex located on the lower middle part of the prefrontal lobe of the brain, associated with the experience and regulation of feelings.

Panic attacks: discrete episodes of severe anxiety associated with marked symptoms of physiological arousal and a sense of impending death.

Panic disorder: the repeated occurrence of panic attacks.

Paranoid thinking: the false belief that others are planning harm against one.

Parasuicidal acts: self-injurious behaviors that are not intended to result in death.

Posttraumatic stress disorder: a mental disorder occurring after exposure to a traumatic event of threatened death or serious injury that is persistently reexperienced and results in avoidance of situations that will recall the trauma and is associated with symptoms of increased arousal.

Pre-schizophrenia: a term initially used to refer to patients who had symptoms similar to borderline personality disorder.

Primary clinician: a psychiatrist or other mental health professional skilled in the diagnosis and treatment of a disorder.

Prognosis: expected response to treatment or the natural outcome of a medical disorder.

Projection: the unconscious psychological attempt to deal with anxiety by attributing one's own unacceptable attributes to the outside world.

Pseudoneurotic schizophrenia: the unconscious psychological attempt to deal with anxiety by attributing one's own unacceptable attributes to the outside world. Same as projection.

Psychoanalysis: a form of psychotherapy based on the psychoanalytic theory of human development and behavior, formulated by Sigmund Freud.

Psychodynamic psychotherapy: a form of psychotherapy based on learning and applying a body of knowledge about complex conscious and unconscious thoughts, feelings, and behaviors.

Psychosis: symptoms of a mental disorder characterized by episodes of significant loss of contact with reality, often accompanied by delusions and hallucinations.

Psychotic episodes: periods of psychosis.

Resident: a physician who is in graduate training to qualify as a specialist in a particular field of medicine, such as psychiatry. The American Board of Psychiatry and Neurology requires four years of postgraduate training in an approved facility to qualify for board examination in psychiatry.

Risk factors: genetic mutations and developmental and environmental events that increase the probability of developing a medical illness.

Schizotypal personality disorder: a disorder characterized by difficulty in developing close relationships associated with odd perceptions, distortions, and eccentric behavior beginning in early adulthood.

Seminal article: an article that significantly influences and stimulates later thinking and research.

Serotonergic activity: involving activity of serotonin in the transmission of nerve impulses.

Serotonin: a neurotransmitter that stimulates or inhibits the activity of neurons in the brain.

Stress–diathesis model: a concept of the interaction of a biological (genetic or developmental) predisposition to an illness and environmental factors or stresses that increase the likelihood of developing the illness.

Tardive dyskinesia: spontaneous movements developing in some patients exposed to antipsychotic drugs. Typical movements include tongue writhing or protrusion, chewing, lip puckering, finger movements, toe and ankle movements, leg jiggling, or movements of neck, trunk, and pelvis. These movements range from mild to severe and may occur singly or in many combinations.

Thalamus: the largest subcortical cluster of neurons, located in the middle of the cerebral hemispheres of the brain, that serves to relay and regulate impulses to and from the cerebral cortex.

References

FOREWORD BY DONALD W. BLACK, MD, AND NANCEE BLUM, MSW

Black DW, Pfohl B, Blum N, et al. Attitudes toward borderline personality disorder: A survey of 706 mental health clinicians. *CNS Spectrums* 2011;16:67–74.

Shanks C, Pfohl B, Blum N, Black DW. Can negative attitudes toward patients with borderline personality disorder be changed? The effect of attending a STEPPS workshop. *Journal of Personality Disorders* 2011;25:806–812.

INTRODUCTION

American Psychiatric Association. Practice guideline for the treatment of patients with borderline personality disorder. *American Journal of Psychiatry* 2001;158(October supplement).

Grant BF, Chou SP, Goldstein RB, et al. Prevalence, correlates, disability, and comorbidity of DSM-IV borderline personality disorder: Results from the wave two national epidemiologic survey on alcohol and related conditions. *Journal of Clinical Psychiatry* 2008;69:533–545.

Gunderson JG, Links PS. *Borderline Personality Disorder: A Clinical Guide.* 2nd ed. Washington, DC: American Psychiatric Publishing; 2008.

Hyman SE. A new beginning for research on borderline personality disorder. *Biological Psychiatry* 2002;51:933–935.

CHAPTER 1: WHAT IS BORDERLINE PERSONALITY DISORDER AND HOW IS IT DIAGNOSED?

Domain 1: Poorly Regulated Emotions

Akiskal, HS. The temperamental borders of affective disorders. *Acta Psychiatrica Scandanavica* 1994;379(supplement):32–37.

Carpenter RW, Trull TJ. Components of emotion dysregulation in borderline personality disorder: A review. *Current Psychiatry Reports* 2013;15:335.

Deltito J, Martin L, Riefkohl J, et al. Do patients with borderline personality disorder belong to the bipolar spectrum? *Journal of Affective Disorders* 2001;67:221–228.

Herpertz SC. Emotional processing in personality disorder. *Current Psychiatry Reports* 2003;5:23–27.

Pukrop R. Dimensional personality profiles of borderline personality disorder in comparison with other personality disorders and healthy controls. *Journal of Personality Disorders* 2002;16:135–147.

Sanislow CA, Grilo CM, McGlashan TH. Factor analysis of the DSM-III-R borderline personality disorder criteria in psychiatric inpatients. *American Journal of Psychiatry* 2000;157:1629–1633.

Shearin EN, Linehan NM. Dialectical behavior therapy for borderline personality disorder: theoretical and empirical foundations. *Acta Psychiatrica Scandanavica* 1994;379(supplement):61–68.

Skodol AE, Gunderson JG, Pfohl B, Widiger TA, Livesley WJ, Siever LJ. The borderline diagnosis I: Psychopathology, comorbidity, and personality structure. *Biological Psychiatry* 2002;51:936–950.

van Zutphen L, Siep GA, Gitta N, Jacob GA, Goebel R, Arntz A. Emotional sensitivity, emotion regulation and impulsivity in borderline personality disorder: A critical review of fMRI studies. *Neuroscience and Behavioral Reviews* 2015;51:64–76.

Zanarini MC, Frankenburg FR, LeLuca CJ, Hennese J, Khera GS, Gunderson JG. The pain of being borderline: Dysphoric states specific to borderline personality disorder. *Harvard Review of Psychiatry* 1998;6:201–207.

Domain 2: Impulsivity

Goodman M, New A. Impulsive aggression in borderline personality disorder. *Current Psychiatry Reports* 2000;2:56–61.

Henry C, Mitropoulou V, New AS, Koenigsberg HW, Silverman J, Siever

LJ. Affective instability and impulsivity in borderline personality and bipolar II disorders: Similarities and differences. *Journal of Psychiatric Research* 2001;35:307–312.

Links PS, Heslegrave R, van Reekum R. Impulsivity: Core aspect of borderline personality disorder. *Journal of Personality Disorders* 1999;13:1–9.

Paris J. Chronic suicidality among patients with borderline personality disorder. *Psychiatric Services* 2002;53:738–742.

Sanislow CA, Grilo CM, Morey LC, et al. Confirmatory factor analysis of DSM-IV criteria for borderline personality disorder: Findings from the collaborative longitudinal personality disorders study. *American Journal of Psychiatry* 2002;159:284–290.

Wang GY, van Eijk J, Demirakca T, et al. ACC GABA levels are associated with functional activation and connectivity in the fronto-striatal network during interference inhibition in patients with borderline personality disorder. *NeuroImage* 2017;15:164–174.

Domain 3: Impaired Perception and Reasoning

Arntz A, Appels C, Sierwerda S. Hypervigilance in borderline disorder: A test with the emotional Stroop paradigm. *Journal of Personality Disorders* 2000;14:366–373.

O'Leary KM. Borderline personality disorder: Neuropsychological testing results. *Psychiatric Clinics of North America* 2000;23:41–60.

O'Leary KM, Cowdry RW. Neuropsychological testing results in borderline personality disorder. In: Silk KR, ed. *Biological and Behavioral Studies of Borderline Personality Disorder*. Washington, DC: American Psychiatric Press; 1994.

Zanarini M, Frankenburg F, Wedig M, Fitzmaurice G. Cognitive experiences reported by patients with borderline personality disorder and Axis II comparison subjects: A 16-year prospective follow-up study. *American Journal of Psychiatry* 2013;170:671–679.

Domain 4: Markedly Disturbed Relationships

Bailey RC, Grenyer BF, Gunderson JG. *Borderline Personality Disorder: A Clinical Guide*. Washington, DC: American Psychiatric Publishing; 2001.

Gratz K, Dixon-Gordon K, Breetz A, Tull, M. A laboratory-based examination of responses to social rejection in borderline personality disorder: The mediating role of emotion dysregulation. *Journal of Personality Disorders* 2013;27:157–171.

Jeung H, Herpertz SC. Impairments of interpersonal functioning: Empathy and intimacy in borderline personality disorder. *Psychopathology* 2014;47:220–234.

Judd PH, McGlashan TH. *A Developmental Model of Borderline Personality Disorder: Understanding Variations in Course and Outcome.* Washington, DC: American Psychiatric Publishing; 2003.

Koenigsberg HW, Harvey PD, Mitropoulou V, et al. Are the interpersonal and identity disturbances in the borderline personality disorder criteria linked to the traits of affective instability and impulsivity? *Journal of Personality Disorders* 2001;15:358–370.

Lis S, Bohus M. Social interaction in borderline personality disorder. *Current Psychiatry Reports* 2014;15:338.

Scott L, Kim Y, Nolf K, et al. Preoccupied attachment and emotional dysregulation: Specific aspects of borderline personality disorder or general dimensions of personality pathology? *Journal of Personality Disorders* 2013;27:473–495.

CHAPTER 3: THE HISTORY OF BORDERLINE PERSONALITY DISORDER

American Psychiatric Association. *Diagnostic and statistical manual of mental disorders.* 5th ed. Washington, DC: American Psychiatric Publishing; 2013.

Brinkley JR, Beitman BS, Friedel RO. Low-dose neuroleptic regimens in the treatment of borderline patients. *Archives of General Psychiatry* 1979;36:319–326.

Goldberg C, Schulz SC, Schulz PM, Resnick RJ, Hamer RM, Friedel RO. Borderline and schizotypal personality disorders treated with low-dose thiothixene vs. placebo. *Archives of General Psychiatry* 1986;43:680–686.

Gunderson J, Singer M. Defining borderline patients: An overview. *American Journal of Psychiatry* 1975; 132:1–10.

Gunderson JG, Links PS. *Borderline Personality Disorder: A Clinical Guide.* 2nd ed. Washington, DC: American Psychiatric Publishing; 2008.

Kendler KS, Myers J, Reichborn-Kjennerud T. Borderline personality disorder traits and their relationship with dimensions of normative personality: A web-based cohort and twin study. *Acta Psychiatrica Scandanavica* 2011;123:349–359.

Kernberg OF. Borderline personality organization. *Journal of American Psychoanalysis Association* 1967;15:641–685.

Knight RP. Borderline states. *Bulletin of the Menninger Clinic* 1953;17:112.

Lieb K, Völlm B, Rücker G, Timmer A, Stoffers JM. Pharmacotherapy for borderline personality disorder: Cochrane systematic review of randomised trials. *British Journal of Psychiatry* 2010;196:4–12.

Linehan MM, Walks CR. The course and evolution of dialectical behavior therapy. *American Journal of Psychothera*py 2015;69:97–110.

Livesley WJ, Dimaggio G, Clarkin JF, eds. *Integrated Treatment for Personality Disorder: A Modular Approach.* New York: Guilford; 2016.

Millon T. The borderline construct: Introductory notes on its history, theory, and empirical grounding. In: Clarkin JF, Marziali E, Munroe-Blum H, eds. *Borderline Personality Disorder, Clinical and Empirical Perspectives.* New York: Guilford; 1992.

Silk KR, Friedel RO. Psychopharmacological considerations in the integrated treatment of personality disorder. In: Livesley WJ, Dimaggio G, Clarkin JF, eds. *Integrated Treatment for Personality Disorder: A Modular Approach.* New York: Guilford; 2016.

Skodol AE, Gunderson JG, Pfohl, B, Widiger TA, Livesley WJ, Siever LJ. The borderline diagnosis I: Psychopathology, comorbidity, and personality structure. *Biological Psychiatry* 2002;51:936–950.

Spitzer RL, Endicott J, Gibbon M. Crossing the border into border-line personality and borderline schizophrenia: The development of criteria. *Archives of General Psychiatry* 1979;36:17–24.

Stern A. Psychoanalytic investigation of and therapy in the borderline group of neuroses. *Psychoanalytic Quarterly* 1938;7:467–489.

CHAPTER FOUR: THE CAUSES OF BORDERLINE PERSONALITY DISORDER

Friedel RO. Dopamine dysfunction in borderline personality disorder: A hypothesis. *Neuropsychopharmacology* 2004;29:1029–1039.

Judd PH, McGlashan TH. *A Developmental Model of Borderline Personality Disorder: Understanding Variations in Course and Outcome.* Washington, DC: American Psychiatric Publishing; 2003.

Millon T. Sociocultural conceptions of the borderline personality. *Psychiatric Clinics of North America* 2000;23:123–136.

Paris J. Childhood precursors of borderline personality disorder. *Psychiatric Clinics of North America* 2000;23:77–88.

Reich DB, Zanarini MC. Developmental aspects of borderline personality disorder. *Harvard Review of Psychiatry* 2001;9:294–301.

Skodol AE, Siever LJ, Livesley WJ, Gunderson JG, Pfohl B, Widiger TA. The borderline diagnosis II: Biology, genetics, and clinical course. *Biological Psychiatry* 2002;51:951–963.

Soloff PH, Lynch KG, Kelly TM. Childhood abuse as a risk factor for suicidal behavior in borderline personality disorder. *Journal of Personality Disorders* 2002;16:201–214.

Torgersen S, Lygren S, Oien PA, et al. A twin study of personality disorders. *Comprehensive Psychiatry* 2000;41:416–425.

Trull TJ. Structural relations between borderline personality disorder features and putative etiological correlates. *Journal of Abnormal Psychology* 2001;110:471–481.

Zanarini MC. Childhood experiences associated with the development of borderline personality disorder. *Psychiatric Clinics of North America* 2000;23:89–101.

Zanarini MC, Frankenburg FR, Reich DB, et al. Biparental failure in the childhood experiences of borderline patients. *Journal of Personality Disorders* 2000;14:264–273.

CHAPTER 5: TRACING THE COURSE OF THE DISORDER

Becker DF, Grilo CM, Edel WS, McGlashan TH. Diagnostic efficiency of borderline personality disorder criteria in hospitalized adolescents: Comparison with hospitalized adults. *American Journal of Psychiatry* 2002;159:2042–2047.

Garnet KE, Levy KN, Mattanah JJF, Edell WS, McGlashan TH. Borderline personality disorder in adolescents: Ubiquitous or specific? *American Journal of Psychiatry* 1994;151:1380–1382.

Gunderson JG, Bender D, Sanislow C, et al. Plausibility and possible determinants of sudden "remissions" in borderline patients. *Psychiatry* 2003;66:11–119.

Judd PH, McGlashan TH. *A Developmental Model of Borderline Personality Disorder: Understanding Variations in Course and Outcome.* Washington, DC: American Psychiatric Publishing; 2003.

Links PS, Heslegrave RJ. Prospective studies of outcome: Understanding mechanisms of change in patients with borderline personality disorder. *Psychiatric Clinics of North America* 2000;23:137–150.

Ludolph PS, Westen D, Misle B, Jackson A, Wixom J, Wiss FC. The borderline diagnosis in adolescents: Symptoms and developmental history. *American Journal of Psychiatry* 1990;147:470–476.

Paris J, Brown R, Nowlis D. Long-term follow-up of borderline patients in a general hospital. *Comprehensive Psychiatry* 1987;28:530–536.

Seivewright H, Tyrer P, Johnson T. Change in personality status in neurotic disorders. *Lancet* 2002;359:2253–2254.

Stevenson J, Meares R, Comerford A. Diminished impulsivity in older patients with borderline personality disorder. *American Journal of Psychiatry* 2003;160:165–166.

Zanarini MC, Frankenburg FR, Hennen J, Silk KR. The longitudinal course of borderline psychopathology: 6-year prospective follow-up of the phenomenology of borderline personality disorder. *American Journal of Psychiatry* 2003;160:274–283.

CHAPTER 6: BORDERLINE PERSONALITY DISORDER IN CHILDREN

Aguirre BA. *Borderline Personality Disorder in Adolescents*. Beverly, MA: Fair Winds Press; 2007.

Bemporad JR, Smith HF, Hanson G, Cicchetti D. Borderline syndromes in childhood: Criteria for diagnosis. *American Journal of Psychiatry* 1982;139:596–602.

Cohen DJ, Paul R, Volmar FR. Issues in the classification of pervasive and other developmental disorders: Toward DSM-IV. *Journal of American Academy of Child Psychiatry* 1986;25:213–220.

Coulston CM, Tanious M, Mulder RT, Porter RJ, Malhi GS. Bordering on bipolar: The overlap between borderline personality and bipolarity. *Australian & New Zealand Journal of Psychiatry* 2012;46:506–521.

Fonagy P, Speranza M, Luyten P, Kaess M, Hessels C, Bohus M. ESCAP Expert Article: Borderline personality disorder in adolescence: An expert research review with implications for clinical practice. *European Child and Adolescent Psychiatry* 2015;24:1307–1320.

Greene RW. *The Explosive Child: A New Approach for Understanding and Parenting Easily Frustrated, Chronically Inflexible Children*. New York: Harper; 2005.

Greenman DA, Gunderson JG, Cane M, Saltzman PR. An examination of the borderline diagnosis in children. *American Journal of Psychiatry* 1986;143:998–1003.

Guzder J, Paris J, Zelkowitz P, Marchessault K. Risk factors for borderline pathology in children. *Journal of the American Academy of Child and Adolescent Psychiatry* 1996;35:26–33.

Hawes DJ. Does the concept of borderline personality features have clinical utility in childhood? *Current Opinions in Psychiatry* 2014;27:87–93.

Koenig J, Kemp AH, Feeling NR, Thayer JF, Kaess M. Resting state vagal tone in borderline personality disorder: A meta-analysis. *Progress in Neuro-Psychopharmacology & Biological Psychiatry* 2016;64:18–26.

Lincoln AJ, Bloom D, Katz M, Boksenbaum N. Neuropsychological and neurophysiological indices of auditory processing impairment in children with multiple complex developmental disorder. *Journal of the American Academy of Child and Adolescent Psychiatry* 1998;37:100–112.

Lofgren DP, Bemporad J, King J, Lindem K, O'Driscoll G. A prospective follow-up study of so-called borderline children. *American Journal of Psychiatry* 1991;148:1541–1547.

Paris J. Childhood precursors of borderline personality disorder. *Psychiatric Clinics of North America* 2000;23:77–88.

Paris J, Zelkowitz P, Guzder J, Joseph S, Feldman R. Neuropsychological factors associated with borderline pathology in children. *Journal of the American Academy of Child and Adolescent Psychiatry* 1999;38:770–774.

Singh MK, Ketter T, Chang KD. Distinguishing bipolar disorder from other psychiatric disorders in children. *Current Psychiatry Reports* 2014;16:516.

Stepp SD, Lazarus SA, Byrd AL. A systematic review of risk factors prospectively associated with borderline personality disorder: Taking stock and moving forward. *Personality Disorders* 2016;7:316–323.

Vermetten E, Spiegel D. Trauma and dissociation: Implications for borderline personality disorder. *Current Psychiatry Reports* 2014;16:434.

Winsper C, Lereya ST, Marwaha S, Thompson A, Eyden J, Singh SP. The aetiological and psychopathological validity of borderline personality disorder in youth: A systematic review and meta-analysis. *Clinical Psychology Review* 2016;44:13–24.

Yeomans FE, Clarkin JF, Kernberg OF. *Transference-focused Psychotherapy for Borderline Personality Disorder: A Clinical Guide.* Washington, DC: American Psychiatric Publishing; 2015.

Zanarini MC. Childhood experiences associated with the development of borderline personality disorder. *Psychiatric Clinics of North America* 2000;23:89–101.

CHAPTER 7: BORDERLINE PERSONALITY DISORDER AND THE BRAIN

Amad A, Ramoz N, Thomas P, Jardri R, Gorwood P. Genetics of borderline personality disorder: Systematic review and proposal of an integrative model. *Neuroscience Biobehavioral Reviews* 2014;40:6–19.

American Psychiatric Association. Practice guideline for the treatment of patients with borderline personality disorder. *American Journal of Psychiatry* 2001;158(October supplement).

Bohus M, Schmahl C, Lieb K. New developments in the neurobiology of borderline personality disorder. *Current Psychiatry Reports* 2004;6:43–50.

Brüne M. On the role of oxytocin in borderline personality disorder. *British Journal of Psychiatry* 2016;55:287–304.

Buckholtz JW, Treadway MT, Cowan RL, et al. Dopaminergic network differences in human impulsivity. *Science* 2010;329:532.

Chanen AM, Kaess M. Developmental pathways to borderline personality disorder. *Current Psychiatry Reports* 2012;14:45–53.

De la Fuente JM, Goldman S, Stanus E, et al. Brain glucose metabolism in borderline personality disorder. *Journal of Psychiatric Research* 1997;31:531–541.

Donegan NH, Sanislow CA, Blumberg HP, et al. Amygdala hyperreactivity in borderline personality disorder: Implications for emotional dysregulation. *Biological Psychiatry* 2003;54:1284–1293.

Friedel RO. Dopamine dysfunction in borderline personality disorder: A hypothesis. *Neuropsychopharmacology*. 2004;29:1029–1039.

Friedel RO, Schmahl C, New A, Distel M. The neurobiology of borderline personality disorder. In: Schmahl C, Phan L, R Friedel, eds. *The Neurobiology of Personality Disorders*. New York: Oxford University Press; 2018.

Gurvits IG, Koenigsberg HW, Siever LJ. Neurotransmitter dysfunction in patients with borderline personality disorder. *Psychiatric Clinics of North America* 2000;23:27–40.

Herpertz SC, Dietrich TM, Wenning B, et al. Evidence of abnormal amygdala functioning in borderline personality disorder: A functional MRI study. *Biological Psychiatry* 2001;50:292–298.

LeDoux J. *The Emotional Brain*. New York: Touchstone; 1996.

LeDoux J. *Synaptic Self: How Our Brains Become Who We Are*. New York: Viking Penguin; 2002.

Leyton M, Okazawa H, Diksic M, et al. Brain regional alpha-(11C)methyl-L-tryptophan trapping in impulsive subjects with borderline personality disorder. *American Journal of Psychiatry* 2001;158:775–782.

O'Leary KM. Borderline personality disorder: Neuropsychological testing results. *Psychiatric Clinics of North America* 2000;23:41–60.

Paris J, ed. *Borderline Personality Disorder: Etiology and Treatment*. Washington, DC: American Psychiatric Press; 1993.

Ruocco AC, Carcone D. A neurobiological model of borderline personality disorder: Systematic and integrative review. *Harvard Review of Psychiatry* 2016;24:311–329.

Silk KR. Borderline personality disorder: Overview of biological factors. *Psychiatric Clinics of North America* 2000;23:61–76.

Skodol AE, Siever LJ, Livesley WJ, Gunderson JG, Pfohl B, Widiger TA. The borderline diagnosis II: Biology, genetics, and clinical course. *Biological Psychiatry* 2002;51:951–963.

Soloff PH, Meltzer CC, Greer PJ, Constantine D, Kelly TM. A fenfluramine-activated FDG-PET study of borderline personality disorder. *Biological Psychiatry* 2000;47:540–547.

Tebartz van Elst L, Theil T, Hesslinger B, et al. Subtle prefrontal neuropathology in a pilot magnetic resonance spectroscopy study in patients with borderline personality disorder. *Journal of Neuropsychiatry and Clinical Neuroscience* 2001;13:511–514.

Witt SH, Kleindienst N, Frank J, et al. Analysis of genome-wide significant bipolar disorder genes in borderline personality disorder. *Psychiatry Genetics* 2014;24:262–265.

CHAPTER 8: COMMON CO-OCCURRING DISORDERS

Aldenkamp AP, De Krom M, Reijs R. Newer antiepileptic drugs and cognitive issues. *Epilepsia* 2003;(supplement)44:21–29.

Becker DF, Grilo CM, Edell WS, McGlashan TH. Comorbidity of borderline personality disorder with other personality disorders in hospitalized adolescents and adults. *American Journal of Psychiatry* 2000;157:2011–2016.

Deltito J, Martin L, Riefkohl J, et al. Do patients with borderline personality disorder belong to the bipolar spectrum? *Journal of Affective Disorders* 2001;67:221–228.

Golier JA, Yehuda R, Bierer LM, et al. The relationship of borderline personality disorder to posttraumatic stress disorder and traumatic events. *American Journal of Psychiatry* 2003;160:2018–2024.

Johnson BA, Ait-Daoud N, Bowden CL, et al. Oral topiramate for treatment of alcohol dependence: A randomized controlled trial. *Lancet* 2003;361:1677–1685.

Oldham JM, Skodol AE, Kellman HD, et al. Comorbidity of axis I and axis II disorders. *American Journal of Psychiatry* 1995;152:571–578.

Skodol AE, Oldham JM, Gallaher PE. Axis II comorbidity of substance use disorders among patients referred for treatment of personality disorders. *American Journal of Psychiatry* 1999;156:733–738.

Zanarini MC, Frankenburg FR, Dubo ED, et al. Axis I comorbidity of borderline personality disorder. *American Journal of Psychiatry* 1998;155: 1733–1739.

Zanarini MC, Frankenburg FR, Dubo ED, et al. Axis II comorbidity of borderline personality disorder. *Comprehensive Psychiatry* 1998;39: 296–302.

Zimmerman M, Mattia JI. Axis I diagnostic comorbidity and borderline personality disorder. *Comprehensive Psychiatry* 1999;40:245–252.

CHAPTER 9: THE KEY ELEMENTS OF TREATMENT

American Psychiatric Association. Practice guideline for the treatment of patients with borderline personality disorder. *American Journal of Psychiatry* 2001;158(supplement).

Fossati A, Novella L, Donati D, Donini M, Maffei C. History of childhood attention deficit/hyperactivity disorder symptoms and borderline personality disorder: A controlled study. *Comprehensive Psychiatry* 2002;43:369–377.

Gunderson, J.G., Links, P.S. *Borderline Personality Disorder: A Clinical Guide.* 2nd ed. Washington, DC: American Psychiatric Publishing; 2008.

Judd PH, McGlashan TH. *A Developmental Model of Borderline Personality Disorder: Understanding Variations in Course and Outcome.* Washington, DC: American Psychiatric Publishing; 2003.

CHAPTER 10: MEDICATIONS

Abraham PF, Calabrese JR. Evidenced-based pharmacologic treatment of borderline personality disorder: A shift from SSRIs to anticonvulsants and atypical antipsychotics? *Journal of Affective Disorders* 2008;111:21–30.

Aldenkamp AP, De Krom M, Reijs R. Newer antiepileptic drugs and cognitive issues. *Epilepsia* 2003;4(supplement):21–29.

American Psychiatric Association. Practice guideline for the treatment of patients with borderline personality disorder. *American Journal of Psychiatry* 2001;158(supplement).

Black DW, Zanarini MC, Romine A, Shaw M, Allen J, Schulz SC. A dose comparison of low and moderate doses of extended-release quetiapine fumarate (quetiapine XR) in the treatment of borderline personality disorder: A randomized, double-blind, placebo-controlled trial. *American Journal of Psychiatry* 2014;171:1174–1182.

Brinkley JR, Beitman BD, Friedel RO. Low-dose neuroleptic regimens in the treatment of borderline patients. *Archives of General Psychiatry* 1979;36:319–326.

Goldberg SC, Schulz SC, Schulz PM, Resnick RJ, Hamer RM, Friedel RO. Borderline and schizotypal personality disorders treated
with low-dose thiothixene vs. placebo. *Archives of General Psychiatry*
1986:43:680–686.

Lieb K, Völlm B, Rücker G, Timmer A, Stoffers JM. Pharmacotherapy for
borderline personality disorder: Cochrane systematic review of randomised trials. *British Journal of Psychiatry* 2010;196:4–12.

National Collaborating Centre for Mental Health (UK). *Borderline Personality
Disorder: Treatment and Management.* Leicester, UK: British Psychological
Society; 2009.

Saunders EF, Silk KR. Personality trait dimensions and the pharmacological
treatment of borderline personality disorder. *Journal of Clinical Psychopharmacology* 2009;29:461–467.

Silk KR, Friedel RO. Psychopharmacological considerations in the inte-
grated treatment of personality disorder. In: Livesley WJ, Dimaggio G,
Clarkin JF, eds. *Integrated Treatment for Personality Disorder: A Modular
Approach.* New York: Guilford; 2016.

Soloff PH. Psychopharmacology of borderline personality disorder. *Psychiatric Clinics of North America* 2000;23:169–192.

CHAPTER 11: THE PSYCHOTHERAPIES

American Psychiatric Association. Practice guideline for the treatment of patients with borderline personality disorder. *American Journal of Psychiatry*
2001;158(October supplement).

Beck AT, Freeman A, Davis DD, et al. *Cognitive Therapy of Personality Disorders.* 2nd ed. New York: Guilford; 2003.

Black, DW, Blum, NS, eds. *Systems Training for Emotional Predictability and
Problem Solving for Borderline Personality Disorder: Implementing STEPPS
Around the Globe.* New York: Oxford University Press; 2017.

Fonagy P, Bateman A. *Mentalization-based Treatment for Personality Disorders:
A Practical Guide.* New York: Oxford University Press; 2016.

Gunderson, JG. *Borderline Personality Disorder: A Clinical Guide.* 2nd ed.
Washington, DC: American Psychiatric Publishing; 2008.

Hoffman PD, Fruzzetti AE, Swenson CR. Dialectical behavior therapy—
family skills training. *Family Process* 1999;38:399–414.

Hooley JM, Hoffman PD. Expressed emotions and clinical outcome
in borderline personality disorder. *American Journal of Psychiatry*
1999;156:1557–1562.

Linehan MM. *Cognitive Behavioral Treatment of Borderline Personality Disorder.* New York: Guilford; 1993.

Livesley WJ, Dimaggio G, Clarkin JF, eds. *Integrated Treatment for Personality Disorder: A Modular Approach.* New York: Guilford; 2016.

McMain SF, Links PS, Gnam WH, et al. A randomized trial of dialectical behavior therapy versus general psychiatric management for borderline personality disorder. *American Journal of Psychiatry* 2009;166:1365–1374.

Miller BC. Characteristics of effective day treatment programming for persons with borderline personality disorder. *Psychiatric Services* 1995;46: 605–608.

Robins CJ, Chapman AL. Dialectical behavior therapy: Current status, recent developments and future directions. *Journal of Personality Disorders* 2004;18:73–89.

Roller B, Nelson V. Group psychotherapy treatment of borderline personalities. *International Journal of Group Psychotherapy* 1999;49:369–385.

Silk KR, Friedel RO. Psychopharmacological considerations in the integrated treatment of personality disorder. In: Livesley WJ, Dimaggio G, Clarkin JF, eds. *Integrated Treatment for Personality Disorder: A Modular Approach.* New York, Guilford; 2016.

Stoffers JM, Völlm BA, Rücker G, Timmer A, Huband N, Lieb K. Psychological therapies for people with borderline personality disorder. *The Cochrane Database Systematic Review* 2012;8.

Stone MH. Clinical guidelines for psychotherapy for patients with borderline personality disorder. *Psychiatric Clinics of North America* 2000;23:193–210.

CHAPTER 12: THE INTEGRATED USE OF
MEDICATIONS AND PSYCHOTHERAPY

Silk KR. The process of managing medications in patients with borderline personality disorder. *Journal of Psychiatric Practice* 2011;17:311–319.

Silk KR, Friedel RO. Psychopharmacological considerations in the integrated treatment of personality disorder. In: Livesley WJ, Dimaggio G, Clarkin JF, eds. *Integrated Treatment for Personality Disorder: A Modular Approach.* New York: Guilford; 2016.

CHAPTER 13: WHEN A LOVED ONE HAS
BORDERLINE PERSONALITY DISORDER

Gunderson, JG. *Borderline Personality Disorder: A Clinical Guide.* 2nd ed. Washington, DC: American Psychiatric Publishing; 2008.

Gunderson JG, Berkowitz C, Ruiz-Sancho A. Families of borderline patients: A psycho-educational approach. *Bulletin of the Menninger Clinic* 1997;61:446–457.

Gunderson JG, Lyoo IK. Family problems and relationships for adults with borderline personality disorder. *Harvard Review of Psychiatry* 1997;4:272–278.

Hoffman PD, Fruzzetti AE, Swenson CR. Dialectical behavior therapy—family skills training. *Family Process* 1999;38:399–414.

Hooley JM, Hoffman PD. Expressed emotion and clinical outcome in borderline personality disorder. *American Journal of Psychiatry* 1999;156:1557–1562.

Judd PH, McGlashan TH. *A Developmental Model of Borderline Personality Disorder: Understanding Variations in Course and Outcome.* Washington, DC: American Psychiatric Publishing; 2003.

Mason PT, Kreger R. *Stop Walking on Eggshells: Coping When Someone You Care About Has Borderline Personality Disorder.* Oakland, CA: New Harbinger Publications; 2010.

Weiss M, Zelkowitz P, Feldman RB, Vogel J, Heyman M, Paris J. Psychopathology in offspring of mothers with borderline personality disorder: A pilot study. *Canadian Journal of Psychiatry* 1996;41:285–290.

Zweig-Frank H, Paris J. Predictors of outcome in a 27-year follow-up of patients with borderline personality disorder. *Comprehensive Psychiatry* 2002;43:103–107.

CHAPTER 14: RESEARCH: THE ULTIMATE REASON FOR HOPE

Flint J, Greenspan RJ, Kendler KS. *How Genes Influence Behavior.* New York: Oxford University Press; 2010.

Hyman SE. A new beginning for research on borderline personality disorder. *Biological Psychiatry* 2002;51:933–935.

Siever LJ, Torgersen JG, Gunderson W, Livesley WJ, Kendler, KS. The borderline diagnosis III: Identifying endophenotypes for genetic studies. *Biological Psychiatry* 2002;51:964–968.

Skodol AE, Gunderson JG, Pfohl B, Wideger TA, Livesley WJ, Siever LJ. The borderline diagnosis I: Psychopathology, comorbidity, and personality structure. *Biological Psychiatry* 2002;51:936–950.

Skodol AE, Siever LJ, Livesley WJ, Gunderson JG, Pfohl B, Widiger TA. The borderline diagnosis II: Biology, genetics, and clinical course. *Biological Psychiatry* 2002;51:951–963.

Resources

ADVICE ON TREATMENT RESOURCES

Borderline Personality Disorder Resource Center
21 Bloomingdale Road
White Plains, NY 10605
888-694-2273
bpdresourcecenter@nyp.org
www.nyp.org/bpdresourcecenter

The Black Sheep Project
509 South 22nd Avenue
Bozeman, MT 59718
www.BlackSheepProject.org

American Psychiatric Association, APA
1000 Wilson Boulevard, Suite 1825
Arlington, VA 22209-3901
Toll-free: 888-357-7924
703-907-7300
apa@psych.org
www.psychiatry.org

**The American Academy of Child
and Adolescent Psychiatry, AACAP**

3615 Wisconsin Avenue, N.W.
Washington, DC 20016-3007
Phone: 202-966-7300
Fax: 202-464-0131
www.aacap.org

Personality Disorders Awareness Network, PDAN

1072 W Peachtree Street NW, #79468
Atlanta, GA 30357
209-732-6001
info@pdan.org
www.PDAN.org

ADVOCACY ORGANIZATIONS

National Alliance on Mental Illness, NAMI

3803 N. Fairfax Drive, Suite 100
Arlington, VA 22203
800-950-6264 / 703-524-7600
info@nami.org
www.nami.org

**National Education Alliance for Borderline
Personality Disorder, NEA-BPD**

525 Lawn Terrace
Mamaroneck, NY 10543
914-835-9011
neabpd@aol.com
www.borderlinepersonalitydisorder.com

**Treatment and Research Advancements for
Borderline Personality Disorder, TARA4BPD**

23 Greene Street
New York, NY 10013
212-966-6514
888-4-TARABPD
TARA4BPD.org
tara4bpd@gmail.com

DISABILITY ASSISTANCE

Americans with Disabilities Act, ADA

US Department of Justice
950 Northwest Pennsylvania Avenue
Civil Rights Division
Disability Rights Section—NYAVE
Washington, DC 20530
800-514-0301
www.usdoj.gov/crt/ada/adahom1.htm

FEDERAL RESEARCH

National Institute of Mental Health, NIMH

6001 Executive Boulevard, Room 6220, MSC 9663
Bethesda, MD 20892-9663
866-615-6464
301-443-4513 (TTY) / 866-415-8051 (TTY toll-free)
Fax: 301-443-4279
nimhinfo@nih.gov
www.nimh.nih.gov

FINANCIAL SUPPORT

Social Security Administration

Office of Public Inquiries
1100 West High Rise
6401 Security Blvd.
Baltimore, MD 21235
www.ssa.gov

GENERAL MENTAL HEALTH INFORMATION

The Carter Center Mental Health Program

One Copenhill
453 Freedom Parkway
Atlanta, GA 30307
800-550-3560 / 404-420-5100
info@cartercenter.org
www.cartercenter.org

Mental Health America, MHA
500 Montgomery Street, Suite 820
Alexandria, VA 22314
800-969.6642 / 703-684.7722
Fax: 703-684.5968

National Institute of Mental Health, NIMH
6001 Executive Boulevard, Room 6220, MSC 9663
Bethesda, MD 20892-9663
866-615-6464
301-443-4513 (TTY) / 866-415-8051 (TTY toll-free)
Fax: 301-443-4279
nimhinfo@nih.gov
www.nimh.nih.gov

LEGAL INFORMATION

The Bazelon Center for Mental Health Law
1101 15th Street, NW, Suite 1212
Washington, DC 20005-5002
202-467-5730
202-467-4232 (TDD)
Fax: 202-223-0490
communications@bazelon.org
www.bazelon.org

MEDICAL AND RELATED INFORMATION

BPD Central
PO Box 070106
Milwaukee, WI 53207-0106
BPDCentral@aol.com
www.bpdcentral.com

Mayo Clinic
www.mayoclinic.com

MEDLINEplus Health Information
c/o U.S. National Library of Medicine
8600 Rockville Pike

Bethesda, MD 20894
888-346-3656
custserv@nlm.nih.gov
www.medlineplus.gov

PubMed
National Library of Medicine
www.ncbi.nlm.nih.gov/pubmed/
custserv@nlm.nih.gov

US Food and Drug Administration
10903 New Hampshire Avenue
Silver Spring, MD 20993
888-463-6332
www.fda.gov

PRIVATE RESEARCH FOUNDATIONS
The Black Sheep Project
509 South 22nd Avenue
Bozeman, MT 59718
www.BlackSheepProject.org

National Alliance for Research of Schizophrenia and Depression, NARSAD
60 Cutter Mill Road, Suite 404
Great Neck, NY 11021
Toll-free: 800-829-8289 / (voice mail) 516-829-0091
info@narsad.org
www.narsad.org

RESEARCH AND TREATMENT PROGRAMS
Gerald Adler, MD
Massachusetts General Hospital
278 Clarendon St., Apt. 2
Boston, MA 02116
617-262-4616

Emil F. Coccaro, MD
Chair, Department of Psychiatry and Behavioral Neuroscience
5841 S. Maryland Avenue
Chicago, IL 60637
773-834-7427

Karen Conterio, CEO
Wendy Lader, PhD, MEd
S.A.F.E. Alternatives
800-366-8288
Fax: 888-296-7988
info@selfinjury.com
www.selfinjury.com

Robert O. Friedel, MD
Distinguished Clinical Professor of Psychiatry
Virginia Commonwealth University
Chief Psychiatric Consultant
The Black Sheep Project
13722 Hickory Nut Point
Midlothian, VA 23112
804-744-5261
BPDDemystified.com

Brian Greenfield, MD
Department of Psychiatry
The Montreal Children's Hospital
McGill University
1001 Boulevard Decarie
Montreal, Quebec H4A 3J1 Canada
514-412-4400

John Gunderson, MD
Director, Personality and Psychosocial Research Program
Belmont Campus
800-333-0338
mcleanhospital.org

Kenneth S. Kendler, MD, Professor
Department of Psychiatry, VCU HS

P.O. Box 980126
Richmond, VA 23298
804-828-8590
kenneth.kendler@vcuhealth.org
medschool.vcu.edu

Otto Kernberg, MD
Weill Cornell Psychiatry at New York–Presbyterian, Westchester
    Division
21 Bloomingdale Road
White Plains, NY 10605
914-997-5714

Jerold J. Kriesman, MD
Mercy Hospital
Allied Behavioral Consultants
11477 Olde Cabin Road
Suite 200
Saint Louis, MO 63141-7137
314-567-5000
Fax: 314-567-3110

Marsha Linehan, Ph.D., ABPP
Professor and Director
Behavioral Research & Therapy Clinics
University of Washington
Center for Behavioral Technology
Department of Psychology, Box 355915
3935 University Way NE
Seattle, WA 98195-5915
206-543-2782
Fax: 206-616-1513

Paul Links, MD
Lawson Health Research Institute
750 Base Line Rd. E.
London, ON N6C 2R5, Canada
519-685-8500 ext. 75694
paul.links@lhsc.on.ca

John C. Markowitz, MD
Columbia University, Department of Psychiatry
1051 Riverside Drive
New York, NY 10032
212-543-6283 / 212-746-3774

Thomas H. McGlashan, MD
Emeritus Faculty, Yale Psychiatric Institute
Department of Psychiatry
300 George St.
New Haven, CT 06511
203-974-7346
www.medicine.yale.edu

Joel Paris, MD, Professor
McGill University, Department of Psychiatry
Institute of Community and Family Psychiatry
4333 Cote Ste-Catherine Road
Montreal, Quebec, H3T 1E4, Canada
514-340-8222 ext. 5338
Fax: 514-340-7507
joel.paris@mcgill.ca

J. Christopher Perry, MPH, MD
Professor, Department of Psychiatry, McGill University
Director of Psychotherapy Research
Department of Psychiatry, Jewish General Hospital
3755 Cote Sainte Catherine Road
Montréal, Québec, H3T 1E2
Canada
514-340-8222 ext. 4643
jchristopher.perry@mcgill.ca

Charles P. Peters, MD
Personality Disorder Program
Sheppard Pratt Hospital Health System
6501 N. Charles Street
Baltimore, MD 21204

410-938-30000
info@shappardpratt.org
www.sheppardpratt.org

K. Luan Phan, MD
Dept. of Psychiatry
University of Illinois at Chicago
1747 W. Roosevelt Rd.
WROB/IJR, Rm. 244
Chicago, IL 60608
kllphan@uic.edu

Christian Schmahl, Prof. Dr.
Head of Clinical Department
Central Institute for Mental Health, J 5
K 3, 21, 3rd Floor, Room 314
68159 Mannheim, Germany
49 621 1703–4021
Fax: 49 621 1703–4005
info zi–mannheim.de
www.zi–mannheim.de

S. Charles Schulz, MD, Professor
Department of Psychiatry
University of Minnesota Medical School
420 Delaware Street SE
Minneapolis, MN 55455
612-626-2935
scs@umn.edu
www.umn.edu

Paul H. Soloff, MD
UPMC Western Psychiatric Institute & Clinic
3811 O'Hara Street Room 868
Pittsburgh, PA 15213
412-624-2100
Fax: 412-246-5410

SUBSTANCE ABUSE

Faces and Voices of Recovery
840 1st St. NE, 3rd Floor
Washington, DC 20002
202-737-0690
Fax: 202-737-0695
info@facesandvoicesofrecovery.org
www.facesandvoicesofrecovery.org

Facing Addiction, Inc.
100 Mill Plain Road
Third Floor
Danbury, CT 06811
www.facingaddiction.org

Families Anonymous, Inc.
701 Lee St., Suite 670
Des Plaines, IL 60016
800-736-9805
Fax: 847-294-5837
www.familiesanonymous.org

Nar-Anon
23110 Crenshaw Blvd., Suite A
Torrance, CA 90505
800-477-6291 / 310-534-8188
wso@nar-anon.org

Narcotics Anonymous World Services
PO Box 9999
Van Nuys, California USA 91409
818-773-9999
Fax: 818-700-0700
www.na.org

National Clearinghouse for Alcohol and Drug Information, NCADI
844-768-0487
www.addiction.com

**National Council on Alcohol and
   Drug Dependence, NCADD**
217 Broadway, Suite 712
New York, NY 10007
212-269-7797
www.ncadd.org

National Institute on Drug Abuse, NIDA
Office of Science Policy and Communications
Public Information and Liaison Branch
6001 Executive Boulevard
Room 5213, MSC 9561
Bethesda, Maryland 20892
301-443-1124
www.drugabuse.gov

**Substance Abuse and Mental Health
   Services Administration, SAMHSA**
5600 Fishers Lane
Rockville, MD 20857
877-726-4727
800-487-4889 (TTY)
www.samhsa.gov

Acknowledgments

I AM GRATEFUL TO THE READERS OF THE FIRST EDITION OF *Borderline Personality Disorder Demystified*. Their enthusiasm for and acceptance of the book have been gratifying and have enabled and encouraged me to prepare this revised edition.

My daughter Linda F. Cox, LCSW, has considerable clinical training and academic and clinical experience in the area of borderline personality disorder. She helped me significantly in the preparation of this edition of *Demystified* by performing literature searches, preparing draft material, reviewing drafts of all chapters, and suggesting minor to major alterations in their content. Preparing this edition in a thorough and timely manner would not have been possible without her assistance and collaboration. My other daughter, Karin, who assisted me with the first edition, also helped me with the revision of this edition. I am unable to thank both of them adequately.

The remainder of my family, especially my wife, Susanne, have been very patient during those periods when I secluded myself in my study to work on this task. I continue to appreciate Ernest Hemingway's famous comment, "There is nothing to writing. All you do is sit down at a typewriter and bleed." I would add, in this context, that one does not do so alone.

It is a rare blessing that an author has the benefit of longtime professional colleagues and friends who take the time from their busy lives to review a book and provide their thoughtful opinions in *two* Forewords that approach the work from entirely different perspectives. I extend my deep appreciation to Donald W. Black, MD, Nancee S. Blum, MSW, and Jim and Diane Hall.

Claire Schulz, who served as the editor for this edition of *Demystified*, has consistently provided splendid editorial assistance and strong support when most needed. Amber Morris, Senior Project Editor, was diligent and highly skilled in discerning flaws in the wording and the coherency of the book's content. Therefore, any deficits in these areas may be rightfully attributed to the author.

My literary agent, Katie Boyle, relentlessly keeps me on the path that is likely to achieve the most effective results.

My patients with borderline disorder, and their families, continue to teach me how to help them more effectively. I am grateful for their trust in me and admire greatly their persistence in their continued efforts to improve their lives.

Finally, I will always remain grateful to my deceased parents, Denise and August, for providing me with all that a son needs to pay forward some of those blessings that have been bestowed upon him.

Index

anger, intense or difficult to control, 5–6, 21
animal studies, 227–228
anorexia nervosa, 152–153
anterior cingulate cortex (ACC), 126, 128, 131–133
antianxiety agents, 176
antidepressants, 143, 145, 152
antiepileptics, 173–175, 183
antipsychotic agents, 42
   atypical, 168–172
   for borderline personality disorder, 166, 179–182
   See also first-generation antipsychotic agents (FGAs); second-generation antipsychotic agents (SGAs)
antisocial personality disorder, 59, 60, 154, 157
anxiety, 4–5, 54
   borderline personality disorder in children and, 99, 101
   as co-occurring disorder, 99, 101, 148
   treatment of, 180–181
approval, strong need for, 17
Aretaeus, 48
aripiprazole (Abilify), 169, 170, 210
attachment behaviors, 121
attention deficit hyperactivity disorder (ADHD)
   borderline personality disorder in adolescents and, 80
   as co-occurring disorder, 59, 60, 104, 106, 146, 210
   hyperactivity and, 147
   impulsivity and, 147
   inattention and, 146–147

atypical antipsychotic agents. *See* second-generation antipsychotic agents (SGAs)
auditory hallucinations, 15
autism, 103
avoidant personality disorder, 155–156

Baillarger, Jules, 48
Bateman, Anthony, 190–191
behavior, neural pathways and, 123
behavioral disorders, resembling borderline disorder in children, 104–107
behavioral domains of borderline personality disorder, 2, 119–122
   impaired perception and reasoning, 13–17, 121
   impulsivity, 7–13, 120
   markedly disturbed relationships, 17–20, 121–122
   poorly regulated emotions, 3–6, 119–120
behavioral problems, borderline disorder in children and, 95–96
Beitman, Bernard, 60, 182, 227
Bemporad, Jules, 99, 100, 101, 103
benzodiazepines, 149, 176, 180
biological causes of borderline personality disorder, 64–65
biological impairment, borderline disorder in children and, 98
Biological Psychiatry, 235
biological risk factors, 66–71
   borderline personality disorder in children and, 108–109
   developmental, 66–68
   genetic, 66, 67

derealization, 16
Descartes, René, 64–65, 118
destructive behaviors, planning
    ahead for, 221
developmental delay, borderline
    disorder in children and, 99
developmental risk factors, 66–68
diagnosis of borderline personality
    disorder
    in children, 97–98, 99–103, 107
    evolution of, 48–49
diagnosis of co-occurring disorders,
    138
*Diagnostic and Statistical Manual of
    Mental Disorders,* 2nd edition
    (DSM-II), 39
*Diagnostic and Statistical Manual of
    Mental Disorders,* 3rd edition
    (DSM-III), inclusion of
    borderline personality disorder
    in, 48, 58, 87
*Diagnostic and Statistical Manual of
    Mental Disorders,* 4th edition
    (DSM-IV-TR), 78
*Diagnostic and Statistical Manual of
    Mental Disorders,* 5th edition
    (DSM-5)
    borderline personality disorder in
        adolescents and, 79
    co-occurring disorders, 138
    diagnostic criteria of borderline
        personality disorder, 20–21
    on factitious disorder, 11
    Intermittent Explosive Disorder
        in, 106
    personality disorders in, 153
    revision of criteria of mental
        disorders, 138

diagnostic classification of borderline
    personality disorder, 229,
    230–231
diagnostic criteria of borderline
    personality disorder, 20–21
Diagnostic Interview for Borderline
    Patients (DIB), 58, 100
diagnostic strategies for borderline
    personality disorder, 230–231
dialectical behavior therapy (DBT),
    61, 189–190
    case example, 205–210
    STEPPS and, 194–195
diazepam (Valium), 42, 149, 176, 180
Dimaggio, Giancarlo, 233
dissociative episodes, 11, 121
dissociative symptoms, 15, 21
distributed processing, 124
divalproate (Depakote), 173, 174
divalproex, 145
dopamine, 125, 130, 177
dopamine D2 receptor, 168, 169
dopamine modulatory pathways, 135
dopaminergic activity, 135
dorsolateral prefrontal cortex, 126,
    133–134
double-blind method, 227
Douglas, Michael, 9
Duke Psychiatric Clinic, 36
dyskinesia, 168
dysthymia
    as co-occurring disorder, 139, 141
    distinguishing between borderline
        disorder and, 141–143

eating disorders, 151–153
    anorexia nervosa, 152–153
    bulimia nervosa, 151–152

fear responses, 126
    neurobiology of conditioned,
        128–129
first-generation antipsychotic agents
    (FGAs), 166–167
    case example of treatment using,
        171–172
    compared to second-generation
        antipsychotic agents, 168–170
    introduced as treatment for
        borderline disorder, 60–61
    side effects, 168
    study of effectiveness in treating
        borderline disorder, 181–182
    symptoms improved by, 183
5-HT2A receptor, 169
fluoxetine (Prozac), 190
flurazepam (Dalmane), 176
Fonagy, Peter, 190–191
Food and Drug Administration
    (FDA), 168, 182
Frankenburg, Frances, 176
Freud, Sigmund, 49
Friedel, Beatrice, 30, 31, 33–35
Friedel, Denise, 24–36
funding of research on borderline
    personality disorder, 235–238
    National Institute of Mental
        Health, 235–237, 239
    private research foundations,
        237

gamma aminobutyric acid (GABA),
    125, 133, 174, 177
gender
    attention deficit hyperactivity
        disorder incidence and, 146
    borderline personality disorder in
        children and, 96–97

personality disorders and, 157
    suicide methods and, 12
gene-environment interplay,
    borderline personality disorder
    prognosis and, 86
genetic factors, in borderline
    personality disorder, 64, 66, 67.
    See also biological risk factors
genetic strategies, 231
Geodon (ziprasidone), 168–170
glutamate, 125, 174, 177
good psychiatric management
    (GPM), 193–194
Greene, Ross, 114
Greenman, Deborah, 100–101
grief reaction, response to loved one
    with borderline disorder, 217
Grinker, Roy, 57–58
ground rules of therapy, 38
group therapy, 160, 195–196
guidelines
    for evaluating borderline disorder
        in children, 111
    for families with loved ones with
        borderline disorder, 218–223
Gunderson, John, 58–59, 100–101,
    161–162, 182, 194, 215
Gunderson/Lyoo study, 215
Guzder, Jaswant, 109

Halcion (triazolam), 176
Hall, Jim and Diane, 220
hallucinations, 13
    auditory, 15
haloperidol (Haldol), 168
heritability of borderline personality
    disorder, 60, 67
    research on, 229
    risk factors, 74

Herschel, Ernst, 48
Heslegrave, Ronald, 84, 90–91
hippocampal formation, 130–131
Hippocrates, 48
history of borderline personality
    disorder, 47–62
  borderline disorder-specific
    psychotherapies, 61
  development of advocacy,
    educational, and support
    organizations, 61–62
  evolution of diagnosis, 48–49
  Grinker and borderline syndrome,
    57–58
  Gundersen and borderline
    patients/borderline personality
    disorder, 58–59
  how became valid diagnosis,
    57–59
  introduction of medications into
    treatment, 60–61
  Kernberg and borderline
    personality organizations, 56–57
  Knight and borderline states, 56
  neurobiological underpinnings of
    borderline disorder, 59–60
  psychoanalytic origins of, 49–57
  recent changes in borders of
    borderline disorder, 59
  Stern and border line group,
    50–55
histrionic personality disorder, 59,
    60, 155
Hoffman, Perry, 220
Homer, 48
Hyman, Stephen, 235
hyperactivity, attention deficit
    hyperactivity disorder and,
    147

hyperreactive, 3
hypersensitivity, inordinate, 53
hypomanic episode, 144–145

impulse control, neural systems of,
    131–133
impulsivity
  anterior cingulate cortex and, 126
  attention deficit hyperactivity
    disorder and, 147
  orbitomedial prefrontal cortex
    and, 126
impulsivity (domain II)
  borderline personality disorder
    and, 7–13, 21, 91
  borderline personality disorder in
    adolescents and, 80–81
  Munchausen by proxy, 10–11
  Munchausen syndrome, 10
  recurrent suicidal behavior,
    gestures, or threats or self-
    mutilating behavior, 8–10, 21
  self-harming behaviors, 7–8
  suicide risk, 11–13
inattention, attention deficit
    hyperactivity disorder and,
    146–147
incidence, of borderline personality
    disorder, 2
infant temperament, borderline
    personality disorder in children
    and, 95, 96
inferiority, feelings of, 54
instruments, for research, 227
integrated modular treatment
    (IMT), 196–198, 202, 233
intensive outpatient care, 163
interdependence, relationships and,
    81

Intermittent Explosive Disorder, 104, 106–107
interpersonal group psychotherapy (IGP), 195–196

Judd, Patricia, 74

Kahlbaum, Karl, 48
Kendler, Ken, 74
Kernberg, Otto, 56–57, 74
Klonopin, 149
Knight, Robert, 56
knowledge, learning about borderline personality disorder, 218–219, 221–222
Kraepelin, Emil, 48–49
Kreger, Randi, 217
Kübler-Ross, Elisabeth, 217

lamotrigine (Lamictal), 145, 167, 173, 174–175
latent schizophrenia, 49, 50
LeDoux, Joseph, 119
levels of care, 163
Librium (chlordiazepoxide), 42, 180
light therapy, 145
Linehan, Marsha, 61, 73–74, 189
Links, Paul, 74, 84, 90–91, 194
Links and Heslegrave study, 90–91
lithium, 145, 173, 175, 183
Livesley, W. John, 196, 198, 202, 233
Lofgren, Donna, 100
lurasidone (Latuda), 169, 170, 209–210
case example of use, 209–210
Lyoo, Kyoon, 215

magical thinking, 16
major depressive disorder

as co-occurring disorder, 3, 12, 59, 60, 90, 139–141, 210
distinguishing between borderline personality disorder and, 141–143
manic episodes, 143–144
masochism, 54
Mason, Paul, 217
McGlashan, Thomas, 74
McLean study of treatment of borderline personality disorder, 87–89
medications for borderline personality disorder, 40, 42–43, 60–61, 75–76, 165–183
antianxiety agents and sedatives, 176
case example, 171–172
in children, 113
clozapine, 172–173
how medications are selected, 177–179
integrated use with psychotherapies, 201–210
medications used, 166–167
mood stabilizers, 173–175, 183
neuroleptics and atypical antipsychotic agents, 168–172, 179–183
neuroscience-based nomenclature for psychiatric medications, 167–168
nutraceutical agents, 176, 183
use of antipsychotic agents, 179–183
memory
difficulty with, 13
emotion and, 124, 130–131
memory pathways, 124

quetiapine (Seroquel), 168, 169
Quinlan, Karen Ann, 32

reality thinking, difficulties in, 55
reasoning, impaired (domain III),
    13–17
  borderline personality disorder in
    adolescents and, 81
reasoning, neural systems of, 133–134
Reichborn-Kjennerud, Ted, 74
relationships
  black-and-white world and, 14
  pattern of unstable and intense
    personal, 17–18, 21
relationships, markedly disturbed
    (domain IV), 17–20, 121–122
  borderline disorder in adolescents
    and, 81–82
  borderline disorder in children
    and, 99
reparenting, 193
research
  advocacy for, 234, 238–239
  anecdotal information, 225–227
  animal studies, 227–228
  clinical studies, 227
  Clozapine Risk Evaluation and
    Mitigation Strategy (REMS)
    Program, 172
  Collaborative Longitudinal
    Personality Disorder Study,
    89–90
  on course of illness, 231
  current funding for, 235–238
  on diagnosis of borderline
    disorder in children, 99–103
  on diagnostic strategies, 230–231
  empirical, 225, 226, 227–228
  on environmental risk factors, 232

on genetic strategies, 231
Gunderson/Lyoo study, 215
how much is performed for
    borderline disorder, 233–235
information gained from, 228
Links and Heslegrave study, 90–91
McLean study, 87–89
most promising areas of, 229
on neurobiological basis of
    borderline disorder, 232–233
open-label clinical research trials,
    175
on prevalence of borderline
    disorder, 229–230
Sharon Glick Miller study,
    212–213
on treatments, 233
where research information
    comes from, 225–235
residential care, 163
residents, 36
responsibility for treatment, taking,
    161, 222–223
Rexulti (brexpiprazole), 169
rigid personality, the, 53
risk factors, causes vs., 65–66
risperidone (Risperdal), 168, 169
Ritalin (methylphenidate), 146
Rorschach test, 37

Schacht, Samuel, 48
schema-focused therapy (SFT),
    192–193
schizoid personality disorder,
    153–154
schizophrenia
  borderline personality disorder
    and, 49–50
  pre-schizophrenia, 47, 49, 50

suicidal thoughts, 142
suicide risk in borderline personality disorder, 11–13
support groups, 160, 196
 family, 221–222
supportive psychotherapy, 40
support organizations for borderline personality disorder, 61–62
symptomatic episodes, 83–84
symptoms of borderline personality disorder, 1, 2–20
 in adolescents, 78–79
 episodic nature of, 83–84
 impaired perception and reasoning, 13–17
 impulsivity, 7–13
 markedly disturbed relationships, 17–20
 poorly regulated emotions, 3–6
 See also behavioral domains of borderline personality disorder
Systems Training for Emotional Predictability and Problem Solving (STEPPS), 194–195

tardive dyskinesia (TD), 168, 170–171
temazepam (Restoril), 176
tests to define borderline personality disorder, need for improved, 229
thalamus, 127
Thematic Apperception Test (TAT), 37
therapeutic alliance, 20, 185
therapists
 as part of clinical treatment team, 204–205
 strategies for locating, 198–199
 See also mental health professionals

therapy
 ground rules of, 38
 play, 114
 See also psychotherapies
thinking
 magical, 16
 paranoid, 11, 15, 38–39, 53, 121
 See also cognitive function
thiothixene (Navane), 168
Thorazine (chlorpromazine), 168
top-down control, 131–133, 134
topiramate (Topamax), 167, 173, 174–175
transference focused psychotherapy (TFP), 191–192
trauma
 borderline personality disorder and childhood, 63–64
 posttraumatic stress disorder and, 149–150
treatment
 of anxiety and panic attacks, 149
 of attention deficit hyperactivity disorder, 146
 of bipolar disorder, 145, 173
 of bulimia, 152
 of depression, 142–143
Treatment and Research Advancements Association for Personality Disorder (TARA APD), 61
Treatment and Research Advancements National Association for Personality Disorders (TARA), 222, 234
treatment of borderline personality disorder, 75–76
 building collaborative relationship among providers, 203–205

About the Authors

Robert O. Friedel, MD, is Distinguished Clinical Professor of Psychiatry at Virginia Commonwealth University (MCV/VCU) and professor emeritus at the University of Alabama at Birmingham (UAB). He received his undergraduate and medical degrees from Duke University, where he was elected to Alpha Omega Alpha honorary medical society. He then completed a medical internship and residency in psychiatry at Duke, with an intermittent two-year period engaged in neurobiological research at the National Institute of Mental Health in Bethesda, Maryland.

Dr. Friedel was the Heman E. Drummond Professor and chair of the Department of Psychiatry and Behavioral Neurology at UAB. He has also served as chair of the departments of psychiatry at Virginia Commonwealth University and the University of Michigan, executive director of the Mental Health Research Institute at the University of Michigan, and senior vice president director of research, and a member of the Board of Directors at Charter Medical Corporation.

Dr. Friedel founded Borderline Personality Disorder Clinics at UAB and at MCV/VCU. His research interests have focused, in part, on developing effective pharmacological treatments for patients with borderline personality disorder and in understanding the biological basis of the disorder. His clinical practice has concentrated mainly on borderline personality disorder.

In 1999, Dr. Friedel was appointed founding editor-in-chief of the journal *Current Psychiatry Reports* (now co-edited with Dr. Dwight Evans). He serves on the Scientific Advisory Board of the National Education Alliance for Borderline Personality Disorder, the Editorial Board of the *Journal of Clinical Psychopharmacology*, and is a member of a number of professional and scientific organizations. Dr. Friedel has published over 100 scientific articles, book chapters, and books. He lives in Virginia.

Linda F. Cox, LCSW, has a background in clinical practice in outpatient and residential mental health facilities and in academic research. Her clinical work has focused primarily on the treatment of adolescents, especially those with borderline personality disorder. She received a BS in Psychology from the University of Virginia and a Masters degree in Social Work at Virginia Commonwealth University. She is Dr. Friedel's daughter.

Karin Friedel is a writer and editor specializing in mental health, with an emphasis in borderline personality disorder. She earned a BS in Economics, with a minor in English, from James Madison University. She is Dr. Friedel's daughter.